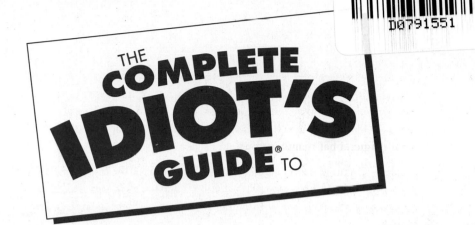

THE COMPLETE IDIOT'S GUIDE® TO

Starting and Running a Bar

by Steve Johns and Carey Rossi

ALPHA

A member of Penguin Group (USA) Inc.

ALPHA BOOKS

Published by the Penguin Group

Penguin Group (USA) Inc., 375 Hudson Street, New York, New York 10014, USA

Penguin Group (Canada), 90 Eglinton Avenue East, Suite 700, Toronto, Ontario M4P 2Y3, Canada (a division of Pearson Penguin Canada Inc.)

Penguin Books Ltd., 80 Strand, London WC2R 0RL, England

Penguin Ireland, 25 St. Stephen's Green, Dublin 2, Ireland (a division of Penguin Books Ltd.)

Penguin Group (Australia), 250 Camberwell Road, Camberwell, Victoria 3124, Australia (a division of Pearson Australia Group Pty. Ltd.)

Penguin Books India Pvt. Ltd., 11 Community Centre, Panchsheel Park, New Delhi—110 017, India

Penguin Group (NZ), 67 Apollo Drive, Rosedale, North Shore, Auckland 1311, New Zealand (a division of Pearson New Zealand Ltd.)

Penguin Books (South Africa) (Pty.) Ltd., 24 Sturdee Avenue, Rosebank, Johannesburg 2196, South Africa

Penguin Books Ltd., Registered Offices: 80 Strand, London WC2R 0RL, England

International Standard Book Number: 978-1-59257-6968
Library of Congress Catalog Card Number: 2007932651

10   09   08   8   7   6   5   4   3   2   1

Interpretation of the printing code: The rightmost number of the first series of numbers is the year of the book's printing; the rightmost number of the second series of numbers is the number of the book's printing. For example, a printing code of 08-1 shows that the first printing occurred in 2008.

Printed in the United States of America

Most Alpha books are available at special quantity discounts for bulk purchases for sales promotions, premiums, fund-raising, or educational use. Special books, or book excerpts, can also be created to fit specific needs.

For details, write: Special Markets, Alpha Books, 375 Hudson Street, New York, NY 10014.

Publisher: *Marie Butler-Knight*
Editorial Director: *Mike Sanders*
Managing Editor: *Billy Fields*
Acquisitions Editor: *Tom Stevens*
Development Editor: *Michael Thomas*
Production Editor: *Kayla Dugger*

Copy Editor: *Jeff Rose*
Cartoonist: *Shannon Wheeler*
Cover Designer: *Bill Thomas*
Book Designer: *Trina Wurst*
Indexer: *Celia McCoy*
Layout: *Chad Dressler*
Proofreader: *John Etchison*

Contents at a Glance

Contents

Introduction

Roadhouse, Cheers, Cocktail, It's Always Sunny in Philadelphia, and *The Club*. These movies and television shows have glamorized bars. Hollywood does get one thing right—the bar business can be a lot of fun. What we don't see is the hard work and long hours required to make a bar successful.

When you own a bar, you own a small business—one that can add to your community by bringing people from all different backgrounds together. The world's first bars, pubs, and taverns were the center of their communities. Weary travelers always knew to find the nearest tavern if they were looking for room and board. In England, town hall meetings took place in pubs. (Now that sounds like a fun city council meeting!)

Today bars are a place where old friends hang out, new friends get to know one another, and some grab a bite to eat. They promote fun in what can be a serious world. If you are reading this, it is your hope to maybe open and operate your own bar to add more fun and excitement to your community. Maybe it will happen next week, maybe next year, or maybe a few years from now, but if your dream is vivid and you're passionate, it will happen.

The bar business is not for the meek or the lazy. To succeed in this industry takes a lot of hard work, drive, and physical labor. Here, we give you a step-by-step guide from conception to your grand opening and beyond. You will understand the importance of décor and music to the overall vision of a bar, know how to find funding to make this exciting dream happen, understand the importance of promotions and advertising, and see how to run a profitable bar.

We want you to understand the bar business inside and out. With this understanding, you will more likely make the first of many decisions that will be right for you. By the time you finish this book, you will have gained in-depth knowledge about your own motivations, the inner workings of any bar, and a solid idea about what it's going to take to make the bar of your dreams a reality. The rest is up to you.

How to Use This Book

This book is divided into six parts:

Part 1, "More Than Where Everyone Knows Your Name," challenges you to think about the many aspects of starting your own bar. With a good, solid gut check, you'll know whether this business is for you.

Part 2, "Getting Started," walks you through the many aspects of seeing your dream become a reality.

Part 3, "Putting It All Together," helps you recognize the importance that the support functions play in building a successful restaurant, from planning traffic patterns to hiring the right people.

Part 4, "Eat, Drink, and Be Wary," helps you plan your food and bar offerings and gives you basic knowledge of liquor, wine, and beer. It will also show you how to order and how to set your prices.

Part 5, "Back-of-the-Bar Business," explains the systems that keep your bar running at optimal levels.

Part 6, "Opening the Doors and Beyond," discusses promoting your business so it achieves success now and in the future.

The appendixes provide additional resources, tools, and reference material that you may find helpful in your quest to operate a profitable bar.

Extras

Throughout the book you will find the following visual references in the form of various tips, warnings, thoughts, and definitions.

Beer Goggles

These boxes give you warnings about situations you may face and advice on how to handle them.

Bartender Knowledge

These boxes include interesting facts and insights from the bar business that will help you understand how it all works.

def•i•ni•tion

These boxes define common terms in the bar business.

Tip Jar

These boxes give you ideas on how to make starting and running a bar easier.

Acknowledgments

I look back at my 10 years in the restaurant business with fond memories. It was as a cocktail waitress and manager that I met some of my closest and dearest friends. It is my experience in the service industry that allows me to enjoy a complicated glass of wine, make a killer margarita, and have the small amount of patience that I do.

Though I'm no longer an active participant in restaurant operations (you have to have a lot of patience, in fact—I don't), I write about nutrition and how to do anything. When my agent Marilyn Allen approached me to write this book, Steve was the first person I called. This book was made possible because he agreed to share his vast knowledge of the bar business with all of you. He deserves the credit.

As for the people in my travels who have helped me, there are too many to name here. One thank you I must make is to my partner, Michael Berg, who weathered all-night writing sessions and endless tape transcriptions in the course of preparing this book.

Thank you,

Carey Rossi

I'd like to thank many people for helping me and guiding me down a proper path. I'm very grateful for the ones around me, all the family and friends, and the business relationships that soon became friends. So here goes!

Family first. For all their support, my mother and father, Leo, Chris, Demetra, Connie, Debbie, Linda, and my dear cousin Carey, who helped with support through the years I've been a part of this crazy industry. And to the girlfriends who put up with me—you know who you are.

Thanks are owed to the associates that I have worked with, from beginning to present: Tim Evans, Todd Love, Bill Wickham, Harvey Izen, Joe Gallager, Mike McCormick, Rod Copeland, Vosso Boreta, John Boreta, Ron Boreta, Chris Coreta, David Spindle, Craig Marlar, Louis Gonzales, Hal Hall, Anthony Seltz, Doug Ahlers, Sean Sontag, Phil Lockheart, Carl Kilaberg, Ted Hane, Jim Stephens, Doug Blair, Tom Nolan, Larry Lanning, Kim Jughard, Denise Kasofsky, Vanessa Cruz, Vanja Terzic, Heather Riccio, Bob Scatchell, and David Field. I must also include my accountant Jackie Leon, my lawyer Steven Dedina, and my liquor salesman and friend, John Santillo. Special thanks to consultant and friend Don Miller, and all the staff and friends that worked through the years on all the different projects.

To all of you reading this with dreams of opening your own establishment, remember to believe in yourself first and your vision—the rest will follow you to your great success. An old wise man once said, "Out of ten bars and restaurants, only three will survive within a three-year period: One because it has great food and cocktails; one because it has great food, cocktails, atmosphere, and theme; and one because it has great food, cocktails, atmosphere, and theme, and a little bit of magic. That magic is you!"

If you're willing to do whatever work it takes to turn your vision into reality and follow the relatively simple formula outlined by that wise man, a saying he was fond of will also hold true for you: "The best is yet to come."

Steve Johns

Trademarks

All terms mentioned in this book that are known to be or are suspected of being trademarks or service marks have been appropriately capitalized. Alpha Books and Penguin Group (USA) Inc. cannot attest to the accuracy of this information. Use of a term in this book should not be regarded as affecting the validity of any trademark or service mark.

Part 1

More Than Where Everyone Knows Your Name

Bars are where you can go to hang out with old friends, meet new friends, and enjoy a sense of community that the digital age has lessened. This isn't any different than the function of pubs and taverns hundreds of years ago; they were the center of city life. Today, however, your neighborhood watering hole could be a Euro-Asian sake bar with appropriate dress required. (So much for come as you are.)

Whether that's your thing or not, it doesn't matter, because a bar is about to be your domain. Turn the page to start making your place the place to be.

Can You Pour the Shots?

In This Chapter

◆ A typical day running a bar

◆ What's involved in running a bar

◆ Find out whether you're up to the challenge

◆ How to get experience

◆ Where to find mentors

Out of 10 bars that open, 7 of them fail in the first 3 years. What's the secret to the successful ones? Some may have great drinks and food and others may have great drinks, food, atmosphere, and ambience. But a successful bar will be a special place because it will have great drinks and food, great atmosphere and ambience, and a little bit of magic. The magic is you.

Think about television barkeeps—Sam Malone from *Cheers*, the group of friends from *It's Always Sunny in Philadelphia*, and Ed Williams from *The Club*. Each brings their own magic to their establishment. All three are great examples of what makes a bar successful (or not, since Williams was ousted in a hostile takeover). But television makes running a bar seem easy. The reality is starting and running a bar is a lot of work. (You're going to be hearing that a lot.)

In this chapter, we introduce you to the responsibility, the hard work, and the privilege that comes with owning a bar—as well as help you determine if you're up for the challenge. Consider this your overview of life as a barkeep. If you read this chapter and are still excited about running a bar, we think you'll do all right … with the help of this book, of course.

A Day in the Life of a Bar

People get into the bar business for the glamour, the fun, and the excitement. They experience these as patrons, so it's understandable that they want to create the same experience for others. But to create that magic, a lot of work takes place behind the scenes.

Bar owners don't show up a half hour before the doors open for business. Like any other business, operations follow a cycle. Orders are placed, and bookkeeping is done. How your cycle runs depends on whether you're a seven-day or four-day operation. No two days are the same. Sure, every day you'll do the bookkeeping and the upkeep—checking the *breakage* from the night before and some other things—but in general, the bar business always varies.

def•i•ni•tion

The amount of empty bottles at the end of the night is called **breakage**. Breakage can also refer to glassware that is broken, food that spoils, or drinks that are spilled.

One thing is the same: your business hours. You have to keep a regular schedule for your purveyors, deliveries, orders, accounting, and so on. Assuming that you're a small business owner, you will probably do most of the following. But if you have managers, they will help with some of the tasks.

A typical day starts at 5 A.M. with the cleaning crew. They have the place done by 9 A.M. Then the first management or bookkeeper comes in between 9 and 10, depending on the size of the place. Whether it is you or another management person, that person checks the alarm, checks the orders that may have been placed the night before or calls in orders, and accepts deliveries. Depending on the size of the operations, you work all day answering phones and fielding questions of all sorts—employment, hours, possibly reservations, purveyors. If you have a bookkeeper or a receptionist (could be the same person), this frees you up to make the deposit and get change from the bank. You can then go out into the community and drum up business by visiting area hotels and businesses, passing out flyers, or other marketing tactics (see Chapter 22 for more).

If you are lucky enough to hire someone to answer the phones during the day, you return to the bar about 90 minutes prior to opening the doors. During this time you might set up the bar, making sure that there are enough mixes prepared for drinks, plenty of ice has been made, candles are on the tables, glasses are clean, garnishes have been cut, enough food is prepped, and so on. Depending on the number of employees, you also may have a short meeting just prior to opening the doors for business to get your staff excited and talk about any specials.

Once you're open, you keep an eye on the business and determine whether the staffing is enough or too much for the business coming in the door. If you're busy, you may roll with the drink orders or provide support for your employees, depending on your establishment. No matter what, you will interact with your customers by talking with them, getting to know them, collecting feedback from them, and making sure you're not liquoring them up. All of these things help you grow your business and ensure that you stay in business.

Tip Jar _____

Short meetings prior to opening or at the beginning of shifts are a great way to facilitate communication between management and the staff. If they know what's going on in the business, your employees will feel connected to it and possibly even have a sense of ownership, too.

The bar will be busy until last call (at least it will if you do your marketing right; see Chapter 22). Once the last customer has left, you close the doors and clean up the bar. You put all the liquor away, drain and wipe down the ice bins, count the money, tip out the employees, clean up other food or drink service areas, mop the floors, and so on. Finally you lock the doors, set the alarm, and go home to sleep a few hours until you begin the cycle again tomorrow.

What It Takes to Be in This Business

It takes a while to become Sam Malone, hiring a couple of cocktail waitresses (Carla and Diane) and a bartender (Woody), eventually selling your bar to a larger corporation, or even franchising it. Before any of that can happen, you need as much control as possible. To do this and succeed, it takes a lot of hard work—mentally and physically. This means that you have to wear many different hats: contractor, interior designer, manager, bookkeeper, sales manager, marketing manager, maybe even bartender. As your business grows, you will hire some of these positions so that you don't have to work all the time. Be prepared to work 16 hours a day. After your business is running smoothly and you're able to hire a manager, your hours will diminish.

A bar owner cannot be afraid, or unwilling, to do hard labor. This type of work will tax all of you. When envisioning your bar, doing math for forecasting profits, setting prices, dreaming up signature drinks or menu items, and managing your employees and customers, your brain will get quite a workout. You might as well let your gym membership lapse, because the manual labor will keep your muscles strong. Cleaning your establishment takes a lot of scrubbing and scouring. You may need to do some construction work to get your space ready. And let's not forget all the cases of liquor you will lift. Actually, if you aren't physically fit now, you may want to speak to your doctor about starting some kind of exercise program. Think about it as training for your dream; it will help you keep your wits about you. And your wits are important because starting and running a bar will affect your relationships.

If you're not married, it will be easier, because new partners will only know your new life. That doesn't mean that you won't feel lonely or think that all you ever do is work—you will. To balance this, you'll want to surround yourself with supportive friends and family. When times seem impossible, you need to know who your cheer-leaders are.

If you're married and have children, starting and running a bar will put a lot of stress on your family life. When you first start out, the workload will take a lot out of you and steal a lot of the time that you would normally spend with your family, especially your evenings. Your spouse will need to be very understanding.

Before you embark on this journey, you need to do a bit of soul-searching. Ask yourself:

- Am I willing to work late hours?
- Am I willing to do hard work?
- Am I willing to work many hours?
- Do I like being around people who drink?
- Do I want to provide a fun atmosphere for people?
- Do I like people?
- Am I willing to take a financial risk?
- Will my family support me?
- Is this business for me?

These questions are true to what the business entails. It's late hours. It's hard work. But just like any other business, it's rewarding … and it's fun.

The key to success—and we talk more about this and marketing in Chapter 22—is promoting the word "fun." You don't want your patrons to get so inebriated that they cannot walk out of your establishment, but you want them to have fun in the meeting place that you have created for them. If they enjoy themselves, they will come back. Think of it as creating a living room for everybody that comes through your bar's front door. We have met many bar owners. Some are fun and come from behind the bar in costume and make their customers laugh. All of them are characters—each very different—but all the successful ones have the same characteristics:

◆ They are outgoing.

◆ They are friendly.

◆ They enjoy the public.

◆ They have a strong work ethic.

◆ They bring a bit of magic to their establishments.

Ultimately, you must be outgoing, friendly, and enjoy the public. If you're not any of those things, you probably shouldn't work in any type of service industry, restaurant or bar. You and your attitude rub off on your clientele; they know when you are not having a good time.

Are You Up to the Challenge?

Serving alcohol to the public is a privilege that comes with a lot of responsibility. Sure, this business is fun, but you also deal with a controlled substance—one that you will be controlling. How's your ability to finesse others to see your way? How well do you multitask? Are you detail oriented? To meet the challenges of being a bar owner you need to have these characteristics. There are patrons who will want to drink more than they can safely handle; there are laws that need to be followed, and there are small details, whether financially or physically, in your business that will need to be tended to.

Running a bar is challenging. You are dealing with the public. You are dealing with law enforcement. You are upholding laws of your city, state, and country (hopefully you are doing this already). You are the party starter. You even become a psychologist and best friend. (And as a result, you may learn more about people than you care to. As a barkeep or bartender, there is no such thing as TMI—too much information.)

> **Bartender Knowledge** _____
>
> Approximately 20.9 million American adults, or 9.5 percent of the U.S. population, have a mood disorder, such as depression, according to the National Institute of Mental Health. Know that this is who your patron might be, especially in light of a 2004 study in the *Journal of the American Medical Association* that found a strong connection between mood disorders and substance (e.g., alcohol) use.

How to Get Experience

People get into the business only so many ways: 1) They have never worked in the service industry but they have money, have seen it, and think it looks fun; 2) They have worked in a bar before; or 3) They have an ego and want their names on a business. Hopefully you've worked in a bar or restaurant before so you know what you are getting into. If not, it's best to experience the in's and out's of this business before you jump in with two feet.

To get hard-knocks knowledge, get a job as a bartender, cocktail waitress, or manager of a bar or even a restaurant that has a good bar business. This will allow you to learn about the industry and see if you like it. Behind the scenes is much different than what you see from sitting on a barstool. Different places can give you different experiences, whether they are privately owned, chains, or franchises. Or you could just hire a consultant or find a mentor.

Privately Owned Operations

If you go to work for a mom-and-pop bar, know this: you'll only learn what they have learned. They most likely went through a lot of trial and error, or run things one way which may not be the most efficient or the most effective. You will see how much work is involved and you will definitely learn some things—good and bad.

Chain Operations

Corporations, or *chain* bars, have ironed out a lot of mistakes. So working for them will teach you a little bit more about the systems that you have to put in place. Then, if you go into a mom-and-pop afterward, you will have a better idea about how to forecast for the future and day-by-day.

If you work for both, you can have both perspectives. But working in a corporation, especially as a manager, allows you to observe and learn how things can be streamlined, which will make it easier to streamline operations in your own establishment. This will also establish credibility, which is especially helpful when looking for investors.

Franchises

If you invest in a franchise, they will teach you the way they do things and give on-going support to help you succeed. Think of it as a crash course in bar ownership. Another benefit to investing in a franchise is that your plan is in place for you, plus you have the benefit of instant name recognition.

But be cautious. Like any investment, purchasing a franchise is not a guarantee of success. You will have certain obligations to the company or franchisor. A franchise typically enables you, the investor or "franchisee," to operate a business. By paying a franchise fee, which may cost several thousand dollars, you're given a format and possibly systems developed by the franchisor, the right to use the franchisor's name, and assistance.

If this type of business seems attractive to you, consider the following components of a typical franchise:

- ◆ **Cost.** Besides the initial investment, what other fees are there?

- ◆ **Controls.** Franchisors typically control how franchisees conduct business to ensure uniformity. Will their controls restrict your ability to exercise your own business judgment?

- ◆ **Contract.** A franchise contract is usually only for a limited time and there is no guarantee that you'll be able to renew it. Does this work with your dream for the future?

def•i•ni•tion _____

Chains are owned and operated by one company, local individuals, or firms. They have centralized marketing and purchasing, which tends to mean lower costs and higher profits. Examples are Fado Irish Pub and John Harvard's Brew House.

Beer Goggles _____

You may think that buying a franchise reduces your investment risk because it associates you with an established company, but it also can be costly to your pocketbook and to your vision. As a franchisee, you may be required to relinquish significant control over your business while taking on contractual obligations with the franchisor.

If you decide to consider franchising, definitely do your homework. The Federal Trade Commission has information on how to enter into the franchise system on its website: www.ftc.gov.

Consultants

You could hire a consultant. This book will help you with narrowing down your concept, finding a location, designing the interior, and many other things, but a consultant can give personal advice. When hiring a consultant, make sure you find out what kind of work he or she has done and whether it matches up with your bar's theme and location (i.e., city). Not only should any consultant you consider have references, you should check those references.

Finding Mentors and Advisors

Who's your favorite bar owner? Is there a bar owner that you would like to emulate? If so, ask him if you could follow him around for the day and see what he does. Or you could ask him to mentor you. If he won't, ask the bar owner if he knows anyone as knowledgeable as he is. Flattery can get you anywhere. It's possible that he will refer you to someone who can advise or even consult you.

Why You Need This Book

By following one of the preceding paths, you will learn what running and owning a bar takes—and what it takes is a lot of hard work. Remember: "The party in progress turns to profit." Crowds will enjoy your atmosphere while your bar becomes like *Cheers*—a place where all walks of life come. Imagine: the lawyer, the constructor, the firefighter, and so on, all coming together and enjoying your place. It is the pride of ownership that really becomes your reward and feeds your profits.

This book will walk you through the process of starting and running a bar, especially if your experience is lacking. Consider it your "party planning guide."

The Least You Need to Know

 ◆ Running a bar requires long hours of hard work.

 ◆ To be a successful bar owner, you need to be outgoing, enjoy the public, have a strong work ethic, and bring a bit of magic to your establishment.

◆ Serving alcohol is a privilege that comes with a lot of responsibility.

◆ You need to have some experience working in a bar before owning your own bar.

◆ Working in a chain bar will help you learn efficient systems and may help you get funding easier.

◆ This business is all about selling fun.

Chapter 2

The State of the Bar

In This Chapter

- Bar history 101
- Challenges facing the industry
- Who's looking over your shoulder?
- Controlled versus licensed
- Knowing the different ABCs

Through the course of American history, alcohol has brought people together, been banned, been sold on the black market, and then come back into good graces—that is, in some states. This controlled substance always faces challenges and as a bar owner, you will, too.

But we can learn from history. In fact, it is Prohibition that gave states the individual power to determine how alcoholic beverages are sold. And it is another prohibition—this time of smoking—that will challenge you to keep your business growing despite the changes to the laws. This chapter provides an overview of the history of bars, the challenges of today's bars, and an introduction to government oversight of selling alcohol.

A Brief History of the Bar

We're not sure where the modern-day bar originated. In Great Britain, public houses or pubs have been around for hundreds of years and still remain an important element in British community life. It's thought that pubs existed in the eleventh century, when travelers were invited to drop by houses and have a tankard of local brew. Since then pubs—and their offspring in the United States, taverns and saloons—have been places where travelers rest and people congregate and enjoy the local brew or distilled spirit.

Bartender Knowledge

"The Red Lion" is the most common pub name and may date back to the 1700s.

The Industrial Revolution also marked the creation of large regional brewers in Britain. These breweries fostered the growth of pubs in their area and would supply these establishments with their brew. But when World War I began, drinking alcohol became a social and moral issue, not just in Britain, but across the pond in the United States. In fact, the United States may have been the first place to demonize alcohol.

In the early 1900s, the Temperance movement was gaining legs in the United States. Wanting to make alcohol illegal, this group led the way to Prohibition. In 1905, three states outlawed alcohol. By 1916, Prohibition was in effect in 26 states. On January 16, 1920, Prohibition was put into effect after the Eighteenth Amendment to the United States Constitution had been ratified and the Volstead Act was passed. This meant that the manufacture, sale, and transport of alcohol were illegal. Our neighbors to the north and south, however, still had legalized alcohol and the distilleries and breweries in Canada, Mexico, and the Caribbean flourished as a result of illegally importing their products to the United States.

A profitable black market emerged during Prohibition. Racketeering occurred when powerful gangs corrupted law enforcement agencies. As for the alcohol, strong distilled spirits became popular because their potency made it more profitable to smuggle.

The cost of enforcing Prohibition was high, and the lack of tax revenues on alcohol affected the government's ability to keep up. Prohibition was therefore repealed in 1933 as a result of the Twenty-First Amendment. The amendment gave states the right to restrict or ban the purchase or sale of alcohol; this has led to a patchwork of laws in which alcohol may be legally sold in some but not all towns or counties within a particular state. The Twenty-First Amendment has shaped today's liquor laws and explains why each state has its own Alcoholic Beverage Control (ABC).

The repeal of Prohibition sparked the revival of nightclubs, which had gone underground as speakeasies. These bars and nightclubs had jukeboxes or live bands to entertain their customers. But in 1953, a Paris club laid down a dance-floor, suspended colored lights from the ceiling, and replaced the jukebox with two turntables operated manually—the goal was to eliminate breaks between the songs. This set the standard for the discothèque.

Nightclubs weren't the rock 'n' roll generation's thing, and therefore faded out. But in the 1970s, the club returned with the disco. Today, nightclubs and bars come in all shapes and themes. And while they are not the public houses of early Britain, their social aspect is the draw in a world full of electronic communication.

What Are the Industry Challenges?

The bar business creates a challenge for itself simply because it deals with a controlled substance—alcohol. And if you are in a license state, the ability to sell liquor may be a commodity. There also are laws that govern smoking and minimum wage that will affect business. Read on to see how.

Liquor License

Liquor license prices have gone up. It is the perfect supply and demand model as more bars, restaurants, and so on continue to open. Now there are brokers just for liquor licenses, since being able to actually get one is difficult in some areas. In the past, these things usually lost their value; now they are an equity proposition. Even if you fail and don't have any liens against you, you can sell your liquor license. If there are no marks against it, meaning it's a clean license, you might walk away with money on your initial investment since you may be able to sell it for more than you paid for it. This is the number-one thing you must have in the business. The only drawback is that, in most cases (remember, liquor laws vary in each state), you have to hold a license for two years before selling it. The fact that a liquor license is equity is the biggest trend in bars.

Smoking Laws

Currently we are undergoing a bit of a legalized prohibition when it comes to cigarettes. Smoking laws are the newest hot topic in the service industry, because many people smoke while drinking. According to Smoke Free USA, California, Connecticut, Delaware, Maine, Massachusetts, New Jersey (casinos exempted), New

York, Rhode Island, Vermont, and Washington have banned smoking in restaurants and bars. Montana banned smoking in restaurants, and smoking in bars will be banned in the state beginning in 2009. Arizona, Minnesota, Nevada, and Ohio have banned smoking in most public places. In addition, a number of cities and counties have banned smoking in restaurants. In one of the most controversial of these bans, New York City banned smoking in bars and nightclubs.

Most thought that sales in the service industry would suffer, but that hasn't been proven. In fact, the Texas Department of Health (TDH) and CDC analyzed sales tax and mixed-beverage tax data during the 12 years preceding and 1 year after El Paso, Texas, implemented their smoking ban in all public places and workplaces (including restaurants and bars). They found that there were no statistically significant changes in restaurant and bar revenues after the smoking ban took effect. These findings are consistent with those from studies of smoking bans in other U.S. cities.

If smoking bans haven't occurred in your city or state, the best thing to do is plan for them to be implemented. This means having patio space as part of your bar or, if you feel strongly that this is an infringement on rights, opening a smoking/cigar bar.

Minimum Wage

Minimum wage laws always affect the service industry. As this book is being written, numerous minimum wage bills are being discussed in state legislatures and in Washington, D.C. Where state and federal minimum wage levels are not the same, the higher of the two wage rates prevails. Twenty-six states have minimum wages that are above the federal guidelines, and cities such as San Francisco and Los Angeles are providing city-mandated living wage rates that increase the minimum allowable wage inside that city's limits even more.

Bartender Knowledge

Kansas is the only state that has a minimum wage that is less than the federal standard.

There's a reason why businesses fight minimum wage increases when lawmakers consider them. Increasing the minimum wage lessens the amount of profit being made. This loss results in either a decrease in profits or an increase in menu prices to make up for the shortfall.

Turnover

Turnover in the service industry is a normal occurrence of epic portions. Industry turnover averages run in excess of 200 percent for hourly employees and exceeds 100 percent for salaried employees. To put these numbers into perspective, if you have a projected staff level of 10 employees and a projected turnover of 200 percent, you will need to hire 20 employees in the next year to stay at 10.

Turnover has affected every segment of the industry and continues to be a driving force behind rising compensation levels, poor operations, and profit erosion.

Beer Goggles

Hasty hiring decisions can increase your employee turnover rate even more because the hire isn't a good fit. You'll also lose time and resources training someone you may have to fire in the future.

The Government's Oversight

Alcoholic beverage control is a bit complicated. Per the Twenty-First Amendment to the Constitution, all states have their own liquor laws. Depending on the state, the governing bodies may go all the way down to the county or city level.

Federal Level

The production of alcoholic beverages is regulated and taxed by the federal government. The Bureau of Alcohol, Tobacco, Firearms and Explosives and the Alcohol and Tobacco Tax and Trade Bureau (formerly one organization known as the Bureau of Alcohol, Tobacco and Firearms) enforces federal laws and regulations related to alcohol, though most regulations regarding serving and selling alcoholic beverages are made by the individual states.

State Level

Besides the normal oversight of business names, also known as fictitious names, some states take a hands-on approach to regulating alcoholic beverages in their states.

After national prohibition ended in 1933, some states decided to continue their own prohibition against the production, distribution, and sale of alcoholic beverages within their borders. Those that decided to continue

def•i•ni•tion

Control states have a monopoly over the selling of alcoholic beverages, such as beer, wine, and distilled spirits. **License states** leave the issue to local jurisdictions, including counties and cities.

the prohibition of alcohol are called *control states*. These states have a monopoly over the selling of alcoholic beverages, such as beer, wine, and distilled spirits. Control states include:

- Alabama
- Idaho
- Iowa
- Maine
- Maryland (Montgomery and Worcester counties)
- Michigan
- Mississippi
- Montana
- New Hampshire
- North Carolina
- Ohio
- Oregon
- Pennsylvania
- Utah
- Vermont
- Virginia
- Washington
- West Virginia
- Wyoming

Other states decided to leave the issue to local jurisdictions, including counties and cities, a practice called local option. These states are known as *license states*.

Bartender Knowledge

Control states belong to the National Alcohol Beverage Control Association (NABCA), which shortens its acronym to ABC. However, license states have Alcoholic Beverage Control, also known as the ABC.

Local Level

Your local government oversees that your location is zoned for serving alcoholic beverages and issues your business license. The local law enforcement makes sure that you are abiding by all the laws of the land, including those of the Alcoholic Beverage Control.

Know Your ABCs

If we were to go through all the various laws that each state requires to serve alcoholic beverages, this book would be a series of volumes. The best advice we can give you is to go to your local Alcoholic Beverage Control (ABC) office (we give each state's ABC contact information in Appendix B) and buy the book of rules and regulations that you will have to follow for your state, county, or town. Read it and commit it to memory as these will be the most important regulations that you will follow as a bar owner (more on ABCs in Chapter 5).

 Tip Jar

A representative from your local ABC will come to your bar and do seminars and presentations on the laws governing alcohol in your area. This is a great way to ensure both you and your employees know the law.

The Least You Need to Know

◆ The Twenty-First Amendment allows states to decide how to control alcoholic beverages.

◆ On a federal level, it is the Bureau of Alcohol, Tobacco, Firearms and Explosives that oversees alcoholic beverage manufacturing.

◆ Depending on your state, your liquor license could be an equity investment.

◆ Keep yourself informed on laws affecting smoking and minimum wage.

◆ The laws set by your local ABC chapter will be the most important for you to commit to memory.

What's Your Vision?

In This Chapter

◆ Imagine your bar, from the logo to the entrance to the exit

◆ Know the difference between a bar, a lounge, and a nightclub

◆ Determine a theme for your bar

◆ Consider whether your vision will succeed

Perhaps you're just starting out on your dream of bar ownership, or you've decided that being a barkeep is what you want to do in your second life after the kids are grown and your 9-to-5 has left you bored silly. Whatever the impetus, it's not enough to simply have the idea to get into the business—you need to get specific.

For instance, even though Steve has helped open and run numerous bars, he still has a dream. He knows the name and the theme or concept for his own bar. He can picture every detail, from what the front of the building looks like to what the customers see when they first walk in, what the waitresses are wearing, and the placement of the bar and even the bathrooms. He hasn't quite found the best location for it, but when he does, he's opening it in a heartbeat.

Hopefully you have a similar vision. You may know the name but have no idea about what anything else will look like. Or maybe you know what type of bar it is but are having difficulty imagining it. No matter what, this chapter will help you hone your vision so you can say, "I'm opening an English Pub on Main Street in Aspen," and know that it will be wildly successful to boot.

What's Your Type?

Before you can open your establishment, you must have a vision for it. Will it be a bar? A *lounge?* A nightclub? Some people classify a nightclub as a place with dancing and entertainment. Some people classify a bar as a neighborhood establishment. For the most part, where your bar is located and the size of your establishment will be a contributing factor to what type of bar you open.

def•i•ni•tion

A luxurious, comfortable place to serve alcohol is known as a **lounge.**

Size can be a determining factor when deciding between starting a bar or a nightclub. If you've settled on a space that is 1,000 square feet, for instance, you are deceiving yourself if you think you are going to open a nightclub, since a nightclub needs a bigger area to create the right atmosphere to succeed.

Bars and Lounges

Besides space constraints and location, another key difference is the atmosphere. The atmosphere of a bar tends to be more laid-back. Consider your neighborhood bar, sports bars, taverns, saloons, and pubs to be the typical vibe of a bar. In the most general sense, a bar is just that: an establishment that has a bar, some chairs, and serves alcohol.

Beer Goggles

Knowing the kind of atmosphere you want your bar to provide can lead you to deciding the best theme. For instance, if you want your bar to provide a romantic and low-key vibe, you shouldn't consider opening a bar where the draw is live rock band performances. Ultimately you spend your time and effort in this establishment; it should reflect you.

Now there are exceptions to this. (Aren't there always?) Bars with comfortable seating and a more polished atmosphere—i.e., cocktail lounges—were mostly found in hotels not so long ago, but these posh destinations are now popping up in areas around the country. Their décor tends to be more refined and they have a cool, hip vibe. Sometimes there is entertainment (hello, lounge singer), or sometimes these bars morph into nightclubs by just moving the seating out of the way and bringing in a DJ. For both bars and lounges, the focus is on consuming alcohol—it is the atmosphere that differs.

Nightclubs

In the 1970s, they were known as discos or discothèques. Today, these entertainment hubs that do most of their business when the sun is down are called nightclubs. They mostly differ from a bar because of the prominent positioning of a dance floor. The atmosphere of a nightclub is all about entertainment—dancing, DJs, bands, and so on. Most require dress codes and have a cover charge to offset the cost associated with the entertainment.

Nightclubs tend to be high-fun zones, whereas bars or lounges allow patrons to relax and enjoy their company and the atmosphere of the establishment more. Now that doesn't mean that bars and lounges can't have dancing, bands, or a DJ; unlike night-clubs, however, they are not integral parts of their establishment.

Music and special lighting—who can forget the disco ball?—help create the atmosphere. The music can be played by a DJ or per-formed by a band, and the type of music is particular to the club or particular to the theme night that the club may have.

Since music creates a powerful connection with patrons, the theme of a nightclub must extend to the music. It should be easy for you to host evenings focused on a specific music genre. In this way, you can grow your business by catering to a variety of different people.

Tip Jar

Besides having a unique theme for your establish-ment, you can run special promo-tional nights to bring in different types of patrons. This drives your business and may even help create regular customers who frequent your bar because of what happens on that night. In the case of nightclubs, you could have blues, jazz, '80s, country, rock, or hip-hop nights.

See Your Bar Clearly

Close your eyes. What do you see? Maybe you see a Mexican cantina, a jazz club, or an Asian-inspired lounge. All of these ideas are themes. The theme includes the atmo-sphere and the décor. As a rule of the thumb: the theme of your bar should start at the front of the establishment and run to the back of the house. Immerse all elements in your theme; otherwise, you may have a great concept in mind but it could fall flat with a simple oversight. For instance, you could serve martinis in an Irish pub, but would they be your specialty? Only if you want to create a disconnect between your crowd and the environment you're trying to create.

If your vision isn't specific and you want to include some disparate elements from the previous examples, it may or may not work. (Can you imagine an Asian-inspired lounge with a roaming mariachi band?) The key is figuring out what themes can work together, and which can work for the neighborhood and city or town you're located in. Here are a few questions that will help you figure out exactly what your vision for your bar is:

◆ *What inspires your vision?* Is it a movie or television show? Is it something that you saw in another town? Is it your favorite vacation location? Is it something that you just dreamed up?

◆ *Who do you imagine your customers to be?* Are they young, old, or both? Are they professionals, college students, parents, or retirees? Are they all of the above, or a mixture of two or three age demographics?

◆ *What is the main hook of the bar?* Is it interaction with the customers? Is it music? Is it entertainment? Is it the drink menu? Is it the ambience?

Bartender Knowledge _____

Different bars will use a different hook to draw patrons. Here's an example many of you will recognize: ever come across one of those outdoor bars along the Las Vegas strip that have a lineup of machines mixing frozen drinks? The draw of these establishments is that they are located in hot climates, serve cold drinks, and have plenty of outside seating and shade.

After answering these questions, you should be able to imagine a theme or a mixture of complementary themes that will carry through your bar. Your vision may be bits and pieces of a few things—hopefully not too many things, because you don't want to cram too many elements into one vision, one dream, or one theme. You want to pick a theme and only have a couple of variables in it. You can't be everything to everybody; you have to choose one or two things that will work.

If you're still having a difficult time narrowing down your vision, focus on the business and the demographics of the area where you are planning to open. By learning the demographic elements, you can calculate how each theme may be received. Ultimately, this will help you narrow down your vision.

Making It with the IN Crowd

Can your location support your theme? What are the age brackets of your location's residents and those of the areas surrounding it? Will people located within a 25-mile radius drive to come to your vision? If so, how many times will they come to it? What is the draw? Will you be able to attract clientele at a high enough rate to be profitable?

All these questions help you understand the elements of success for doing business in your area. These are the local elements, and they come into play to make sure that your theme works. The only way you are going to really understand the climate for business in your area is by doing your homework.

Beer Goggles _____

Your bar can fail if you don't perform your research. It's easy to think that since you've lived in a particular area for years you know all about its residents and their habits. Honestly, you will have a better understanding of exactly who your potential clientele is if you research your location as if you were an outsider. This information drives your bar's theme and makes your dreams of running a bar a successful reality.

You could have the best idea—but it could be in the wrong spot. What works somewhere else isn't necessarily going to work in your spot, and that is a proven fact. Even franchises and corporations have picked up and left places because their business didn't work in that location. So what exactly do you need to know? Population demographics, what bars and restaurants are in your area, what bars and restaurants were in your area in the past, and what your locale needs that is missing. All of this information will come into play when you write your business plan, which will be discussed in Chapter 7.

Who Are Your People?

Finding out the types of people that make up your location and the surrounding areas is one of the easiest and most important things for you to research. Nothing is worse than having a fabulous idea for a bar, only to open it in a location where the residents have no interest in the concept or no desire to want to experience it.

The first step is to get census data. Most of this information can be found on the Internet (see Appendix B for websites that can provide demographic information). Your Chamber of Commerce should also provide some insight into whom the patrons of your town are. Things that you should keep in mind when researching your area's population:

◆ Young vs. old

◆ Professionals vs. working class vs. retired

◆ Families vs. singles

◆ Students vs. nonstudents

◆ Employed vs. unemployed

◆ Gay vs. straight

◆ Year-round residents vs. tourists

By researching these variables and deciding on what target you're truly trying to reach, you can figure out whether you will attract a good customer base. This is important. If you have the best concept in the world, but there is not enough of your target demographic group locally, then you are less likely to open a successful business. You don't want to depend on people from the outlying areas to come into the city. Your bar should appeal to both populations inside and outside the city limits.

Bartender Knowledge

Since you're entering the service industry, get acquainted with your city's Convention and Visitor's Bureau, if it has one. The bureau can provide helpful information about the influx of people who come into your city as well as provide recommendations to meeting planners about businesses to patronize while their attendees are in town.

Your great concept might work in Seattle or Miami, but that doesn't mean it will work in your area. So research not just your population, but also the types of people who visit your city. Find out what conventions, festivals, tourists, and so on, come into town and when. Again, this is all easy information to get by asking your Chamber of Commerce, Tourist Bureau, or Convention and Visitor's Bureau.

Know the Competition

You could have the best theme and vision and still fail. Lots of reasons contribute to why new owners fail, but one of the most common is that they don't research or realize that there is competition.

So how do you find out who the competition is? It's time to do some fieldwork. To really understand your competition you need to experience your competition. Also, don't cast a small net when determining who that is. Restaurants with bars will be competitive to your establishment. Think about your area. For instance, does it have an El Torito or a Chili's restaurant? We mention both of these chain restaurants because they run successful bars with good drink recipes, good atmosphere, and good value to the customer.

Visit all the bars in your city (or at least in the general radius of your desired location if you are in a really big city). When you do, pay attention to the establishments':

- Theme

- Atmosphere

- Décor

- Menu (food and drink)

- Prices

- Clientele

- Employees

- Value

Another way to determine your competition is to ask people where they go for a drink and why. This is the kind of word of mouth that you will hope to get once you open up your bar. Knowing who is getting that buzz now helps you understand who you are truly competing with when you are fighting for business. It also allows you to analyze whether you are going to complement, compete against, or be different than businesses already in your city.

If you try to duplicate something that a competitor is doing, depending on the town, one of you or both of you are going to fail because you're going to split the crowd up in aiming for the same market. It's okay to have competition; competition is healthy. But when you're going to do that, you need to be capitalized properly and have a strong theme and design and layout to make it work for you and the location.

Tip Jar

Just because he's your competition doesn't mean he should be your sworn enemy. A little friendliness can go a long way in terms of saving time and energy. For instance, if you don't know the owners or the managers at a competing bar, you'll spend time visiting his bar to check the drink pricing. But when you engage in a little friendly competition, this information could be a phone call away.

Get a History Lesson

If you don't have partners, bring in someone you trust who knows the area. Good consultants also know what has worked and what hasn't in a city. Since you bought this book, we are assuming you're going it alone. And just as we've been stressing the importance of research, we'll tell you how important it is to have information, more information, and still more information.

Here's what you should find out about the location where you would like to open your bar. The answers will give you an idea of whether there is potential for growth opportunities.

- What types of bars have been in the area before?

- Are they out of business? Why?

- How long were they in business before closing?

- How have the area's demographics changed?

Fill the Void

Once you know who your competitors are and were, it's time to find out what the people want. The best way to get that information is to go out among your demographic. While you still are going to analyze the market and figure out what your city or town is missing, this fieldwork will allow you to hear from others what they would like to see in their area.

Beer Goggles _____

When asking people around town what they think is missing, record it; file it; and then look at all the data you have collected so far about the market, the competition, and the history of the industry. When viewed with everything else, your brother's idea to open a Brazilian dueling drum bar may not be such a hot idea. It may be missing from the town—but that doesn't mean it needs it.

To bring something to the area, you need to research what the city or town is missing. This way, you could bring an element to the area that it doesn't have and thus provide a service that was previously nonexistent.

A good example is when a little bar called Chillers came to Palm Springs, California, filling a void in its downtown area. In this high-traffic area of the resort city, nightclubs were predominant. Yes, people could have a drink in the afternoon at the family-owned Mexican restaurant or at the sports bar, but both were located at opposite ends of the downtown strip.

Chillers offered their frozen drinks in the bustling center of the main thoroughfare, required no cover charge or dress code (which was fabulous since most people ran around in their bathing suits, cover-ups, and flip-flops), and sold ice-cold drinks in a hot location. Palm Springs had never seen anything like it, and it did well because its theme catered to what the city needed—a casual bar amidst the action of downtown.

After researching what the area is lacking, you may find that it just needs a *better* pub, tavern, or nightclub. You may think you can improve upon what someone else isn't doing well. If this is the case, you'll really need to be on your game, as ultimately you want to outdo your competition. You need to be better in all respects—design, theme, and service—and all matched to the area's needs. If your concept isn't better than your competition, why would customers choose you?

Find Your Identity

Now you should know your potential patrons and present competitors, and the types of bars that have been in your area and are missing from your area. With this information, you can determine if your vision will succeed. If you didn't have a clear vision before this process, you may have found out that your multiple themes of the Mexican cantina, the jazz club, or the Asian-inspired lounge each fill the void. Or you may have even decided to combine the lounge idea with the jazz club.

There is another realization that you may have come to—your dream bar will not be accepted in your location. If this is the case, you need to weigh out what is more important to you: the drive to open up a bar in a particular location or the drive to open up a specific bar. If the location is the important thing to you, then you need to adjust your theme so that it will succeed in that area. If the theme is the important factor, you have to find an area whose demographics it appeals to.

Ultimately, you want to make money. To do that, you need to be realistic and bring your bar idea to a place that is most desirable. Don't think that if you build it, they will come. If you bring something into the community that is not acceptable, no one will come.

The Least You Need to Know

- ◆ Your bar's theme determines its atmosphere and décor.
- ◆ The vision for your bar should come from what inspires you, who your customers are, and what the bar's hook is.

◆ Your bar can have two different themes; just make sure they complement each other.

◆ The more information you obtain about your area, the more chance of success you have.

◆ Knowing the type of business your community is lacking can help you determine your bar's theme.

◆ Identify whether you have the drive to open a specific bar or to open in a specific location; you might have to choose.

Part 2

Getting Started

Did your mother ever tell you that you could go out and play once your homework was done? Starting a bar isn't much different. You must do research; you have to write reports; you have to do *math*.

Running a bar is fun, but starting a bar is a lot of work. It requires you to talk with lawyers, accountants (who can do the math for you), city and state officials, and law enforcement. Doesn't match up to the party people you thought you would be rubbing elbows with? Don't write them off too early. Not only will they help you get your party started right, they may come enjoy the festivities.

But first, there's business to do …

Chapter 4

Building Your Business Plan

In This Chapter

- ◆ Why success needs to be planned
- ◆ Figuring out what you want to accomplish
- ◆ How to project sales
- ◆ Finding the money to start
- ◆ Deciding whether to partner up
- ◆ Identifying financial angels

Let's say you decide to drive cross-country. You may toy with the adventure to take off on the highway and see where it leads you. If you need to be at your final destination by a certain time, however, you'll probably lay out your journey: the roads you'll take and the number of hours you'll drive each day. Starting a bar is no different than navigating through the United States—you'll be more successful with a plan.

Just like embarking on your cross-country trip, starting a bar is a journey. During both you learn about yourself and the world around you, and it may be difficult. Having a plan makes the experience a little less painful. Sure you could just drive, but in the business world this approach costs time and money. (Do you really have a plethora of both? Probably not.) This chapter will help you develop a business plan so you don't get lost on the way to creating a successful bar.

Creating Your Road Map for Success

Planning the "party in progress" that will be your bar requires direction. When you create your business plan, you decide what steps you will take to make your bar successful. The best thing to do is to write it down. Recording what you want to accomplish with your bar gives you a starting point. Think of your business plan as your road map to success. It lays out your business objectives, market analysis, timeline, contingency plan, costs, expected income and cost of sales, and marketing plan.

By writing down your intentions, you discover what is expected of you while starting your bar, and you can make decisions accordingly. This allows you to stay on course, which is especially important since it's easy to veer off track in this business. Avoid becoming a casualty of the "Be something to everyone" syndrome. A well-done plan keeps you focused on the end result—the neighborhood bar, the ultra-lounge, or the wine bar—and helps you make the right decisions for your business.

Consider the business plan the beginning of putting hard work into your business. Taking the time to lay out this plan of action will help you know exactly how to proceed. You could look at it like a very detailed to-do list for the next six months to five years.

Listing Your Business Objectives

Now comes the age-old question: What do you want to accomplish with your bar? Make money, yes. Have fun, yes. How? That's where your business objectives come in. These to-do items are called objectives. They should be SMART: Specific, Measurable, Actionable, Realistic, and Timely. Once you have decided on your objectives, you need to establish the strategies to achieve each one. From there you can break it down even further by listing the tactics or the actions you must take to attain the strategies.

Beer Goggles

Be careful not to gulp down more than you can swallow. If you set too many objectives, your odds of accomplishing all of them are small. Cap the number of objectives you set out to do at six.

Following are some examples of objectives that you may want to accomplish when running a bar:

- Make a profit the first year

- Increase sales by 3 percent in the second year of business

- Keep liquor costs under 30 percent of revenue

- Keep labor costs under 15 percent of revenue

Researching Your Market

Remember all that work you did in Chapter 3—finding out your potential patrons and present competitors, and what types of bars have been in your area and are missing from your area? It all comes into play here. Writing out your analysis of this legwork helps keep everything in perspective not just for you, but for potential investors or partners that you may bring into your business.

Creating a Marketing Plan

Here's the part of your plan that explains how you're going to fill all those barstools and get people drinking and having fun. In this section of your business plan, you will outline your marketing strategy, media budget, and miscellaneous marketing tools. (You will learn more about how to determine the best plan of action for your establishment in Chapter 22.)

Realize that your marketing plan will be evolving constantly because it will reflect the needs of your business. The best way to organize this section is by month, quarter, or even year because it will reflect the ebbs and flows of business in your area.

Doing the Math: Projecting Your Income and Expenses

Your projections will be the most scrutinized part of your business plan. You need to plan, then check and double-check your financials. In this section, you project what your start-up budget should be, how much capital you need, and what your estimated sales and profits will be. You also include a *break-even analysis*, payback periods, funding plans, sources and uses of funds, projected pro forma and financial statements, and other pertinent financial data.

When starting a new business, the most important section of a business plan is your start-up projections and your projected pro forma, which is what you guess your income and your expenses will be. Your estimation of these important figures should be conservative—low income and high expenditures. Besides the pro forma and the start-up protections, you need to include a timeline, a growth plan, and a contingency plan.

def•i•ni•tion

The **break-even analysis** is a common tool used to evaluate the economic feasibility of a new business and is based on two types of costs: fixed and variable. It helps determine the point when the revenue is exactly even to the costs.

Projecting Start-Up Costs

Determining how much capital you need to open your doors is easier than you might think. Just look at the steps necessary to start your bar. Research the cost of each item and ask vendors, suppliers, and other bar or restaurant owners what the fair price is for each item.

Bartender Knowledge

The more items you research for your starting cost projection, the more accurate the projection will be and the smaller the chance for surprise costs during the process.

Don't leave a stone unturned; take account of everything. This includes necessities such as payroll, electricians, plumbers, equipment, glassware, rent, and so on. It should also incorporate possible luxuries such as interior designers and consultants. If you don't find yourself asking, "Can I afford this?" throughout this process, then you probably don't have your business cap on. Remember, you are planning to spend *your* money. Make sure you spend each dollar effectively and efficiently; if not, you need to reevaluate and make the necessary adjustments.

Projecting Your Pro Forma

Time to get out your crystal calculator and foresee the future profitability of your bar. Of the many numbers to look at and consider, the six that potential investors will want to see are:

- Projected sales
- Projected food and liquor costs
- Projected labor costs
- Projected controllable expenses
- Projected facility costs
- Projected profitability

Forecasting sales by calendar months, or seasonal adjustments according to your area's population because of special events or tourism influx, can explain why some times may be more profitable than others. It can also help you avoid unforeseen cash-flow problems and manage your operation more effectively. Considering the ebbs and flows of business in your area helps your projected pro forma paint a more accurate picture of your bar's potential financial picture and provides an essential tool in managing it.

While it's wise to expect the unexpected, a well-constructed marketing plan, combined with accurate sales forecasting, can allow you to spend more time honing your vision rather than responding to unforeseen day-to-day developments.

This all sounds well and good, but how do you forecast sales when you don't have past sales data to look at? Start by asking yourself a few questions based on the market research you've done:

- How many customers do you plan on serving each year?

- How many new customers should you gain each year?

- How many customers might you lose each year?

- How much will each person spend at your establishment?

- Are there months that your business may have an increase in traffic? A decrease?

If you feel that you can, try to specify the number of drinks and amount of food that each customer may consume. By determining the volume of product as well as the value of the sales, you can plan for storage and labor. For instance, your bar has a Brazilian theme and your signature drink is the *caipirinha*. You forecast that 50 percent of your customers will drink at least two of these drinks and the capacity of your bar is about 200. This drink will affect food costs, liquor costs, and labor because of the amount of limes and signature rum used in it as well as the time it takes to squeeze the limes each time the drink is made. It isn't as quick as putting some ice in a glass and pouring.

def•i•ni•tion

The **caipirinha** is a cocktail popular in Brazil. It is made with lots of fresh limes and sugar cachaça (pronounced cah-SHAH-sah), a type of white rum distilled from sugar cane.

Your Growth Plan

Because each year you are in business is different, you need to make some sales forecast assumptions—factors or circumstances that could affect your sales. If possible, give these changes a value so you can quantify their impact on your business and also explain why you gave each factor that value so that others reading your plan can understand better and decide whether you are being realistic. Common sales assumptions that you can make are:

- A large convention is coming to town or possibly leaving your town

- Road construction happening near your location

♦ Natural disasters like tornadoes or hurricanes

♦ A new competitor is successful

> **Bartender Knowledge** _____
>
> When forecasting sales, it's easy to be overly optimistic and put the figure you need for the bar to be viable in your forecast. Consider whether it is physically possible to achieve the sales you're forecasting. This means taking your assumptions seriously (e.g., don't show increasing sales during a low-volume month in your city).

After building your sales forecast, have someone challenge it. By getting an experienced person, such as your accountant or one of your advisors, to review the whole document, you can eventually finalize it. If you spend a lot of time refining the forecast, you won't get the other stuff done, like opening your bar.

And while the projected pro forma had you reaching into the immediate future for numbers, this section of your business plan will have you consulting with your accountant and the ghost of bar profits future to see what your business could do in the next one, three, and five years.

The Timeline for Profit

Part of setting objectives for your bar is that they need to be timely—and that includes the opening of your business and when it becomes profitable. Making money is still the ultimate goal of this endeavor, and here is where you will lay out what's going to happen and when. That's why it's called a timeline.

Contingency Plan

Besides taking into consideration the sales forecast assumptions, your contingency plan should discuss the possible challenges, issues, or barriers that your bar could encounter. These things could be economic, personal, or liability issues, or other risk management challenges. A bar is a high-risk business. Stating plans to minimize your risk will help you weather the storm no matter how it blows in the door.

Funding Your Journey

Besides being a map and a large to-do list, your business plan is also the document that you submit to get funding. Keep in mind when you write your business plan that others will read it and look for different things. You may read your business plan to keep your vision at the top of your mind, while a potential investor might read it to learn who the founding management is, and what the potential growth of the business is. Others who may read your business plan are:

◆ **Bankers.** They look for data that will ensure that you'll be able repay the loan. This includes what your qualifications are and whether you can personally guarantee the loan. In general, they don't like to lend money for a high-risk business such as a bar, but you never know.

◆ **New management or potential partners.** We understand this seems odd, but if you are shy on experience and you're trying to recruit good people, your stellar business plan can help bring the experience you need on board. These people will want to see how they can contribute to your operation.

◆ **Vendors, purveyors, or service providers.** They need to know what your potential growth will be. Hey, if your business grows, so does theirs; it's a win-win situation. They may also know people who invest in bars. If they like what they read, they could spread the word to people with dollars, lots of them.

You won't need to share every component of your business plan with everyone. But if you're trying to secure some form of funding, which is probably the case, you need to send a comprehensive version of the plan to the money folks, whether they're potential partners, bankers, investors, or venture capitalists.

Most people know that this is a high-risk business, which makes it all the more important that your presentation is slick. Any savvy investor wants to show your business plan to their accountants and lawyers. You not only want this person to give you money for a risky venture but trust that you can provide a profitable return. The more buttoned up and professional your plan is, the better. This includes making sure that all your math is correct and that your i's are dotted and your t's are crossed. Remember, you are not just trying to impress the investor, but his or her advisers as well.

To Partner Up or Not

Usually, people partner up to help finance the venture or bring needed expertise to the business. When choosing a partner, you can decide to team up with someone with cash who wants to work on the business, someone interested in staying away from the operations but who contributes capital and gets a percentage of the business, or someone with industry knowledge who's willing to put in sweat equity. The latter is usually paid a salary with benefits in the future.

> **Bartender Knowledge**
>
> Partners with experience can help in the operation of the bar. A chef can be a great partner not only because of his culinary expertise but also his purchasing experience. A chef can ensure less waste of food and profits.

No matter whom you decide to team up with, make sure the partnership is drawn up in a legal contract. This way all parties involved are aware of the terms of the agreement.

Finding Your Financial Angel

Private or angel investors are the largest pool of capital in the United States. When you have exhausted your personal financing options, such as friends, family, and personal credit lines, they're a resource you can try to tap into. Typically they can be found through networking with others in the industry, but they can also be found in many investment clubs. Angel investors tend to invest smaller amounts of money in individual companies than venture capitalists do.

> **Tip Jar**
>
> If you want to keep the peace, be open-minded. You chose your partners for a reason; respect their decisions and opinions. You can all learn from each other—you just may need to bend a bit.

A trade group called Angel Capital Association helps investors determine good investments and explains the role of investing to those looking for capital. You can find these people through others that you know in the service industry, such as other owners, vendors, suppliers, bankers, lawyers, accountants, and so on.

Choosing an angel investor is a great opportunity for you to gain an advisor, so do your research. The best investor for your bar contributes significant experience, knowledge, and networking opportunities, as well as the cash you need to grow your business. Always be aware of who you're talking to about your bar because you never know where your angel may be lurking.

Tapping Into Capital

Made popular during the dot-com boom of the 1990s, venture capitalists fund more than just technology. They could fund your idea for a bar if it's compelling enough. Usually a venture capital firm is made up of multiple investors that have a pool of professionally managed funds. Money is invested on behalf of the firm.

When it comes to start-up money, venture capitalists are not the way to go. Since they want to turn their investment around quickly for profit, they would prefer to invest in a bar (if at all) after your establishment has been proven as viable and it is ready to grow.

As with angel investors, you can find venture capitalists through networking. In both cases, do your homework. Do a background check on the persons interested in funding your interests.

The Least You Need to Know

- ◆ You need to write a business plan if you want outside funding and if you want to succeed.

- ◆ When projecting numbers, be conservative—low income, high expenses.

- ◆ Pay attention to and plan for your sales-forecast assumptions.

- ◆ When writing your business plan, keep in mind who else will be reading it.

- ◆ If you decide to take on partners, make sure your agreement is drawn up and executed in a contract.

- ◆ Always keep your eyes open for potential financial angels.

Chapter 5

Step Up to the Bar Legally

In This Chapter

- ◆ How to hire an accountant
- ◆ Finding the lawyer for you
- ◆ Licenses and permits, oh my!
- ◆ Deciding on your business structure
- ◆ The benefits of a payroll company
- ◆ The ABC's of liquor licenses

Your bar is more than just a party in progress. Sure, that's the fun part, but it's also a business. And when you're starting a business there's a lot of serious stuff: real estate, accounting, legal matters, insurance, human resources, and much more. If you expect your establishment to succeed, you need to learn about all of the above. You need to make sure you learn to navigate the big world of regulation precisely. Consider hiring professionals to advise and teach you throughout the process.

A new establishment is exciting, not only for you as the owner, but also for your area. And do you know why? Because it means more money for them. New bars need permits, licenses, and forms, and are required to meet certain requirements. Owning a bar can be like crossing a minefield of laws and rules, particularly because you're selling a controlled substance.

This chapter deals with the legalities of owning a bar. You will learn how to make your life easier by hiring the right accountant, lawyer, and payroll company, and get the licenses, permits, and insurance you need. And you'll discover which of the various types of business structures will fit your establishment.

Hiring Professionals

When you start a business—any business—money is a concern. If you can save some money by doing things yourself, great! But there are two professionals that you need to hire early on—an accountant and a lawyer. There is also a service that will simplify your life—a payroll company.

Finding an Accountant

Accounting is math, and how hard can math be? Very, especially when you deal with profit, loss, and money. If it isn't obvious that you need to hire one, let us tell you everything an accountant will do. He'll help you set up your *chart of accounts*, review your numbers periodically, and prepare all of your necessary federal, state, and local tax returns. Not to mention, he'll provide accurate financial numbers—a necessary tool so you can judge your bar's performance—and help you manage by enabling you to make decisions that will maximize your profitability, increase cash flow, and establish benchmarks to compare with future sales.

def•i•ni•tion

A **chart of accounts** is the list of general ledger account numbers that subdivide into associated titles using basic accounting equations.

Business finance isn't as simple as balancing your checkbook. It's too important for you to do in between securing licenses and permits, determining décor and menu items, finding purveyors … we think you get the picture. Hiring an accountant to help set up your financial system is one of the most important things you can do to ensure your business succeeds. Here's how to find the right accountant for you:

1. Decide what you need, what you desire this person to do, how long you will need to work with this person, and what your financial quirks and preferences are.

2. Find candidates by getting referrals from associates and looking at directories or listings in industry trade magazines and websites.

3. Look at the candidates you found and compare them to the needs you identified in step 1. Place those candidates that match your needs on the to-interview list.

4. Interview each and decide whether you like her, have a good impression, and trust her with your business financials. If not, move on to the next candidate.

Finding a Lawyer

The bar business is not only a high-risk venture financially, but also legally. So waiting to hire a lawyer until the police are at your doors, ABC has cited you, or neighbors have noise complaints is not a smart move. Find yourself a good lawyer or law firm that wears many hats, because many situations require a professional's services, from basic zoning compliance and trademark advice to formal business incorporation to lawsuits and liability.

When it comes to assembling your legal eagles, should you opt for a big firm or a small one? A solo practitioner or small firm may not be able to handle your lawsuits, negotiate your lease of office or retail space, file a trademark, defend you in an ABC hearing, and advise you on terminating a disruptive employee.

Now a large law firm may be more expensive, but they usually have a number of lawyers who specialize in a multitude of areas. This means that you go to them for any of your legal needs. Another possible perk to using a larger law firm: they may be willing to introduce you to financing sources, or you may be able to use their name as a reference when seeking partnership arrangements.

Your lawyer will help you make many decisions about your business. Make sure you hire the right person or firm. Interview them as you would any potential employee by asking them:

Tip Jar

The American Bar Association's National Lawyer Regulatory Data Bank allows you to see if any disciplinary action has ever been taken against lawyers you are considering hiring.

Bartender Knowledge

At the very least, make sure that your lawyer, whether from a small or big firm, can handle these four areas: contracts, business organization, real estate, and taxes and licenses. You will need your lawyer for these issues from the beginning.

◆ **What is your experience?** Don't be afraid to ask direct questions about a law-yer's experience. For example, if you are worried about being able to handle ABC indiscretions, such as serving someone under 21, ask if he has ever had to go in front of the local or regional liquor board. Your attorney should have worked with restaurants and bars in the past.

◆ **How broad is your network?** Your lawyer should be able to recognize what your problem is and fix it himself. However, he should also know when your problem needs a specialist. If your attorney's network isn't large, he won't be able to readily consult with a specialist. And you shouldn't have to hunt for a new lawyer each time a different legal issue comes up.

◆ **Do you represent other restaurant and bar owners?** As mentioned above, your attorney should be familiar with this industry and its legal environment.

◆ **How hands-on are you willing to be?** You and your staff need to know about many legalities. Find out whether your attorney is willing to talk with your man-agement staff about ways to avoid potential problems and to keep everyone abreast of new developments in the law, espe-cially in the area of sexual harassment.

Beer Goggles

Feeling uneasy about the attorney sitting before you? Then walk away. You should be able to communicate openly and freely with your attorney at all times; if you feel that you cannot trust her or that the two of you are traveling on two different planes of reality, keep looking.

◆ **How do you bill?** Most lawyers will charge a flat fee for routine matters, such as forming a corporation or LLC. Be sure to ask if the flat fee includes the lawyer's out-of-pocket expenses, such as filing fees and overnight courier charges, and find out when he expects the flat fee to be paid. If a lawyer asks you for a retainer or deposit against future fees, make sure the money will be used and not held indefinitely in escrow.

Finding a Payroll Company

Hiring a payroll company allows you to spend time running your business rather than trying to master everything involved in payroll. Most small businesses process paychecks internally, but in the hands-on bar business, this may not be a cost-effective solution. Processing payroll can cost you hours each pay period in addition to the expenses of accounting software and training. Doing it yourself also means that you need to keep in touch with ongoing changes in personnel, deadlines, and tax requirements. That's why a payroll company is a good solution if you have 10 or more employees.

Payroll services offer a valuable alternative to in-house processing. They can provide a less expensive, simpler means of paying employees, filing taxes, and performing other tasks. In the service industry, payroll becomes a bit more tricky when figuring tips into their taxes. Payroll companies know how to handle this and other tax regulations that come up.

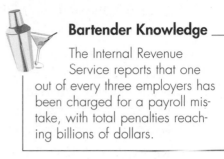

Bartender Knowledge

The Internal Revenue Service reports that one out of every three employers has been charged for a payroll mistake, with total penalties reaching billions of dollars.

Basic payroll processing services include calculating paycheck and tax obligations for each employee, printing and delivering checks, and providing management reports. Paychecks are usually issued on a weekly or bi-weekly basis. When choosing a payroll company, evaluate them on these criteria:

- Turn-around
- Efficiency
- Accuracy
- Ease of use
- Bonded
- Customer service

Deciding on a Business Structure

We bet you're thinking, "Structure? I'm opening a bar. The only structures I need are liquor laws and business hours." Unfortunately the party in progress has tax implications. That's why you need to entertain what business classification you want your establishment to take:

- A sole proprietorship is owned and run by one person. This structure is the simplest and cheapest to set up, but it can cost you tons in lost tax advantages and increased personal liability.

- A partnership is a business relationship between two or more people who have agreed to share their talents, profits, and losses in specific portions. Like a sole proprietorship, it can have tax and liability issues.

◆ A corporation (C-Corp) exists separately from the owners. It's legally like a person in that it can be sued, own property, or acquire debts. The set-up costs can be expensive; however, the benefits are better tax advantages and reduced liability compared to either sole proprietorships or partnerships.

◆ A limited liability company (LLC) combines the best of many structures, but check with your local advisors to see if and how this structure would benefit you. An LLC combines some of the benefits of a partnership with some of the benefits of a corporation.

◆ A Subchapter S-Corporation denotes a corporation under state laws with the option to incorporate on a federal level. What you decide has many tax implications. It is confusing and should be discussed with your tax and legal advisors.

As you can see, a lot must be decided, and the ramifications of making the wrong decision can be costly. Make sure you find an advisor you trust who can walk you through the process.

Registering Your Business

When you're embroiled in the excitement of starting a bar, it's easy to ignore the need for licenses and permits. Doing so can be a detriment to your business. But believe it or not, failing to obtain licenses and permits—and doing it from the beginning—is one of the most common mistakes new owners make.

Take, for instance, the owner of a bar called Copycats in Palm Springs, California, who didn't have her liquor license in time for her grand opening. Her club was based on the theme of celebrity impressionists. Instead of waiting to open her club when her liquor license was secured, she opted to get a beer and wine license and open her doors. While her theme was a good one for her area, she wasn't able to serve the needs of her customers. Repeat business was difficult to come by because people remembered that she didn't have a full bar. This mistake may have cost her the business.

And so the moral of that story is to time your licenses accordingly to ensure success—not just with your patrons but with the government entities that you will be dealing with.

State and Federal ID Numbers

You will need two types of identification for your business to the taxman: an Employer Identification Number and a Sales Tax License.

◆ **Employer Identification Number (EIN).** An EIN or a Federal Tax Identification Number is used to identify a business. You may apply for an EIN in various ways—phone, fax, and online. Check with your state tax board to see if you need a separate number. Most likely if your state has income tax, you'll have to register with them, too. Contact your state's Department of Revenue or Treasury Department to do so.

◆ **Sales Tax License.** Since you will be selling a product, you may have to charge sales tax depending on your state. If this is the case, you need to obtain a sales tax license known as certificate of resale, seller's permit, or a certificate of authority. A license or permit is important because in some states it's a criminal offense to undertake sales without one.

State Board of Equalization

You may also have to register with the Board of Equalization, depending on your state. This is a nonjudicial board whose functions are to review appraisals to see that all districts are assessed at a uniform level of value and to raise or lower the taxes to achieve this purpose. Ultimately it is their job to make sure that a uniform basis of taxation is achieved. Also referred to as Board of Tax Review or Board of Appeals.

Licenses and Permits

Without your licenses and permits in place you cannot open your doors. There are numerous stories of businesses that missed their opening deadline because their permits and licenses had not come. Do your homework and plan ahead when applying for the following.

Business License

When you get your business license, you should get every permit you think you will need to grow your business seamlessly. Check into cabaret or dance permits if you want to have bands. The reason that you want to think about these permits now, before you actually incorporate things like live music or dancing into your bar, is that later the city could come after you because you didn't get the permit in the first place. Another reason is that laws change. If a dance permit is already on your business license and zoning changes, your business has been grandfathered to still allow dancing. Think about the future when deciding on your permits.

You can get this through your city's business license department. This license grants you permission to run a business in your city. When you file your license application, the city planning or zoning department will check to make sure your area is zoned for the purpose you want to use it for and that there are enough parking spaces to meet the codes.

Fire Department Permit

You need to get a permit from your fire department because your premises will be open to the public. In most cities, you have to get this permit before you open for business. In addition, you might have to schedule periodic inspections of your business to see if you meet fire safety regulations. If you don't, they'll issue a citation. Bars tend to be subjected to especially close and frequent scrutiny by the fire department.

Occupancy levels are determined by the fire marshal. He makes sure your building meets the fire codes, calculates occupancy based on the layout of your building, and checks things such as sprinklers, smoke detectors, number of exits, better lit signs, handicap access (to the bar as well), bathrooms, spacing for the front door, panic hardware on those doors, location of exit doors that spill out to a main thoroughfare, and so on. If you're building a place from scratch or remodeling an existing location, you need to keep all these things in mind. However, if you are taking over an existing business your occupancy may be grandfathered.

def•i•ni•tion

Occupancy is the number of people that a building can safely hold.

For example, let's say you decide to buy an old favorite watering hole in your city. Because it has been around so long, it doesn't have a fire sprinkler system that is required presently, and it has a second room that only has one way in and out. If you decide not to add the sprinkler system and/or add an exit door to the second room, the fire marshal can decrease the occupancy of the bar, which means less revenue. Now as the new owner, you may have not had the $38,000 to do these things and bring the building up to current codes. In fact, you may not want to endure the expense, especially if you don't own the building. But because you are located in a spot that allows you to work within grandfathered codes, the fire marshal can deem that you will have to serve fewer people at a time, which limits your profits.

At what time you bring in your fire marshal depends on whether you are remodeling or building a new place. The city planning board will tell you what will be required. Then when you build it out, the marshal will do her walk-through and approval. She will go through your attic, look at your wiring, and make sure it is up to code. If you are properly fire coded, it will coincide with your liability insurance. Many neighborhood bars that have been around for years and years have been grandfathered. But some laws say that safety changes need to be made.

Health Department Permits

If you plan to sell food, you need a county health department permit, which requires an inspection of your bar. What does the health department look for? Surprise! Cleanliness. But besides that they will check for proper temperature of dishwasher, ice scoop, bacteria transfer, how things are stacked, if your cordials or sweet mixes are screened and capped, documentation on the wall, warning signs, and the occupancy level posted in plain sight. Those are all checklists that are at the planning department. And this is important: you need to have all inspections done before your grand opening.

Sign Permit

Some cities have sign ordinances that restrict the size, location, and sometimes the lighting and type of sign you can use outside your business. To avoid costly mistakes, check regulations before you go to the expense of having a sign designed and installed.

County Permits

County governments often require essentially the same types of permits and licenses as cities. If your bar is outside any city or town's jurisdiction, these permits apply to you. The good news: county regulations are usually not as strict as those of adjoining cities.

The Big Kahuna: The Liquor License

The most important license for a bar owner is the liquor license, as it allows you to sell alcoholic beverages to individuals from a particular place. No one can sell alcoholic beverages or allow consumption in a public place without getting the appropriate license. Unfortunately, how to get your liquor license is not cut and dried.

One of the first things you need to do is get comfortable with your state's Alcoholic Beverage Control (ABC). And here's why: the location of your bar determines what you need to do to get your liquor license.

Alcohol is a controlled substance. Regulations dictate how it is bought and consumed. To make sure that you serve it within the restrictions set by your region, go to your local ABC office and buy the materials that outline all the bylaws, rules, and regulations. (Each state distributes this information differently. For some states, you may find it on the agency's website.) It's worth every penny and each minute that you sit down to read these rules. Any infraction on your liquor license diminishes its value and places you at an increased liability.

Bartender Knowledge

Within the United States, each of the 50 states has a state Alcoholic Beverage Control (ABC) agency that is unique for regulating the wholesale distribution and retail sale of alcohol. All states have some form of restrictive system; there are no unrestricted free markets for selling alcohol.

Your local ABC determines the fee of the license, the *liquor license quota* for your area, how the licenses are awarded, and the qualifications needed. For instance, in the state of Wisconsin, the basic qualifications for getting your liquor license are: you must be of legal drinking age, you must have resided in the state for at least 90 days prior to applying, you must have a seller's permit issued by the department of revenue, and you must have completed a responsible beverage server course.

def•i•ni•tion

Liquor license quotas are based on population and the number of licenses that are in effect in the community.

When getting your liquor license, consider the time it takes to get it. For instance, in the state of California it takes 45 days to post the liquor license. But each state is different. Then the process may go something like this (again depending on what your local ABC dictates): after being posted, there is a two-week waiting period while the application is published in a local daily paper or a weekly newspaper to see if there are any objections in the community. Anyone can contest it for any reason. It is then brought to the licensing authority, which may be the local ABC board, city council, council licensing board, town board, and so on, where they decide whether this is a viable case or vote on whether to grant the license.

The other thing to be aware of is that the ABC can put conditions on the license for any reason (traffic, noise, etc.), but usually you don't have a problem as long as your location is zoned properly, which you can find out by going down to your local city hall planning department. (We will discuss zoning in Chapter 6.) Do this no matter where your location is. And make sure that the laws are not negating that zoning because of prior problems with that location. It is important that you do all of this research prior to buying or leasing a location, as it will keep headaches away in the future. By this time, you will have your pro forma, location, and everything in line; you need to make sure that your city and the ABC grants their blessings.

Having a liquor license is a privilege. So you better dot your i's and cross your t's if you want to own one.

Working with Locals

City officials and ABC are the most important people that you want to know about before you are going into business. You need to know what you are getting into. Your police chief can also enforce the ABC.

Getting Insurance

Insurance is a big deal and a big expense. You might experience sticker shock during this process. As you can imagine, insurance companies love high-risk, high-liability businesses like bars.

You probably want to find a broker that works with many different agencies. They can vie for your business instead of just dealing with one company. Because there aren't too many brokers that handle bars and restaurants, you have to do research. It's a good idea to ask your neighbor who handles his liability insurance.

Here's something that you would never think would happen: your insurance may dictate your theme. If you have food and you are a restaurant first and a bar second, your insurance will be lower. If you are just a bar, watch out. A lot of possible liability reasons exist: dancing, live music, and so on. All of these things come into the characterization of what you are and determine the price for your insurance. So you have to have a good broker and research that broker and insurance. It can put a big damper on what you want to create.

The Least You Need to Know

- Hire a lawyer and an accountant that you trust and that can help you in all aspects of the business.

◆ Choose your business organization carefully—it can make a difference in taxes and liability.

◆ Make sure you get all your licenses and permits before opening your doors.

◆ Get any permits you think you may need in the future so you can grow your business seamlessly.

◆ You should go to your local ABC office, buy the book of regulations, and read the whole thing.

◆ Owning a liquor license is a privilege.

Chapter 6

Location, Location, Location

In This Chapter

- ◆ Playing in the zone
- ◆ To build or not to build
- ◆ Open your mind
- ◆ Re-imagining space
- ◆ What to look for
- ◆ Looking toward the future

Location shopping for your business involves much more than quiet neighborhoods and good schools; in fact, it is just the opposite—your bar shouldn't be near either of these. Where your bar is located is one of the single most important factors to ensuring your success. You can have a fabulous idea, but in the wrong location it can fail.

There is a successful Mexican restaurant and bar in downtown Palm Springs that serves killer margaritas. Downtown Palm Springs, however, is its second home. The owner first opened the same themed restaurant about 20 miles east of its current location. Although the population was growing in that area, the restaurant didn't do well. The owner decided to give it another chance on the Palm Springs downtown strip. His business grew; in fact, he bought the building he originally leased and was able to expand his business, all thanks to a better location and an awesome drink.

In this chapter, you'll learn how to find the perfect place to house your bar and whether you should or shouldn't build. Keep an open mind, because we'll also talk about tweaking your vision to fit a location that's good for business. Time to find your dream place.

What to Look for in a Location

Looking for a location is a lot like looking for a home. If your theme starts taking direction as you walk through a place, consider that an a-ha! moment. It's a good sign that the location will work for your concept.

But just as if you were buying a home, you need to do your homework about the neighborhood and the amount of repairs and remodeling that the place requires. If the property helps you adjust your theme, that is very powerful. By adjusting your theme, you can increase the probability of making money in your location. Ultimately, you should look for the following in a successful location:

◆ Theme and location complement each other

◆ Traffic patterns

◆ Visibility

◆ Amount of space

◆ Accessibility

Theme and Location Complement Each Other

You must determine if your theme will work within a town, an area, a street, a specific block, and so on. You need to weigh where you want to go with your theme. The area may not support having what would be your key demographic. At that point, you should weigh which is more important to you: opening a bar in a particular location or opening a bar with a specific theme. As discussed in Chapter 3, if the location is more important, then you need to adjust your theme for the location. If the theme is more important, you have to find a different location supportive of your theme.

You want your theme in the most desirable place for your population base. Whether it's in an upscale, trendy, yuppie, or college town, you want to bring an appropriate theme. If you're bringing something into the community that is not appropriate, no one will go to it.

Traffic Patterns

Whether you're considering a walk-up (there is a lot of foot traffic to it) or drive-up (one can only drive to it) destination, ask yourself: is there enough traffic to bring customers to my business? You want to open where a lot of people can see your business. Sometimes you can get the information publicly in the form of *traffic counts*, but you can also sit in your car for a while and observe the traffic for yourself.

Traffic counts are very important numbers. For instance, you don't want your bar in an area that has no traffic at night. This leads us to our next point: traffic counts don't mean squat unless that traffic occurs at times that will help your business grow. If you are surveying a location, make sure that you are getting data on an hourly basis.

Understanding the traffic, its origin, and its destination is very important. Knowing why traffic is flowing from one area to another gives you a better idea about whether people will stop in to your establishment or not.

def•i•ni•tion

> **Traffic counts** are exactly what they sound like: the average daily number of cars or pedestrians passing a particular location within a 12- or 24-hour period. A traffic survey can be conducted by a real estate firm, demographic firm, planning commission, or highway department, or you can conduct it yourself.

When evaluating a drive-up destination, contact the city planning commission to find out which intersections have the highest and lowest traffic counts and which roadways are the most and least used. The city or county transportation or roadworks department also has this information or will know where you can get it. If choosing between locations, lean toward the higher numbers when everything else is equal.

After this, you still may decide on a location that is off the beaten path (with low traffic counts), but realize that you'll really need to be on top of your game to create the energy and magic to drive people to your bar. It's very hard to do that, especially your first time as an owner. It's easier to work with volumes of people around you than have a drive-up destination that is out of the way and hope that the theme brings people to you.

Start at a location with volumes of people to see if you have the magic and the ability to make your theme work. Then after you've proven both—and you actually like the business—you can consider opening off the beaten path. But again, you still need to find the perfect location.

Visibility

A great location isn't great unless you're seen by the right people at the right time. The greatest visibility happens when your site is (a) on a heavy traffic pattern, (b) at the right time of day, and (c) around people who fit your target market. Usually, these are high-rent sites, but they can be well worth the price.

For instance, we know one California pub that is on a busy one-way street. The traffic moves south and the establishment's entrance is south-facing—away from the traffic pattern. When the owner came to town, he bought the whole building that housed an Italian restaurant and a high-end hamburger joint that failed. The pub went into this vacant space. After a while of not seeing the bar flourish, he decided to make some changes. He brought in live entertainment so walk-in traffic would hear the place and come check out the scene. He creatively put all the flags of the world up outside so besides hearing the place customers would see the colors even when driving by.

He took elements that were missing and put them there. The result was success in the worst location. Eventually, he didn't renew the lease of his tenants and created a patio. Now his pub occupies the whole building.

This man is a good example of someone who had a somewhat flawed location and still made the best of it.

Tip Jar

When looking for a location, identify the problems and determine whether they can be solved.

Amount of Space

Before you began the location search, you envisioned your place and what it would be—nightclub, pub, and so on. If you want to open a neighborhood bar that maybe has some live music and dancing, a location may determine whether that is possible or if it should be a smaller bar. For instance, if you have a place that is 5,000 square feet, you are deceiving yourself if you think you are going to open up a neighborhood pub that just serves drinks. That space is too large for what should be a somewhat friendly atmosphere—not to mention that you would probably have to sell an enormous amount of alcohol just to make rent.

Accessibility

It's frustrating to be unable to get to a party when you know you're missing all the fun. You need to consider whether your customers will be able to easily get to your establishment and the fun you're creating. That's why it is so important to consider *ingress* and *egress*. Analyze both to find out how they will affect sales—in the present and future. You can play with this by placing entrances near a competitor or someone who can feed into your business, especially if they are a high-volume business. In fact, you may provide more value and more fun than that person. Ultimately, you want to make sure that customers can flow out of, and especially into, your bar easily.

It's important that you do your research about the traffic patterns around your location. What may be a great location with lots of traffic and parking today can turn into a widened street with medians and minimum parking tomorrow. Again, you need to check with the city and the department of transportation to see if any impending projects will hamper the traffic flowing to your business.

def•i•ni•tion

Ingress and **egress** are words that denote ease of entrance (ingress) to and ease of exit (egress) from an establishment.

Traffic barriers, such as the aforementioned medians, can cause a consumer to consider going elsewhere because they have to slow down. The following common traffic barriers can affect your customer traffic flow in various ways:

- Rivers and bridges
- Railroad crossings
- Traffic congestion
- High-crime areas
- Road construction
- Median strips

Beer Goggles

Avoid median strips! Fifty percent of your traffic will look for businesses that are easier to access on their side of the road.

Finally, consider pedestrian traffic or foot traffic. This can make a huge impact on certain themes in certain locations. Much like vehicle traffic, you must consider factors such as the time of day, theme of the bar, and target audience to determine whether the foot traffic is of value.

What Type of Location Is Best?

If there was a clear-cut answer to this question, then all bars would succeed … maybe. Besides considering whether a location fits your theme, you should consider whether it fits your needs. You need to consider these things: zoning laws, stand-alone or attached buildings, and whether to lease or build.

Zoning Laws

Zoning determines what kind of business can occupy areas of a city. Your city planner and your city's planning commission determine what areas can be zoned for what types of business. For instance, city zoning laws may not allow bars within a specific distance of churches and schools.

Zoning laws don't just regulate your type of business, but the activities that those businesses entail—think serving alcohol, dancing, and playing live music. Zoning laws also pertain to parking, signage, water and air quality, noise, and visual appearance of the business (especially in historic districts). In addition, some cities restrict the number of particular types of businesses in certain areas, such as allowing only two pubs or one nightclub in a particular region.

Unfortunately, zoning laws are not always transferable. Knowing that, don't assume that you are allowed to do a certain activity simply because the previous tenants did it, for a couple of reasons. The first is that laws change. Businesses already in a space can keep doing what they were doing, even if the activity violates that new zoning law (a system referred to as "grandfathering"). When a tenant with a grandfathered exception leaves and new occupants come in, the new business will normally have to abide by the new law. Another possibility is that the previous tenants may have a zoning variance, or an exception to zoning laws. This won't apply to you if you take over the lease.

Stand-Alone vs. Attached Buildings

Another important factor in considering location is whether to locate your bar in a stand-alone or an attached building. This is important because you need to consider your neighbors. For instance, if you are running a nightclub, being attached to a successful romantic restaurant may not be the best choice.

Lease or Build

How much money do you have? Enough to build your bar from the ground up, literally? Most likely not, and that is okay. In fact, it may be great. Usually the second or the third person to go into a location will stay because all the *buildouts* have been done. This helps because it lowers start-up costs and, depending on your capitalization, it can help you put more money toward other things, like your grand opening budget. When you buy into an existing place, you just need to upgrade. When you build up a new place, you can spend hundreds of thousands of dollars.

If you buy an existing business—name, theme, everything—then some things are grandfathered in and you don't have to worry about the upgrades to meet certain codes, or if there are upgrades, they may be minimal. When buying into a new place, you need to budget for improvements to the building if the landlord isn't willing to do those improvements for code enforcement.

def•i•ni•tion

Buildouts are construction needed to create a bar. These normally stay with a building—luckily, since to build them yourself can be costly.

If it's within your means and if building is something you really want to do, the process usually includes these steps:

Tip Jar

Even franchises and corporations can pick the wrong location. The places they vacate are the best locations to take over because they are usually ready to go.

- ◆ Check with the zoning board to ensure that the zoning at your proposed location allows a restaurant or bar (depending on whether you are serving food). If not, it isn't the end of the world. Zoning restrictions can be changed. Contact your lawyer or real estate business broker for assistance.

- ◆ Obtain a site approval from the planning board or commission.

- ◆ A public hearing takes place at which time people can voice their objections concerning your business and plan. Try to find out about any possible objections before the meeting so you can address them appropriately during the meeting. At the hearing, the board considers environmental impact, traffic impact, community impact, and more.

- ◆ A plan review meeting is held with a building department official and a fire department official present. They review the plans in detail for structural integrity, fire code compliance, occupancy capacity, and more.

- ◆ Make a formal application for a building permit. After a building permit is issued, construction may begin.

- ◆ The building inspector makes periodic announced and unannounced inspections of the construction or renovation to ensure its compliance with codes.

◆ When the construction is complete, both the fire inspector and the health inspector make a final inspection.

◆ When everything meets the required codes and guidelines, a Certificate of Occupancy (C of O) is issued to the owner of the business.

Bar Hunting

Now that you know the things to look for when pegging a successful location—the importance of zoning laws and whether it is better to build or take over an existing building—it is time to go bar hunting. We will discuss what to do when you walk through a building. You probably won't find a location perfect for your theme, but if you change the way you look at structures, anything is possible.

Open Your Mind

You need to adapt your theme to the bones or the structure of the building. It's best to be open-minded during this process. You have to be adaptable. If not, you may not be able to open this bar. If you can adapt, however, you come closer to not just opening a bar, but opening a successful one.

Re-Imagine the Space

Everyone has probably been in that successful Chinese restaurant that was once a Taco Bell or a McDonald's or a Chili's. And as a customer you can tell the history of the place because all of those companies have distinctive characteristics in their structures. But that restaurant's owner allowed himself to see past the previous golden arches. He adapted his vision to incorporate the structure of the existing building. If he hadn't, he probably wouldn't have been successful. You will need to adapt, too.

Let's say that you go into a defunct bar and you don't have capital. In your head, you have the vision for a high-end place, but this space used to be a country and western bar. You would need to gut the place to create the atmosphere that you want. It will cost a lot more money to do that; but if you change your theme and vision a bit to adapt to what has been left behind, it can save you some money.

Now that isn't to say you should change your vision to open a high-end country and western bar just because you found a space. But consider how you can use some of those elements of the building in your vision so you are not gutting the place.

For instance, when Steve and his partners were starting South Beach, he had to look at the bones of the building and the capital that he had. As mentioned previously, he has a name of a bar that he still wants to open someday, but it didn't match the bones of the building he had. (One of the partners owned the building.) It would have taken a lot of money to convert the space to match his dream theme. Instead, he looked at the building's character—it had been a Rusty Pelican, a seafood restaurant with a wharf theme—and figured out how he could adjust his vision and make it work with the building. Sure, he could have gutted the whole structure, inside and outside, but why spend the money? Instead he changed the existing structure just enough so that it didn't look like what was there, and he altered his vision so that this nightclub's theme worked from the moment the valet took your car all the way to the back of the house.

Ultimately, you want to be able to walk into a place and say, "You know what? This *was* an Irish pub. But the stage is in a good place; the booths are real nice; I can make this into a cool jazz club." You should be able to visualize your theme as you walk through the place.

Options Are Good

When looking for locations, make sure you have options. It will help if you are continuing to look for capital. If you give yourself three location options—one buildup and two existing—then you can see what types of capital are needed for your plans. If one is too over the top, shelf it for your next venture when you may have more capital to play with. When you're successful and wealthy, you can say, "Okay, now I'm going to start my other vision."

Planning for the Future

When look at a location, take a hard look at whether you can grow into the space or if there is room to expand. While none of us have a crystal ball that can tell us whether we will experience runaway success or a complete failure, we all hope for the former. And the space should allow you room to grow a bit.

To make sure that the location can give you what you need and possibly a bit more (the keyword here), ask:

◆ Does this facility allow me to expand my business if I want or need to?

◆ Do the existing utilities meet the needs of my business?

◆ Are there enough qualified potential employees in the area?

◆ Is there enough parking for employees and customers? Will there be if the business grows?

◆ What are the terms of the lease? If I decide to buy, is there room to expand the building if I need to?

◆ If smoking laws are not in effect in my area, will it be easy to comply with these laws if they are enacted, say, by having a smoking area outside? Or will I need to build a deck or a patio?

It's important that you ask yourself these questions to keep the future in mind. It is much easier to plan ahead and grow in a space that can serve your needs now and in the future than to move a successful business later.

One last note about finding locations: do your research and trust yourself. You can be misled by a real estate agent. The best barometer is yourself. This is part of doing your research. Walk the area, walk the block, and see how things are evolving around you. Then decide whether you would like to evolve your business there, too.

The Least You Need to Know

◆ In a successful bar, theme and location complement each other.

◆ The amount and the timing of traffic around a location are critical; study them.

◆ Learn to re-imagine spaces to fit your needs.

◆ Your best adviser is sometimes within. You have to sell yourself on this idea, not a realtor.

Chapter 7

What's in a Name?

In This Chapter

- ◆ The importance of a name
- ◆ Identifying who you are
- ◆ Make sure it isn't taken
- ◆ Creating a logo
- ◆ Protecting who you are

We'll wager that after you read this chapter, you'll analyze bar and restaurant names forever. Because what's in a name? In the case of the service industry, the name of your establishment should unlock the secret of what a customer will experience inside.

In fact, all you have to do is hear the names from the "2004 Best of New York Bar" list from the *Village Voice* and see what their honor was: Waikiki Wally's for best pyrotechnic drink; The Boysroom for best gay bar that you don't have to be gay to enjoy; MUD for best coffee empire; Brooklyn Social Club for best former Italian social club that is open to nonmembers; and Big Nose, Full Body for best wine shop. We haven't decided which one was our favorite, but our imaginations run wild envisioning the décor in these establishments, who their clientele are, and what kind of drinks and food they serve.

In this chapter, we will help you come up with that all-expressive name and tell you how to make it come to life in the form of a logo. We'll also tell you how to protect it so it will follow you if you choose to expand your business.

The Importance of the Name

Think about successful restaurant and bar names and logos, such as Rainforest Café, Cheesecake Factory, Coyote Ugly, and Duets. All of them illustrate the theme of the establishment. In the case of the two bars in these examples, Coyote Ugly elicits the feel of the movie—a bare-bones place that has hot bartenders dancing on the bar—and Duets is a bar that has duel pianos playing together or dueling against one another. Another bar example that started as a bar and morphed into a bar/restaurant is Saddle Ranch, a country-themed bar with two locations in Los Angeles that is known for its mechanical bull. Even the bull's operators have become a draw. In all of these examples the name gives people an idea of the theme and the atmosphere of the bar.

Tip Jar

Consider how the name can be used as an Internet address, and check to see if the name or a variation is available as a domain name.

Identifying Who You Are and What You Do

You want the feel and the theme to match the name of your establishment. The creativity of the name can be the excitement. Or your theme may continue to evolve as a result of the name.

A name can be many things. It can describe the atmosphere, the feeling the place elicits, the entertainment, the color, or it could just be the name of a person. For instance, inside the MGM Grand Hotel and Casino in Las Vegas there is an ultra-lounge called Tabu. The cocktail tables are low with couch seating and lights shining on the tables where later in the evening the cocktail waitresses dance on top. The name is dark and mysterious and the décor matches it. Another example is the frozen drink bars, Chillers and Fat Tuesdays. The former name describes not only the drink, but the laid-back atmosphere of the bar, and the latter describes the fun party nature of a Mardi Gras, with the colorful frozen drinks and the walk-up destinations.

When picking a name, one word works better than two words, and it's easier for your logo. It's easier to remember than two words, unless you make it the name of a commonly known place—for instance, South Beach. In this case, we modeled it after the elements of Miami's South Beach—the trendiness, beautiful models, and food. We picked the theme and the name based on the bones of the building we had to work with.

Oh, the pressure to come up with a perfect name! You might know that you want to call your bar Mike's English Pub. But if you haven't a clue where to begin, never fear. Like everything else in this book, we will walk you through the process of coming up with some great names that you can research and make sure no one else has snagged. Go through this process without editing yourself—that will come soon enough. Follow these steps:

Beer Goggles

Places make great names, but if expansion is your goal, it may limit you geographically.

1. Write down all the words you can think of that describe your theme. They can be places, adjectives, nouns, and even verbs. Also think about the senses—what you want your customers to see, hear, smell, and feel while in your bar.

2. Think of the names of some of the products that you will be selling and write down their names.

3. Break out the thesaurus and look for synonyms of all the words you have written down.

4. Use a language conversion tool to translate some of the words that are connected to your theme into French, German, Italian, Russian, or Spanish.

5. Edit your list. Read aloud all the words and cross out all the words that don't resemble the theme of your bar.

6. Now it's time to whittle your business names to only the ones that may work. The goal here is to walk away with five names that match your theme. Use these questions to start making cuts:

    ♦ Is it easy to remember and pronounce?

    ♦ Will it appeal to your target audience?

    ♦ Does it tell you what the bar is?

    ♦ What is the first thought or reaction you want people to have toward the name?

    ♦ Does it clue people in to what the theme is?

    ♦ Is it a place?

    ♦ Is it broad enough to appeal to other geographic areas?

This should help you eliminate some names and hopefully shorten your list. Eventually you want to have five names to research and make sure no one else has. If these questions have you eliminating a lot of names, go back to the drawing board.

Checking on Already-Owned Names

Before you register your name with the county or state, you will want to investigate whether the name you want is already in use. This is a good time to call that lawyer you hired. He can run an extensive search on your business name to determine whether it is being used by another business and whether it is trademarked. You should have a few options, as more often than not, names have been taken. Whatever you do, don't start using your business name without this step. It can cost you money in legal fees and possibly in lost business if you need to change your name.

Symbolizing Your Business

Once you have decided the name of your bar, it's time to decide on a way to present it to the world. It's an important aspect of your business because it's an extension of your theme and becomes your physical identity to those who haven't experienced your bar yet. Really consider your logo to be the statement to the world of what your establishment is. It's the cornerstone of your marketing efforts, which we will discuss in Chapter 22.

Have your logo created by a professional. There are many elements to the design process, and many things need to be considered when choosing a logo, because it will reflect the quality of your business.

Professional or DIY

Your logo is the cornerstone of your business's physical features. It serves as the face of the company and is the first image customers see upon introduction to your products or services. The logo should be professionally designed and reflect the quality of your business. A lot goes into the design process and a lot needs to be considered when choosing how to design a logo. A professional has experience and knowledge to take your ideas and create a variety of logos that are appropriate for your theme, your target audience, and your business. Their charges may vary based on the type of logo and the time it takes to create it.

Now, if you choose to do it, be honest with yourself. Are you creative? Are you knowledgeable about the traits needed in logo design? If this is the option you prefer to take, know that there is some help out there for you. A search of the Internet will generate thousands of websites that offer logo design software. And if you kind of like what you designed but want to polish it, you can take it to a designer. They won't get mad, we promise.

Beer Goggles

When hiring a logo designer, make sure that she is listening to your ideas. If she is imposing her vision and it doesn't jive with yours, find someone else.

Logo Design 101

Everyone thinks that they can be creative or have good taste when it comes to design. If everyone did, then the world would be a prettier place. That being said, a few design elements are always important for getting a great logo. The first is simplicity. Whatever image you decide on is okay as long as it is made as simply as possible. Logo color should be bold but kept to no more than four colors; otherwise it can be too distracting and, in some cases, unreadable.

The second element of logo design is that you should be able to resize the logo without harming its integrity and reducing its resolution. Remember that you will be using this for business cards, leaflets, brochures, flyers, table tents, menus, signage, possibly on billboards, and on the Internet, too. The logo should also translate to black and white, remaining legible and clear.

When it comes to bar logos, the first picture that comes to mind is some sort of glassware or liquor bottle. But designing your logo is more than just image. Keep in mind that you want the colors to relate to your menu (whether it is a drink menu or a food menu) and your décor. When choosing fonts, also known as typefaces, look for ones that have the characteristics of your theme. For instance, a whimsical curly font probably won't fit with a sleek, dark, modern beer bar.

Bartender Knowledge

Deciding on what logo will work will be an emotional decision for you; your first response to what you either are shown or design yourself is a good barometer to what will work or not.

When it comes to choosing your logo, go with your gut. You are going to know what expresses your vision best.

Registering and Trademarking Your Name

When you first start your business, it will be locally operated. Therefore, you need to register your business name of Fictitious Business Name with the state. You must also register your business with the county as per the Trade Names Registration Act—that is, unless you have chosen to set up your business as a corporation and your bar carries the same name as the corporation. Some states have you register with the Secretary of State or other state agency, but in most states you will register at the county level. Call your county clerk's office to find out its procedures, requirements, and fees.

The next step is to trademark your name and logo. When you are spending a lot of money, it may be tempting to skip this step as well as the step where you check to see if someone already owns the name. But not doing this also has financial consequences that could cost you more. Here are the pros to trademarking your name:

◆ You will have the exclusive right to use your name within a certain geographic area. Anyone else who uses your registered mark will be infringing on your right and you may be entitled to monetary damages.

◆ The preceding works the other way, too. If you don't register and there's a registered owner of the same or similar mark, then that person can come after you for possible monetary damages at any time.

◆ It gives you the option to expand, whether as a franchise or multiple locations owned by you. Think about the pleasure and feeling of accomplishment you'll have when your name is all over the United States.

◆ You'll get protection. We're not talking about the guys down at the docks driving the dark sedans. State governments may provide additional protection in an infringement if the name is registered with the state. Federal registration notifies the rest of the country that you are the owner of the mark, even if you don't do business nationally, yet.

Your lawyer helps you with this process, from the beginning of the search to filing the paperwork. He asks you numerous questions about how you plan on using your name. One thing that you might want to think about is: will it just be limited to the bar or do you think that someday you would consider launching a product with the same name?

In addition, you will have to provide your attorney with the following documents:

◆ Partnership agreement, if applicable

◆ Incorporation papers, if applicable

- Exact copy of the mark you want to register

- Real-world examples of how the mark is actually used on goods or in the offer of services, such as magazine advertisements or brochures advertising the bar

- If concurrent registration of the mark has previously been allowed, an example of the other concurrently registered mark

def•i•ni•tion

A written communication from the U.S. Patent and Trademark Office indicating that a patent application has been allowed is called a **notice of allowance**.

- Copy of past or present certificate of registration and/or *notice of allowance*

- Opinions, reports, or decisions of the Patent and Trademark Office on past applications or registrations of the mark

The Least You Need to Know

- Your name tells others what to expect at your bar.

- When picking a name, one word is better than two.

- Do your homework and make sure no one is using your name before you start using it.

- Create a logo that you can design your bar with.

- Register and trademark your name so no one can use it.

- Protect your name so it can grow and expand with your business.

Part 3

Putting It All Together

When a bar is well-conceived, well-organized, and well-operated, it's like a houseboat during Spring Break. It's in the right location, which in itself is the catalyst to the party. Then the party progresses and gets better because of the attendees. The people create and generate an energy that moves the party along.

By setting up your own party-in-progress in the right place with the right elements to attract the right crowd, you will create an excitement that will give your bar momentum.

Chapter 8

Planning the Experience Outside In

In This Chapter

- ◆ Creating the nucleus
- ◆ Luring the customer
- ◆ Controlling the experience
- ◆ Having the top design
- ◆ Becoming a master of light
- ◆ What bathroom attendants do

In science, a nucleus is a positively charged dense center of an atom. It keeps the atom going. In the bar business, you want to create your own nucleus—excitement—to keep the party progressing.

Create a nucleus by controlling your customer's experience before he steps into your establishment—and also make sure he does. Remember, your job is to be the perfect party host by creating a fun and exciting atmosphere. In this chapter, we will help you attract the customers' attention, lure them to your establishment, and create an atmosphere that fosters nucleus movement and eventually growth.

Outside Looking In

We keep talking about "the party in progress." A good party creates excitement even before you walk into it. If you want your bar to do this, start by evaluating the experience from the curb up. Think of it like *curb appeal* in real estate. You want to create that for your bar. How you do that depends on whether your location is a walk-up or a drive-up location.

def•i•ni•tion

Curb appeal is the first impression that a building gives from the street.

No matter what the destination, some things universally make for curb appeal. Your sign is important; it should draw people in and reflect your theme. It should be your logo, unless it is cost-prohibitive or city permits will not allow it.

Then look at the front of your building, especially the front doors. It's important to keep this area spotless and clean even if it's not your side of the sidewalk. Who cares if part of it is the city's or another owner's; you want to make sure everything around your establishment is clean and well kept. Walking in the door, the carpet should be vacuumed, the plants should be taken care of, and the door host or cashier area should be clean.

Make sure there is a nice ingress and egress flow. Who wants to try to make their way through a crowd to get in or even try to figure out how to get attention so they can get in? If your building is busy and you have a line, you want to have ropes set up prior to the minute you open up so people know which way to go in and which way to go out. Keep the flow in and out proper and organized.

You must be meticulous from the curb up; everything should be just right. People notice little things—any trash on the floor, the approachability, and so on—and they want the experience to be enjoyable from the moment they see your bar. And so do you.

Worth the Drive

In a drive-up, you physically have to drive, park, get out, and walk up. No sidewalks, stores, or retail shops are connected to it. There's no foot traffic alongside it.

A good example of creating excitement for a drive-up is a popular nightclub from the 1980s called Pompeii. This stand-alone location in southern California had a volcano out front that would erupt, similar to the Mirage Hotel & Casino on the Las Vegas Strip. When you approached the building from the highway, you could see the laser light show piercing through the long, tinted windows that wrapped around the front of the building. A valet greeted you at the front of the building and opened your door when you stopped. You walked into the building on a red carpet and underneath a canopy of fire torches. It was a dramatic entryway. On busy holiday weekends, there would be a VIP line wrapped around the volcano, and the regular line wrapped down toward the highway.

Customers should experience your bar before they reach the front doors. If it is a drive-up location, you should plan your customers' experience to happen as they're driving up. That means you need to design the outside areas—driveway, valet, even where the line is going to be—to reflect your theme. All of this is important for curb appeal.

Stroll In

For a walk-up destination, you must create what the people want. And creating the experience for each person before he or she walks in the doors can be a lot of fun.

One way of doing this is live music. People hear the music and it attracts their attention, so they look. If it's music that they like, it may draw them closer to see people inside or, if you have a patio, people on the patio enjoying food, music, and libations.

Another way of drawing people is with your theme and décor. For example, we know of a bar that is located on the second floor of a building on a busy downtown street. A spiral staircase and music playing draws your attention upward. When you look up, you see a motorcycle hanging, with the logo incorporated into it. It makes you want to take a look. The bar is like a museum of different motorcycles. You're drawn to the place because your interest has been piqued and you're a bit fascinated.

If your location is a walk-up, make sure the potential patrons get a part of the experience before they walk in the doors—especially if you have a patio and are located on the main thoroughfare. When people see others enjoying the experience, that is

Bartender Knowledge

When trying to attract people to your bar with music, try to select a music style that resonates with everyone if your theme will allow it. For example, everyone understands 1980s music, the young and the old, and it's clean music.

Tip Jar

Patios serve two purposes: they show outsiders the fun that they could be having in your bar and they allow you to comply with smoking laws.

the draw from the curb. You want people to walk in and say, "Hey! What's going on here?" so your door host can answer: "Live entertainment, Disco Inferno on stage now, and there will be a DJ later." They may ask more questions, such as "Do you serve dinner or a late-night menu?" or "Could we see a menu?" or "Is there a cover charge?" And just like that, their experience has begun.

Control the Experience

You want to control the experience and perception of the guests even before they step in. To do this, you need to establish a nucleus.

The nucleus is the energy you create for the bar. It starts early and builds throughout the night. Direct this in a variety of ways: VIP passes, happy hours, and seating of customers as they come in.

Bartender Knowledge

VIP passes or cards establish a nucleus by filling your bar or club by a certain time or, in the case of the cards, by filling it with regulars. Passes save the user from paying the cover charge if she comes to the club by a certain time. Cards allow regulars to pay a one-time or yearly fee and gain certain privileges, like not waiting in line.

You need a good greeter—whether he or she works as a hostess, a door host, a valet, or a bartender. Remember: the first impression is everything. You only get one chance to make a first impression.

You don't want people to walk in like lost puppy dogs; you want to grab them, entertain them, and bring them to the bar or their table. If you're running an Irish pub, have a cocktail waitress or a bartender say "Hey, how are you? Welcome to Flaherty's!"

Or, if you run a nightclub, the hostess leads guests to a table. After the guests are seated, the hostess should immediately make eye contact with the server to make sure these people will get good service and won't get forgotten in a corner.

A good hostess and your crew work hand in hand to manage your nucleus. By having her seat the customers, she's balancing the areas around the dance floor and balancing the service areas. This ensures that customers receive proper treatment, namely good service and etiquette. This also allows each server to balance their stations and manage the guests' experience.

Know where you're going to put them ahead of time—don't play a guessing game. Creating a nucleus in your favor for the rest of the evening is a building-block game.

The goal is to even out the workforce in each section, which keeps the help happy, and the entertainment (DJ or band) will work the crowd better because they're evenly placed throughout the room. That's what it means to create your nucleus.

Another way that seating helps create a nucleus is by fostering a positive perception in the passersby. Let's say that your location has large windows. You don't want people to drive by and think your bar is empty. By using a hostess or a cocktail waitress to lead guests to all the tables against the window first, you position the nucleus of your crowd properly to encourage more people to come in. Now when people drive by, it will look busy.

Creating Ambience

Ambience is the positive environment that causes the nucleus to multiply. Based on your bar's theme, your design, lighting, music, and uniforms will determine the success of your bar. If you tie all of these things together so they interact smoothly, you will stand out from your competition.

Décor

Your theme and building will dictate your décor. Your choice of colors and textures can help you create a space that is rich and multidimensional. Really play up your theme. For instance, when Steve opened the nightclub South Beach, the bones of the building were big wooden beams with a very wharflike feel. With the theme of South Beach in mind, he painted the whole place (including the ceiling) with purple and other vibrant colors. The structure of the booths and chairs and even lounge chairs had the Art Deco lines of Miami's South Beach.

Tip Jar _____

Make your bar the focal point of your décor. By doing that, you draw the customer to it. The result is more sales.

Ambient Lighting

Lighting is just as important as your décor. You must have proper lighting safely illuminating walkways and exits. But lighting also plays a crucial role in the interior look of the establishment. We've seen some great interiors and poor lighting.

Lighting can transform a space. For instance, placement on the wall—low, high, or at midrange—has different effects. Place the lighting high when displaying pictures, or behind something to accent a wall. You can shine lights on curtains to separate sections. The key is to light every corner of your establishment.

If your lighting is too bright, you lose ambience; if it's too dark, you can't see the menu. Sort out your lighting before you open. Layers of lighting also help create the atmosphere. Think of photos of 1940s nightclubs, where each table had a light. Go into establishments today; see if they have candles on each table to provide a glow and movement to the room.

Beer Goggles

Before you get into that major do-it-yourself project, price and itemize everything. Need 25 lamps? Are fans incorporated into your theme? Are they specialty fans? Itemize so you know the cost before you do it all; otherwise, you can easily go over budget.

Tip Jar

The fire laws require all lighting be hardwired in— that is, plugged directly into the outlets. You're not allowed to use power strips or extension cords. Consider this when determining what fixtures to put in your place.

How do you make all of this possible when you thought good lighting was a couple of lamps? First, go to a lamp store and become familiar with lighting options. See how they distribute light. Take notes.

Then, if you don't have money, take a look at schematics of the electrical plan. If you don't have one, you can go to the city planning office; they have the building permit, which usually includes a floor plan and an electrical plan. The plan will show you where the outlets are located. Now evaluate how you can pull power to overhead or wall lighting. Also decide types of lights you want to use elsewhere. Hire an electrician and tell him your ideas, and show him the electrical plan. He'll tell you whether it is feasible or not.

Now that you have your electrical plan and know where all your outlets are, after enlisting the help of an electrician, you can return to the lighting store with a purpose. See how much your vision costs and then go to the web and check for cheaper prices.

Lighting a dance floor is another dimension. At that point, you may need to hire a lighting consultant. because a mirrored ball isn't going to be effective in a large night-club. The light show becomes entertainment.

Uniforms

Your employees create the guests' first experience in your bar. They introduce your theme and your décor. Not to mention, what they wear helps set the tone of the environment. Neighborhood bars may have their employees wear t-shirts with the bar's logo on them with either jeans or black pants, eliciting a casual atmosphere. A sports bar may have their employees wear sports jerseys depending on the season. In a night-club, the cocktail waitresses are usually scantily clad.

You will need to think about uniforms for each layer of your staff, from your hostess to cocktail servers to food servers. You may also want to change the uniforms depending on the time of day. For instance, food servers more trained to service someone who's dining versus having cocktails need a more professional outfit—a standard in the industry as far as dining. The cocktail servers, the girls serving cocktails after 9 P.M., would have a whole different look.

Ultimately with uniforms think of the theme of your establishment, but also consider some other things. Sex appeal is one of them. Depending on your bar, skimpier clothing may draw a customer in. Look at the restaurant and bar Hooters. They're known for their orange short-short, tight-tank-top-wearing waitresses. In this case, the uniforms are the center of the theme.

Another issue is color. You want to match the décor. In the earlier South Beach example, bartenders wore purple shirts. Colors were very coordinated, because Miami's South Beach is a colorful place. Think of choosing uniforms as painting a picture. You have created the masterpiece that is the décor and the final pièce de résistance is to place people in it. They enhance the picture and make it better. This is one of the final decisions before everything comes together.

Music

Choose what music to play in your establishment by evaluating your demographic. We discussed earlier how music creates energy and excitement to draw people into your bar. Knowing who you want as your customers helps you choose music that will attract them. For instance, if you want an urban clientele, you may play hip-hop and rap music. If you want to draw in college students, you may play a mixture of hip-hop, alternative rock, and popular rock. If you want to attract the cool and hip, world music might be the way to go. Ultimately, your music should still fit into your theme.

Bathrooms

The bathroom, believe it or not, is also part of the experience and the party in progress. Everyone pees, right?

Your theme and décor shouldn't stop at the restroom doors. One great example of a theme translating into the bathrooms is the ESPN Zone chain of restaurants. Each stall has a television tuned to one of the ESPN networks. But décor isn't the only thing to consider about your restrooms.

You also want the bathrooms to be nice, beautifully designed, and *clean*. How many times have you gone into a beautiful place only to go into the bathroom and find papers on the floor and the soap and towel dispensers empty? That's a bad experience. Keep this chaotic area clean and orderly by scheduling regular checks and instilling an employee mind-set that each time they use the restrooms they make sure they're tidy.

If you run a high-end bar or nightclub, you should schedule bathroom attendants on Friday and Saturday nights. They add class to the atmosphere, but as an owner you know that having bathroom attendants is the trick to keeping law and order inside the bathroom. Bathroom attendants stock the towels and toiletries, provide hairspray, mouthwash, gum, cologne, perfume, or anything else to make the customer's experience a nice one. And at the same time, make sure it is clean and orderly.

Your bathroom attendants should also make sure that nothing naughty is going on. If the police department suspects drug use in your establishment, you can let them know that you monitor the bathrooms. Put a radio on these people so if something does develop, like a fight, security is notified immediately and can respond swiftly.

You would hire bathroom attendants either as employees or as independent contractors. They usually make very good tips. You have to hand-choose these people, because there are not a lot of them; you have to really search.

The Least You Need to Know

- Curb appeal doesn't just apply to real estate; it's also the lure that gets your customer in the door.

- Lighting can make or break the ambience you are trying to create.

- Uniforms should complement the décor.

- The bathroom is also part of the experience; don't neglect it.

The Importance of Floor Plans

In This Chapter

◆ Carving out the bar

◆ Making way for the entertainers

◆ Deciding where everything will go

◆ Getting ready to pour

◆ Keeping the work flowing

◆ Setting up the kitchen

Think about the roads and the highways that you travel on each day. For the most part, everything flows nicely. Everyone drives on the right side of the road and there is order. Unfortunately, people don't move around a bar in this type of matter. Thank goodness! That would make for a boring establishment.

Your floor plan should facilitate easy ingress and egress and movement by placing your bar, stage, and dance floor in places that best suit your bar's theme and needs. Whether you're taking over a defunct bar or looking at four walls, it's easier to achieve this than you might think.

Carving Out the Bar

Your bar is your focal point. When your customers walk into your establishment, they should see the bar in all its glory. And your entrance will determine where the bar is.

You want the bar in a good position. Very similar to walking into a diner by yourself and going to the counter, you want your customers to do the same thing. Bar size and setup are important; it should coincide with the size of the room. You don't want a huge bar and nowhere to sit. You want it proportioned properly.

You also should consider bar storage. For instance, if you're taking on a defunct establishment and the bar has those old-style hanging cabinets above it, do you need storage above your head that blocks the bartender and back end of the bar? It might open up the room to take that storage out and just have the back bar—the area behind the bar—for storage. Some people see taking that out to be a major change. But it is more important to see the back of your bar and give it more definition so you can entice the customer to sit at it. Find other storage for liquor.

Tip Jar

Use the wall behind the bar to entice your customer. Successful ideas include the use of flat-screen televisions, waterfalls, or even liquor bottles displayed in a cool manner.

Bartender Knowledge

To create energy in your establishment, place your bar so it is open to and accessible from anywhere in your establishment. If you have two, one could be an indoor/outdoor (if it's a walk-up destination) or two separate bars.

The bar's placement contributes to the theme and the patrons' enjoyment. If you're building up from four walls—taking an empty shell and decorating the interior—then you have the liberty of designing a bar that best suits your theme. For example, take a bar in Las Vegas, Rum Jungle. Their bar is placed right where you walk in and divides the room into a dining room and bar. The bar goes all the way up to the ceiling with different types of rums, and in the middle they have a runway where girls can dance between the liquor. The bar here is part of the show and helps define the theme.

Depending on how you use it as a focal point, you can plan your seating around it. You can provide tier seating from the farthest point from your bar and stage to allow everyone to see and experience the epicenter of your establishment. The bar's focal point and the use of tiers are especially important if you are taking over a defunct establishment. Utilizing these things can help make people come in and see your place is not the business that used to be there.

To understand the importance of a bar to the energy of the establishment, just look at some of the floor plans of popular chain restaurants, such as P.F. Chang's and the Cheesecake Factory. Everything is wide open to create energy. Both open floor plans use the bar as a focal point with the seating all around. You can eat and drink at the bar, and at the same time, if you want a table, you can still see the bar and what excitement it might have behind it.

The Floor Plan

If the bar is the focal point, the stage and dance floor are the center of the fun. If you're thinking about bringing in local talent, stand-up comedy, or other forms of entertainment that don't involve dancing, you should still plan for the possibility of a dance floor. You never know how your business will evolve, and if you think about it, it is easier to do in the beginning rather than when the time comes. Place the stage now, as if it would expand into a dance floor later, and plan for at least two ways around it. Or put the stage in a corner, where there's tables around it, and eventually those tables could be moved back.

Depending on the point of entry and the location of the kitchen, your stage and dance floor should stand opposite your bar. You want to be able to walk around the dance floor on at least three sides. If your place is large enough to allow seating on all four sides, that's incredible; but seating on at least two sides is good, and on three sides is great. What you don't want to do is make your dance floor an afterthought by placing it in the corner and having the stage across the room.

Tip Jar

If your flooring is all wood and you place your stage properly, it is easy to create a dual area. Put tables down for eating, and at a certain time, move the tables so it's the dance area. This especially works well for small places.

Ultimately, thinking about traffic patterns in your establishment, you want to make sure that the dance floor and stage don't butt up to the kitchen, or really even the bar (though it has been done). Servers carrying food and drinks among dancers is a nightmare. On the other hand, servers carrying food in front of the entertainment can be rude, depending on what the talent is. You should take all that into consideration, because work paths are important. They affect the effectiveness and the efficiency of your staff as well as the safety of the staff and the customer.

Lining Up the Bar

How you organize your back bar is called your line—in kitchens and bars. It's where your equipment will be placed. The line in your bar depends on how many *wells* you have. And the number of wells you have is determined by the size of the bar. How many wells can you put in? A good-size well is 4 feet wide. If you have a good-size bar (about 12 feet), you could have two bartenders working out of two wells. You can't put too many people in a small place—they'll bump into each other.

def•i•ni•tion

The **well** is where bartenders make the cocktails and servers place drink orders and garnish the cocktails. A well consists of the ice bin, speed rack (where the most-used liquors are kept for quick access by the bartender), and three sink areas for washing glasses.

You should have a service well on the side close to the wall so you have two wells and two service areas for each side for each bartender. So when a waitress comes up, it's cordoned off as the station.

You could determine the number of wells you can have by occupancy. Ultimately you don't want the bar to be a pressure cooker because customers are three to four deep waiting for drinks. But you can take a little pressure off the main bar by setting up another bar across the room to offset traffic. Doing this allows you to give better service to your clientele.

Before you bring in another bar, see if you fill the place up and you feel the customers are not getting the service they need. Or even on the other side of the bar, when a waitress goes to the well, if she's not getting enough help from the bartender because he is serving his own customers. If you get to a point like that, you can put in a portable bar on the other end of the room and just serve either shots or beer and wine from there.

Meeting the Bartender's Needs

As for what the bartender needs to pour drinks all night: your well liquor will be in your speed rack, which is usually in front of him. And behind him, the call liquors (see Chapter 12) are on the shelf below, and premiums are displayed above. Glassware is stacked against the back wall or off to the side; those used immediately will be in front. Unfortunately, margarita and martini glasses are not stackable.

Beer Goggles

Don't get lured into buying cool-looking glassware that isn't stackable. If you buy the wrong glassware, you'll use more space.

Anticipating that you will run out of something at the beginning of the night will determine how much the bartender or the barback, the person who assists the bartender but does not pour drinks, will need to replenish during the evening. Before opening, take a look at the levels of liquor in your bottles. You might see one down almost to a quarter or eighth of a bottle; bring a bottle from the liquor room to have on hand as a backup.

Bar Logistics

Unfortunately, no matter where you place the bar, you're going to walk through some people when you're restocking it or refilling the ice bins.

Ideally you have a walk-in cooler you can open up behind the bar, the ice machine to the side, and so on, so you're all self-contained at the back wall of the bar. This allows bartenders to replenish the bar throughout the night without having the workflow go through the party you have created.

But it doesn't usually turn out that way. The reason is space. Even if you're building up, installing a walk-in behind the bar adds another 6 to 9 feet to a bar that's probably already 12×5 feet, so your bar really sticks out. Not necessarily the best thing.

Every situation requires different positioning; the best arrangement is behind the bartender—if there's room.

Setting Up the Kitchen

If you're taking over an existing kitchen, placement is already determined for you. If you are looking at four walls and you can decide where the kitchen will go, place it on the same wall as your bar, so your bar will butt up to the kitchen. It makes things very convenient. For instance, it can put refrigerators and walk-ins closer, which can make for an efficient use of space.

Your theme and its menu will determine the actual setup of your kitchen. If you are serving typical bar fare of fries, burgers, and chicken wings, your kitchen will be set up differently than if you just served desserts or sushi. Another factor in kitchen setup is if you have a chef or not. Chefs are very particular about how their kitchens are arranged and what equipment their kitchens have. We will discuss kitchen equipment more in Chapter 10.

Beer Goggles _____

If you hire a chef, do it early in the process. You don't want to create a kitchen that your chef hates.

The Least You Need to Know

- ◆ The bar should be the focal point of your establishment's floor plan.

- ◆ The closer the bar is to the kitchen or the back of the house, the better.

- ◆ Dance floor and stage areas should have two to four sides of seating around them.

- ◆ Always consider workflow when deciding where the bar, kitchen, and stage should go in relation to each other.

- ◆ How many wells you have determines your actual bar size; you can always add more if you need them.

- ◆ The kitchen line will change to fit your menu and the preferences of a chef.

Equipping Your Venue

In This Chapter

- ◆ Gotta have it
- ◆ Looking at all the party glasses
- ◆ The perils of keeping equipment
- ◆ To buy or to rent
- ◆ Finding the goods

When you're sitting at the bar sipping your drink, do you ever look at the equipment? You really don't need much to have a good working bar. Technology has made things simpler—guns that measure shots, blenders that easily and quickly blend frothy drinks, and so on. But for the most part, you can make do with just a well and some glassware.

The bar isn't just the focal point—it is the place where everything happens, regardless of the establishment's theme. So what do you need to make the magic happen? What will you need so your staff can provide stellar service? These are not scientific problems; they are commonsense questions that you should ask yourself before equipping your bar.

This chapter will tell you what you need to run your bar smoothly, from Ansel Systems to walk-ins. We will also discuss whether to rent or buy.

What You Can't Live Without

We all have something we can't do without, whether it's our family's baklava recipe or our favorite pet. It's the same way with a bar.

At the Bar

Do you at least have a bar? You know, that big counterlike thing that people either stand or sit at? That's your first must-have item. You might as well open something else if you don't get it.

You will need all the small things that good bartenders have—wine openers, beer openers, zesters. But we are going to focus on what your bar needs to function properly. We start with that bar. It houses the other ultra-important components of the bar: the well station that includes, but is not limited to, a *speed rack*, ice bin, and a three-lined sink for cleaning dirty dishes. Without a true bar, these things are out in the open.

def•i•ni•tion

A **speed rack** is a rack at thigh level where the most-used liquors are kept for quick access by the bartender.

That basic setup with an addition of glassware will get you pouring drinks. Add a gun (distributors such as Pepsi and Coca-Cola will provide the gun if you buy their product) with mixers such as cola, diet cola, lemon-lime soda, ginger-ale, tonic, and soda water and productivity just went up a bit.

Now it is time to shake up your bar offerings by adding reach-in refrigerators. These are also essential because they keep mixes cool and can increase your selection by housing bottled beers (and tap, if needed), white wines, champagne, and mixers such as Red Bull. They can also add a bit of service, as you can place glasses in them to chill. Mmmm … nice frosty beer mugs. You should also have a good, quiet blender behind the bar.

You could easily open your bar with these few pieces of equipment. But if you have money, consider installing the chiller refrigerator; the metered well gun, to keep spillage to a minimum; the top-of-the-line blender, if you serve many blended drinks; a mini dishwasher; and lighted glass reach-in refrigerators to display your cool items.

Your bar can be as pimped out or as basic as you want. Remember to let your vision, your space, and your pocketbook guide you through this process.

In the Kitchen

If you decide to serve food, your bar will determine what your kitchen looks like. A kitchen that is in a small neighborhood pub will be very different than a nightclub that serves an early dinner. That doesn't mean one is better than the other. It does mean you should know what you need.

If you have a small space to work with, consider creating a menu that allows you to design your kitchen so it has as little storage space and equipment needs as possible, while staying within the parameters of your theme.

To figure out exactly what kind of equipment you need, list your menu items and what equipment is necessary to make each one. For example, if you run a sports bar and want to serve traditional sports bar fare of fries and chicken wings, you would need a potato cutter, a freezer (if you choose to use premade), and a fryer to make the fries. To make the chicken wings, depending on how you made them, you would either use a fryer or a conventional oven, or even a grill, and you would need to store the chicken in a walk-in refrigerator.

When you finish, you will have a list of all the equipment you need for your kitchen.

Tip Jar

Can you barely make toast? If so, consider prepackaged foods for some of your menu items. This probably won't work in a high-end club, but for your neighborhood bar it may just save you time and effort.

What to Serve It In (or On)

If you have decided to serve food, then you also must purchase wares: silverware, dishware, cookware, flatware, stemware, and the like. Some kinds of wares work better with certain kinds of food, but ultimately they should reflect your theme and the food that they present.

When looking for wares, consider whether they will work for you by asking these six questions:

- ◆ Do they fit with your theme?
- ◆ How big or small are they? Do they make sense with your portion sizes?
- ◆ How well will the ware hold up to wear and tear?
- ◆ Is the ware easy to clean? And is it easy to pick up?
- ◆ How much will it cost?
- ◆ How easy will it be to replace if it breaks?

As for ordering, your projected sales volume, restaurant size, theme, and the type of ware you need all play a role in how much you need to order. Don't forget to order a box or two extra in case of breakage.

Should It Stay or Go?

Taking over a defunct bar may seem like a great idea in order to save money on build-outs and some décor items, as well as the large equipment items, such as the *Ansel System*, the *hood*, and the grease trap. But you should proceed cautiously.

def•i•ni•tion

A **hood** is the ventilation system. The **Ansel System** is the fire suppression system required by the fire department. Both are located in the ceiling of the kitchen and stay with the building.

If the place is grandfathered for fire codes, make sure the kitchen is grandfathered, too. If the city wants you to upgrade it because you're the new owner, and you have to post or notify the community that ownership is changing hands, that is a lot of money that is not set forth in your pro forma. For example, maybe your hood isn't large enough, or your Ansel System is not up to date. They might want you to update all of that. Or you might need a grease trap, which can be very expensive.

Be aware of extra expenditures in the working areas of your bar—behind the bar and behind the equipment—that you might need to purchase to bring the location up to code. In fact, that could be a contingency to your purchase of the place. In other words, if you're going to buy the place, make it a contingency that all these things are passed, or that money gets put in escrow to bring everything up to code.

Now if everything is up to code, you need to get the remaining equipment. If the bar is still intact with a speed rack and ice bins and three-sink basins, look it over using the tips for buying used equipment (see the following section) and see if it stands up.

Buying or Renting?

If you are lucky enough to take over a location that was a defunct bar or restaurant, then most of the built-ins are probably still there. And instead of deciding whether to buy or rent, you might be thankful for the cost savings of not having to purchase an Ansel System or a hood. But for everything else, you will have to decide between buying and renting.

Basically you want to buy. You just have to decide whether you buy new or used. The answer is both. Buying used, you will get it for a fraction of its usual cost: 10 to 50 cents on the dollar at a kitchen outlet or a restaurant supply house. And it is a great way to get what you need if you are a small place. But buyer beware—you'll still be buying used equipment, so look at it closely by …

- Determining whether the piece is dirty or just old. Dirty can go away with elbow grease; the wear and tear of old can't go away.

- Testing the piece to make sure it's mechanically sound before buying it. And sort of like buying a used car, have someone who knows equipment look at it.

- Determining whether the manufacturer is still in business. If not, parts will be hard to find for repairs. Don't buy it.

When you're building out or you're doing an extensive remodel, sometimes it is better to buy new—especially refrigeration, because the compressors tend to break. Another reason to buy new is that you have the manufacturer's warranty and depreciation value. So when the equipment starts to depreciate you can use it as a write-off in your accounting and your tax purposes.

If it is a new place and you just buy certain items, you can try to shop for used items. Say you need a four-burner stove. There's an old saying: no one will go back into your kitchen, look at the stove, and say, "Oh, that's a 1999 stove. I can't eat here anymore, it's not this year's model!" The moral: if it looks the same, pumps out the same amount of gas, and works, who cares?

When considering each piece of equipment, ask yourself:

- How much money am I willing to spend?

- Will it fit in my kitchen or bar?

- How much food or beverage do I need this equipment to produce?

- Will it do the job I need it to do, in terms of quantity and quality?

- Is it essential?

- Is it safe?

- Does it look good and will it be easy to clean and keep sanitary?

- Does it come with a warranty and can it be serviced locally, easily, and affordably?

- Is the equipment cost-effective and can I get it up and running without a ton of expense for utility hookups?

You should know a few things about buying equipment. First, you're responsible for the maintenance. Usually lease agreements have upkeep schedules as part of their terms. Also, the equipment is now all yours, so you're stuck with it despite normal wear and tear. Under a lease, if use takes its toll, you just lease another one. While we don't recommend leasing a whole kitchen or bar of equipment, do realize what you get into when you buy equipment.

Finding Suppliers

Every metropolitan area or major town has lots of restaurant suppliers. If yours does not, you may need to travel 50 to 60 miles to the nearest one. But not to worry if you live far away from everything—there's always the Internet.

In the old days, there used to be auctions. When restaurants and bars closed down, restaurant suppliers came in and bought the entire place—the tables, chairs, salt shakers, ovens, couches, anything that wasn't fixed to the building. Then you would go in and bid on them.

Today, the suppliers still go in and take everything out of the building and the landlord isn't owed any money. But instead of auctions, you just go in and buy it at a retail or wholesale location.

When Steve was designing the South Beach nightclub, he went looking for seating. He went to a restaurant and bar wholesaler and bought five loveseats and four couches that used to sit in an Arizona nightclub. He spent $50 each for these white leather and purple couches and loveseats. He then had them re-upholstered for $350 each. At the most, it cost him $400 to have great furniture to work with. So you can get some amazing deals.

The Least You Need to Know

- You can equip your bar as low or as high tech as you want.
- Let your menu guide you to selecting equipment for your kitchen.
- Order enough variety of glassware that you meet the customers' expectations on drink presentation.
- Plenty of used restaurant and bar supplies are available; shop around for exactly what you want for the price you want to pay.
- If you can, buy your equipment.
- Always rent the ice machine; it's the most unreliable piece of equipment in a bar.

Assembling Your Team

In This Chapter

- ◆ How many people?
- ◆ The key players
- ◆ Say hello and say goodbye
- ◆ The supporting cast
- ◆ Get on the training wagon

Working in a bar can be fun. Each night you run a party in progress. Like great parties, much of the success lies in inviting the right people—those with good personalities, senses of humor, and integrity. (Remember, you are running a business; it isn't all about the party girl.) And as the host each day that you open, it's your duty to get the party started. In the bar business that means hiring those people to join you and become your co-hosts—in other words, your staff.

All bars need people, and since the business has a high turnover rate you will hire lots of people in your career. A successful business owner excels at finding fabulous people and retaining them. Which leads us back to the people: good (friendly) chemistry between your employees can make for a fun—there's that word again—workplace.

In this chapter, we help you decide who you need on your hosting team, what positions they play, and how to find them and make them work for you. We also discuss some of the unpleasant sides of being the boss—drug-testing and firing.

Determining What Staff You Need

How many people does it take to run a bar? Three, 5, 15, maybe even 25. The joke doesn't work when there is no clear-cut answer, or the answer is: it depends. Unfortunately, many bar owners have no idea how many people it takes to run their theme bar properly. They probably know how many people they need to keep labor cost in check depending on what the business is doing. But they don't quite understand how many people it takes to execute their vision, giving the customer exemplary service by making sure each point of the customer's experience from the moment they walk in until the moment they leave—including their time in the restroom—is absolutely stellar.

So now our joke becomes a serious quandary: how many people does it take to ensure a stellar time for each guest? To determine this, pull out those traffic counts from Chapter 3. You need to figure out which times of the day your traffic will be the busiest.

 Beer Goggles

You will lose employees in the first few months for a variety of reasons: they don't like you, they move, they don't show up at all, and so on. Hire 20 percent more staff than you think you'll need so you're not caught short.

Hiring the right people is challenging and time-consuming, but worth it. The type of people you hire can either sink your business or help it soar. If you make bad hires, you will be constantly looking for people, training them, and, if they don't work out, firing them. Ugh! What about working on the vision? What about the fun? Hire good people and you'll have both. Do it right from the beginning. We'll tell you how a little later in this chapter, but we still need to figure how many people you need to ensure that each guest has a good time.

First determine which positions are critical (meaning you can't run the bar without them). Depending on your theme, you need to hire certain positions and possibly fill some yourself. For instance, in a small neighborhood bar that doesn't serve any food, you may only need to hire a bartender (if you can't pour drinks or to back you up) or a cocktail server depending on the layout and size of your place. But if you're opening a nightclub that serves food, you will want to hire a chef and a sous chef, or a kitchen manager and a cook, bartenders, *barbacks*, cocktail servers, and a hostess. Make a list of all the positions that your restaurant concept needs with a general outline of duties.

As the owner, you may think you can do everything and still save some money. The hard truth is, depending on your concept, you can't. Someone must support your staff on busy nights so they can focus on the task at hand: keeping the party progressing. That's why you may want to consider hiring a management team depending on the size and theme of your bar.

def•i•ni•tion

Barbacks provide support to the bartenders by stocking and cleaning the bar area, as well as any other tasks that might arise behind the bar, such as cutting garnishes and taking drink orders.

The management team consists of you (the owner) or a general manager and the assistant manager. It can also include area managers, such as a bar manager and a kitchen manager. These people call the shots and are experts in their respective areas of responsibility. If you are in a partnership, these positions may be filled by partners in the bar. The team is responsible for training the staff, building employee morale, improving operational performance, and more. They can help fill space if you are short and provide experience where you have none. Think about these positions when you make your list of critical positions.

Now the next step is to refer back to those traffic counts that you did when you decided on your location. For each day of the week, graph the traffic flow at your location. For each hour in each day, write down what positions you need to fill. Depending on your bar's theme, you may have 3 people during a low-volume hour and 10 people during a high-volume one. By doing this, you ensure that all your bases are covered during the busiest times of the day and the week. You are also keeping labor costs in check.

Tip Jar

Staff your bar using your chart for the first two to three weeks that you are open. This will allow for additional training, operational practice, and team camaraderie to flourish, even if you are slow.

This system won't be right on the money; no system that tries to predict human nature ever is. This schedule of positions is not set in stone and can be adjusted as you become more familiar with your business.

The Key Players

Depending on your theme, you may need to hire all or a few positions. Anyone working in a bar needs to be 21 years of age. For all positions, you should look for experience and check employment history, references, and, if you can, speak with past co-workers. If you can, go to their place of work and observe them. Here's what each one does and a few hints about what to look for.

Bar Manager

Bar managers do just what the title implies: manage the bar. And depending on the size of your operation and your theme, she is an essential player in your establishment. This person does all the ordering, hiring of bar staff, taking inventory, and making sure costs are in line. This position may be filled by one of the partners. If you must hire this person, however, take great care during the interviewing process.

Some states require background checks conducted by the Liquor Board. Interview candidates three times. The first interview will weed out the undesirables, the second will establish rapport, and the third one should follow the background and references check. This final interview should test her knowledge and allow you to understand how she would handle situations. Test her verbally. Following are some situations that you can ask her to respond to. They may differ based on your establishment.

Bartender Knowledge

Consider hiring a lead bartender instead of a bar manager. This way it gives you a chance to see the individual in action—her work ethic and ability to work with customers and staff. If possible, go watch her work at her current place of employment. Note their attitude toward her surroundings, her proficiency and efficiency, and interaction with others.

- A fight breaks out involving multiple people. What do you do?

- The bartender is angered by a nagging customer and the customer is demanding that the bartender apologize or she will never come back. How would you resolve this?

- Friday night happy hour is in full swing and the barbacks tell you that the ice machine has stopped working and the ladies' room toilets are backed up. What's your plan of action?

- What would you do if you suspected that a bartender was stealing?

- The drawer is short $74, and the bartender says he can't understand why. How do you respond?

- A big-name artist is scheduled to perform and the house is packed with people to see her. She cancels the performance. How do you break the news?

- The fire marshal is on his way and the bar is over capacity. What do you do?

Bartender

Bartenders are key employees. They serve your clientele, dole out your inventory, and have their hands in the till. Putting together and maintaining a qualified bartending staff will help determine the success of your establishment. It is better to operate short-handed and rely on the people that you felt great about hiring than to hire someone unqualified or inappropriate for your bar. Make sure you make the right hire.

Here's what you should consider in a bartender (and in some cases all employees):

◆ **The application.** Is it neat? How correct is it? This can reveal how professional the candidate is and what his attention to detail is.

◆ **His availability.** Screen for how many hours he needs to work, how much money he needs to make, if he has reliable transportation, and if there are any scheduling conflicts.

◆ **The references.** Contact them; talk to them. Not doing so can be a huge mistake.

◆ **His experience.** During the interview, determine how his work experience qualifies him for the position you have.

◆ **His aptitude.** Test his knowledge with questions about mixology, products, and alcohol awareness.

◆ **His demeanor.** Is he able to remain calm, composed, and in control during busy times?

◆ **His flexibility.** We're not talking about his ability to touch his toes. We're talking about how willing he is to learn. Avoid hiring bartenders who think their learning days are behind them.

Tip Jar _____

Some states require bartenders and cocktail servers to have alcohol awareness certification or food safety accreditations. Check with your state liquor board.

Chef/Kitchen Manager

Whether you need to hire a cook, chef, or kitchen manager depends on the type of establishment and the type of food. If you will just have a kitchen in the back of a bar, then you should hire a cook. If you have a higher volume of food and a more complicated menu, maybe a kitchen manager.

When hiring a cook, make sure his experience is in the types of food that you want to serve. His training should be from working hands-on in kitchens. With a cook, you will do the purchasing and your menu will probably be small enough that the cook will also do the prep work.

If you're running a high-end establishment, you may be on the hunt for a chef. This person should have attended culinary school and worked under other chefs. They should have some expertise in the type of food that you want to serve. He functions as a kitchen manager, doing purchasing, overseeing prep, organizing the kitchen, creating the menu, managing inventory costs, and hiring all kitchen staff.

Cocktail Servers

A cocktail server serves cocktails and nonalcoholic beverages to customers. She has knowledge of bar supplies and common drinks and makes suggestions to customers. You may want to require a high school diploma or its equivalent and some experience. She has good tray balance and is friendly and energetic. She also needs to be smart. A good cocktail waitress can remember what everyone she serves is drinking.

Hostess/Doorhost

This is the first person your guests will meet. He or she should be perceptive, genuinely nice, fun, happy, and positive. The first important thing your hostess does is greet everyone and make them feel welcome. The second is evenly distributing guests around the place to create a nucleus and ensure that all guests are serviced properly. He or she may also be in charge of ringing up the cover charge, if there is one, or checking identification if it is a 21 and older establishment. No past experience is required.

Talent/Entertainment

Your talent and entertainment are usually independent contractors that audition to perform in your bar. You may want to ask for references just so you know how reliable they are.

DJ

If you're going to audition a DJ, have him come in and perform on a slower night. If you have a house DJ already, ask that person to come in to listen to the performance and see how the person works the crowd. Hopefully, the potential DJ will drop off sample CDs or DVDs so you can see how the *beats per minute* (bpm) will work and see if he can carry the music across into the next song without bringing down the bpm. If you want to keep the energy high, you want a high bpm. You don't want him inserting a slow song just as the energy is going.

You also want to know what type of music he plays and if he plays only a certain genre, such as hip hop, or if is he willing to play what the house wants. That is important for keeping the atmosphere and theme in check; your DJ has to play the program that best suits the theme.

def•i•ni•tion

Beats per minute, also known as bpm, is a measure of the music's tempo. The higher the number, the faster the song is.

Live Entertainment

Live entertainment can be auditioned early evening or you can give them a slow night to come in. Usually they supply a promo packet, inside of which is a CD/DVD of their performance, song list or their program, and a picture of the band. Listen to the CD and decide whether you want to try them out for one night free to give them a chance. If you like what you see and the crowd likes what they see, then you will probably rehire them for another night and maybe continuous nights, like Thursday nights. Sometimes you can agree upon a price and present a contractual agreement to the band. It could also be a limited engagement, say six weeks, at a certain price.

If you run a larger place that features live entertainment weekly, you might work with an agent. You tell that person what type of music you want and they send in different bands each weekend.

Dancers

Dancers, if part of your theme, are usually contract labor because then you don't have to carry workman's comp or insurance on them. They must sign a waiver for liability issues. Audition dancers to see if they hold a count to the other dancers that you are auditioning and to see if they fit in with the theme. You may think it's an easy job, but it isn't. It looks fun but they work their tails off. You should give them breaks—they're not machines up there.

The Support Staff

The following positions are essential to a smooth-running bar.

Bookkeeper

When hiring, you want to look for someone who is punctual and who can come in and open up and do the day's activities: answer questions, take reservations, receive incoming orders. This person also handles lots of labor questions from the people that work for you. She enters anything into the general ledger from the night before and reconciles cash receipts. This person is the pulse of the business during the day. If you own a small place, you may want to be the person who wears this hat.

Janitorial Company/Cleaning Crew

The cleaning crew is the best set of employees to contract out. Base your decision on how many days you are open—the day you are not open is one of the days that you're cleaning.

Cleanliness is so important because the smell and the aroma from behind a bar can be horrid—not to mention it gets sticky. (When you have a busy place, people drop things.) We have had terrible cleaning crews, and we have had phenomenal ones, too. If you don't have a good and reliable crew, then find one. Usually you will have a one-month trial with a company. If they are fabulous, sign a contract with them for a year so they are in place.

If you don't have a clean place, your patrons will notice. Over time, if your place isn't kept clean, it starts to look shabby.

Say Hello and Goodbye

Hiring and firing are two of the most difficult things about running a business. When finding employees, you are looking for someone who will fit into the vision you have created and not disturb the balance of the staff. When you don't do things correctly, firing someone takes double the effort because you need to take the time to counsel them and document their actions. In many ways, you end up wishing they would be a part of that high turnover rate that the service industry experiences. But they usually drive out the good employees first. Make sure you do it right the first time.

Interviewing

Selecting employee Sally Stellar over Peter Problematic is not an easy task, but if you go through all the steps in the interview process and set your BS radar on high alert, then you may find the right employees for your bar.

We discussed many things to do during the interview process when we discussed bartenders. And those steps apply when you are hiring for all positions. Here's what else you should do:

- **Take notes.** During an interview, write down your observations of this person. It is against the law in some states to write on a person's resumé or application, so you may want to develop a form to facilitate this. There is an example of this in Appendix D.

- **Maintain eye contact.** It is said that a person's eyes can reveal their confidence, truthfulness, and character. Someone who has difficulty maintaining eye contact may be providing insight into his personality—that is, unless you're staring him down and making him feel uncomfortable.

- **Ask open-ended questions.** To conduct an effective interview, pose questions that are challenging and difficult to answer without a lengthy response. The more penetrating the question, the tougher it is to answer, and the more you'll learn by asking it. Here are some questions to get you started:

  - What's the worst thing your former employer could say about you? What is the best thing?

  - What would you do if you caught a fellow employee stealing from our business?

  - What are your major job-related weaknesses? Strengths?

  - What do you like most about working in a bar? What do you like least?

  - If you could change one thing about yourself, what would it be?

  - If you could change one thing about your former manager, what would it be?

Tip Jar _____

Have an assistant perform the first interview and, if he likes the candidate, bring you in at the end of the interview. That way when you do the second interview, the candidate and you have already met.

Some questions you cannot ask, but you need to know the answers. Here's how you can get the information you need without breaking anti-discrimination laws:

- ◆ You Need to Know: Age

  You Can Ask: Are you 21 years of age or older? (to determine if the applicant is legally old enough to work in a bar)

  You Can't Ask: How old are you?

- ◆ You Need to Know: Citizenship

  You Can Ask: Are you legally authorized to work in the United States on a full-time basis?

  You Can't Ask: Are you a native-born citizen of the United States? Where are you from?

- ◆ You Need to Know: Disability

  You Can Ask: Provide the applicant with a list of job functions and then ask: How would you perform them?

  You Can't Ask: Do you have any physical disabilities that would prevent you from doing this job?

- ◆ You Need to Know: Drug and alcohol use

  You Can Ask: Do you currently use illegal drugs?

  You Can't Ask: Have you ever been addicted to drugs?

Drug Testing

No one, especially a bar owner, wants to hire someone who may be prone to using drugs or alcohol while at work—especially if someone has a problem with the latter. As a result, you will probably want to try to test employees, present and future, for drug and alcohol use. These tests are not always legal, and the following provides some information that you need to know if you want to conduct one.

The U.S. Supreme Court has held that collecting both blood and urine are minimally intrusive and, when conducted in a place where the potential employer can observe them, are not harmful to the job applicant or employee. In other words, it could be an invasion of privacy for an employer to require a job applicant to provide a urine sample while other people are in the room watching. If there are concerns that an applicant will tamper with the sample, the employer may be allowed to have one other person of the same sex as the applicant present when the sample is given. There are also labs across the country that you can contract with to administer the test. We can't stress enough how vital it is for you to consult with an employment law attorney before instituting any drug/alcohol testing policy for your business.

Just like the rules that govern selling alcohol, each state has its own laws that concern workplace drug testing or monitoring. In many states, employers have the right to test job applicants for drugs or alcohol provided the applicants know that the testing is part of the interview process. And in most cases, testing can't be conducted until the position has been offered.

Laws also dictate how someone can be tested, whether it is using urine, saliva, blood, or hair samples and whether it is done at "approved" laboratories or not. They also protect employees from being tested without their knowledge. How is that possible? Well, an employer may not pick up stray pieces of hair that an applicant inadvertently left on a chair during the interview and test them for drugs unless the applicant

Beer Goggles _____

Test one, test them all. You may find yourself with legal problems if you test only certain applicants for a position. You must treat all applicants the same.

knows the employer is doing so. Some states allow for the employer to retest applicants or employees at the expense of the employee if he tests positive for drugs or alcohol. You should also check your state laws to find out if you are required to report results. It may be that you only have to tell someone his test was positive.

If you decide to drug test your employees, take these steps to ensure its legality:

◆ Establish a written policy governing when the testing takes place and how it is performed. This may help resolve any future questions as to whether a particular test should be conducted, or whether it was conducted properly.

◆ Establish what type of drugs you will tested for.

◆ Develop a written policy outlining what will happen to an applicant who tests positive for drug use. This type of planning can alleviate future issues concerning how applicants with positive results are handled.

Benefits of Assessment

Once you've hired your stellar employees, make sure they stay great by scheduling regular reviews. The first review should occur after the person has been working for you for at least three months. By then they should be in the swing of things.

Reviews always sound negative, but they shouldn't be. They are a tool to keep the lines of communication open between you and your employees. Tell them what you're seeing: the good and the bad actions. Always speak to the behavior that people are exhibiting and use "I" statements. For example, say "I notice that the people sitting at the bar are really quiet on the nights that you work." Don't say, "You're really boring behind the bar." At the same time, use this time for feedback on your performance as a boss. Remember it is difficult to retain good people in this business. By letting them critique you on your job and how they believe you can do it better, you encourage them to continue to work for you rather than your competitor down the street. Ask them to do this after you have talked about their work. It's okay for them to strike out at you because they were hurt by their review, but it isn't okay for you to do so.

Bartender Knowledge

Don't take what your employees say personally. It isn't your job to be their friend. You're the boss. It's your job to run your business so it's profitable and efficient while still having a good time. This is a fine line to walk, but do it successfully and you will be respected. Better yet, everyone will have money in their pockets.

When to Say "Goodbye"

Owning and running a business can be an enriching experience, until you have to fire someone. Firing an employee is a difficult thing to do, even when you know it is the best thing for your staff and for your business. But in the service industry, it can be particularly difficult because working in the bar fosters personal relationships.

The first thing you should ask: is the firing for a valid reason? Your state will determine what is valid. For example, Minnesota has laws that prevent an employer from firing employees who testify against the employer in minimum wage compliance disputes, who participate in a union, or whose wages are being withheld for child support or other garnishment reasons. In addition, employers may not "penalize" employees for performing jury service and may not "retaliate" against employees for filing workers' compensation claims, safety complaints, wage complaints, or for reporting (or refusing to participate in) illegal activities. In California, employers violate state law if they fire an employee for testifying as a witness, or for disclosing the amount of his wages to another party.

To make sure that your employees know what is expected of them, include a list of company policies for the employee to sign, and keep it in his file. This way your policy states that if there are violations of these policies, the employee may be fired. But to make this a valid fire, create a paper trail of the employee's performance reviews, and make copies of all negative reports or warnings you have issued to the employee. It's much easier to protect yourself later if you can show that on more than one occasion you issued the employee a written warning that his job performance or attitude was subpar.

Secondly, look at your motives for firing this person. Is it because he hasn't been doing his job? Or is it that you just don't like him? You cannot get personal when it comes to firing someone. It can come back and bite you in the butt in various ways—tarred reputation or legal action.

Once you have decided to fire an individual, follow these steps to make this unpleasant experience happen seamlessly:

- Comply with all legal requirements, such as having the last paycheck ready.

- Meet with the person in a private place or when other employees are not around to see the person.

- Arrange for any supervisors to be present at the meeting to back up your reason as to why he should be fired.

- Be direct with your reasons for firing the employee.

- Ask for the employee's keys or access cards to the building.

- Take care not to disparage the employee in front of his former co-workers.

Here's an example of what not to do: When Carey was working as a first assistant manager at a restaurant, the general manager didn't like a waitress who had worked at the restaurant for years—longer than the manager had. She was a great server, had a ton of regulars, and got along with the employees. However, she and this particular manager didn't quite click.

The waitress went on vacation and covered her shifts. She filled out the *swap sheet*, but didn't make sure that a manager signed it, which happened often. One of her replacements didn't show up. The general manager decided to fire her for it and did. His reasoning was that because a manager hadn't signed off on the swap, it was still her shift and this amounted to her not showing up for a shift, a loosely fireable offense.

def•i•ni•tion
_____

A **swap sheet** is a form that employees fill out when they are having others cover their shifts. A manager signs to approve the swap. An example of this form is in Appendix D.

Carey had worked in this particular location for many years before going into management and so had a personal relationship with this waitress. And because of her position, she had to be the witness to this termination, even though she didn't agree with it. Long story short, the waitress went to the regional management, there was an internal investigation, and she got her job back. And rightfully so. If this had been a smaller business, the waitress would have had to hire a lawyer to get the same result. The whole incident changed the atmosphere of the work environment.

Training

Start training new employees on their very first day. The more they know about your business and the better they are trained, the more efficiently and more excitedly they will work. This will make for a more fun atmosphere, because the more proficient employees are at their tasks, the less stressed they get when it's busy. Stressed employees don't provide good service and don't fit into your vision of every guest having a fabulous time.

Get Oriented or Introduce Yourself

An employee's first day should be an orientation. It allows you to get off to a great start. No longer are you and the employee on a blind date, as you should have met at least twice before this day.

Orientation is an employee's first real impression of you and the business, but it isn't about you. It's about being there for the new employee. It shouldn't be her first night of training, but the night before or a night when the same crew she will be working with is scheduled. Orientation should include:

♦ A brief history of you and the business

♦ A tour including introductions to the staff

♦ An explanation of benefits, rules, regulations, and expectations

♦ Scheduling and payroll guidelines and processes

♦ Filling out the required forms in the employee personnel file

A good orientation should be one to two hours in length and should provide an opportunity for the employee to ask questions.

Get on the Training Wagon

Training in the service industry is essential to ensure that employees know how to deliver your products and services per your hospitality, quality, service, and cleanliness standards and guidelines. It is also imperative to ensure that cash is handled properly, accounting and marketing are done to your standards, and virtually every other one of the hundreds of tasks is effectively completed.

Training is about tasks. It occurs when one person instructs another on the steps to completing a given task. Normally, the best way to train is to have a trainer tell the trainee how to do a task while they perform it. Then the trainee gets a chance to practice the task. Once the trainee is proficient in practice, he gets to perform the task with the trainer watching. The trainer gives the trainee feedback on his performance of the task. The trainee practices some more. The trainer follows up again and provides more feedback on possibly how to improve. This cycle of practice and follow-up continues until the trainee is an expert at the task.

Using the preceding described training may not seem feasible when you're busy, but this tactical and systematic approach will ensure your employees know what they are doing.

The Least You Need to Know

- Your employees keep your bar party progressing.

- When determining staffing needs, let your bar type and traffic counts lead you in the beginning.

- Your state may require you to drug test your employees.

- Go through all the steps it takes to interview someone: multiple interviews and checking references and aptitude.

- If you need to fire someone, make sure it is warranted and that you have all the legal stuff buttoned up.

- Take the time to train your employees right to ensure that each customer is serviced properly.

Part 4

Eat, Drink, and Be Wary

Remember Norm from the television show *Cheers?* He was the regular who sat at the end of the bar. All bars have regulars: Jim, Jack, the Captain, and Samuel, as in Beam, Daniels, Morgan, and Adams, respectively. These men have lent their names to bourbon, whiskey, rum, and beer. Get to know them and some of their more haughty friends, known as wine, so you can bankroll the daily party you're putting on.

In addition, you may want to learn how to cook. Food can help keep your guests safe as they travel from your place to theirs. If that happens, you may get your very own Norm.

Chapter 12

Mixology Explained

In This Chapter

- Meet brandy, gin, and whiskey
- What to pour
- What to offer
- Liquid inventory
- It's cocktail time
- Perfect the pour

Gin versus vodka, cognac versus brandy, scotch versus whiskey. Do you know the differences between the aforementioned substances? Most do not. But as a bar owner, the more you know about them the better you will be at training your staff, possibly creating your signature drink, and most importantly serving your guests.

By the way, the answers to the above: gin is *distilled* with juniper berries and vodka is distilled from grain. The next two were trick questions: cognac is actually brandy and scotch is a whisky made in Scotland. There are other more subtle differences that this chapter will address specifically.

Meet Jim, Jack, and the Captain

People are particular about the liquor that they drink. As a bar owner you will decide to stock your speed rack with *well brand* brandy, gin, rum, tequila, vodka, and whiskey (American and Scotch). Just as your patrons will know their favorite brands and will probably *call* them, you should know a thing or two about the liquors you serve and the brands you pour.

def•i•ni•tion

Distillation is the vaporization of an alcoholic liquid by heat; the condensation of its alcohol content is then collected and sometimes placed in oak barrels, pots, or columns.

A **call** drink is when the liquor is defined; for example, a Tanqueray Martini, a Captain and Coke, and a Patrón Margarita. When someone doesn't call their liquor, the drink gets made with the **well brand,** or the liquor that is in the well.

Brandy

What do you get when you mash fruit and distill it? You get brandy. Most brandy is distilled from young white wine grapes. Like wine, brandy is produced wherever the grapes are grown and aged in oak barrels. For instance, cognac comes from France, and Metaxa is from Greece. Many European brandies are made with fruit—German Kirsh is made with cherries, and French Mirabelle is made with plums. To do this, extract or fruit concentrate and sweetening syrup is added to the brandy base that contains the alcohol. The different fruits used are listed on the labels: apricot brandy, cherry brandy, peach brandy, blackberry brandy.

Bartender Knowledge

Seventy-five percent of the brandy sold in the United States is distilled in California. Made from California grapes, these brandy distillers must meet rigid standards.

When it comes to brandy, you'll probably sell cognac the most. Normally drunk as a late-night aperitif, it is the most famous of brandies. It's important to understand that all cognac is brandy, but not all brandy is cognac. A brandy may only be called cognac if it is distilled from wine made of the grapes that grow within the limits of Charente and Charente Inferieure Departments of France in the Cognac region. Even though they may be shipped from the city of Cognac, brandies cannot be legally labeled cognac unless they're distilled from wine in these areas.

Gin

Gin is what a true martini is made of. It is the base of the gimlet, the drink of the retirement community set. But this spirit is one of the most famous drinks—gin and tonic—and maybe the most misunderstood. Gin is a hard alcohol that is flavored by juniper bush berries.

This dry alcohol is rarely drunk straight and it's the base of many drinks, such as the ones previously mentioned. A good gin has a smooth but strong juniper flavor.

While it is thought that a Dutch physician invented gin in the seventeenth century, it wasn't until almost 200 years later the current style of gin was perfected in England. Today it is known as London dry gin. Unlike brandy, gin can have the name London or Dutch without being made in the region.

The gin you drink today is very simple and in some cases it's the same recipe that brands distilled when they began. For instance, the Beefeater London dry gin is the same recipe they used when they started in the nineteenth century. To add some pizzazz and market gin better, brands have incorporated other flavoring or improved distillation. An example of this is Bombay Sapphire. It's flavored with almonds, angelica, coriander, licorice, and lemon zest. Gin can also come in top-shelf varieties. These ultra-premium liquors are usually made in small batches and from whole fruits that can help give them a balance of tastes.

Rum

Imagine white sandy beaches and clear waters and fruity drinks with umbrellas in them. Most likely you are sipping rum. Rum is any alcoholic concentrate made from the fermented juice of sugar cane, sugar cane syrup, sugar cane molasses, or other sugar cane by-products, distilled at less than 190 *proof*. Even though it is produced wherever sugar cane grows, the Caribbean islands are the only place that makes enough rum to export worldwide. This rum is very distinctive as a result of the base material used, the method of distillation, and the length of maturation. Generally, the islands where the Spanish language is spoken, such as Puerto Rico, produce light, dry-tasting rums. The English-speaking Caribbean islands produce dark, heavy-tasting rums.

def•i•ni•tion

Proof is the amount of ethanol in an alcoholic beverage; it's usually twice the percentage of alcohol. Pure alcohol is 200 proof, meaning 100 percent alcohol. A combination of half alcohol and half water is scored as 100 proof or 50 percent alcohol. Proof is a measure of alcoholic strength, not necessarily of quality.

A little more on each type:

◆ Light-bodied, or white and gold rum, varieties have only a very light molasses taste. White is extremely popular. Gold rum is a mixture of light and dark rum and has a sweeter, more pronounced molasses taste. These are often made in Puerto Rico and the Virgin Islands.

◆ Heavy-bodied, or dark rum, varieties are much darker and sweeter, having a more pungent, heavy molasses taste. They differ from light rums because they are fermentated slower and have a special maturation process. These rums are often made in Jamaica, Demerara, Martinique, Trinidad, Bermuda, and New England.

Tequila

When you think about tequila, you either have flashbacks to the worst hangover you ever experienced, or you think of Mexico. Both thoughts are warranted.

First of all, you need to understand that good tequila tastes a bit tart and leaves the tongue clean and tingling. Tequila is made from distilling the fermented juice or sap of the mescal plant, which is a species of the agave plant. This cactus takes 12 to 13 years to mature. When harvested, the bulbous core is taken to the distillery and cooked in pressure cookers. Then it is cooled, shredded, and pressed to release the juices. Fermentation is completed in huge wooden vats. And finally, the fermented juice is then twice distilled in traditional copper-pot stills.

What does this have to do with the worst hangover you ever experienced? Well, if those wooden vats are burned to caramelize the tequila, giving it that gold color, it adds more sugar to the tequila. It is that added sugar that is responsible for your hangover. Good tequila is almost clear.

As for thoughts of Mexico, tequila is that country's primary spirit. In the 1970s, it became the fastest-growing liquor in sàles. It is the base for margaritas and can be sipped straight. In fact, the style of the tequila will determine whether it should be in cocktails or enjoyed alone. Bianco (silver), Reposado, Anejo, and Joven (gold) are the four different styles that tequila is available in. Bianco is totally unaged; Reposado has been aged 60 days to one year; Anejo is aged for at least a year; and Joven isn't aged at all but instead has coloring and flavoring added to it to make it "taste" aged. Aging tequila not only softens its flavors but

Tip Jar

Get to know your tequilas by having a tasting. The quality and taste of tequila can make or break your margaritas—the most popular of tequila drinks.

also diminishes some of its unique characteristics, so while a nice Anejo Tequila might be more gentle and relaxed for sipping, a Bianco tequila will be best for cocktails.

Vodka

If you followed the adventures of the most fashionable bar hoppers in *Sex and the City*, you're familiar with the hippest drink of the 1990s, the Cosmopolitan. This vodka-based drink is a good example of the beauty of vodka. Neutral in taste, vodka can be mixed with almost anything and not overtake or really influence the taste of the drink. It could be why Red Bull and vodka is popular among the just-turned-21 set.

Made from root plants such as rye, wheat, potatoes, molasses, beets, and a variety of other plants, vodka is made by fermenting and distilling the simple sugars from a mash of one or all of these ingredients. The key to vodka distillation is the pot or column that the clear, colorless spirit emerges from. Pot-distilled vodkas will have some of the aromatic and flavor elements of the mash it was produced from, while a column-distilled vodka is more neutral and characterless. In both cases, vodka is not aged for a significant time. It can, however, be flavored or colored with a wide variety of fruits, herbs, and spices.

Vodkas made in the United States are considered neutral spirits, so distilled, or so treated after distillation with charcoal or other materials, to remove distinctive character, aroma, taste, or color according to the Bureau of Alcohol, Tobacco, Firearms and Explosives. There are only very subtle distinctions between brands—alcohol content and price. However, in Poland, vodka is purity-graded: standard (zwykly), premium (wyborowy), and deluxe (luksusowy). Russian vodka that is of superior quality is labeled osobaya (special) and is usually exported.

As mentioned before, since vodka is a neutral liquor it lends itself to flavoring. In recent years numerous flavored vodkas have entered the markets, with fruit flavors being the most successful. But this isn't just an American phenomenon; Russian and Polish vodka makers have been marketing dozen of flavors. Here are some of the better-known ones:

- Kubanskaya: Vodka infused with dried lemon and orange peels.

- Limonnaya: Lemon-flavored vodka.

- Okhotnichya: Flavored with a mix of ginger, cloves, lemon peel, coffee, anise, and other herbs and spices. It is then blended with sugar and a touch of a wine similar to white port.

- Pertsovka: Pepper-flavored vodka.

Whiskey

Meet Jim (Beam) and Jack (Daniels). These whiskeys, like vodka, are distilled from a fermented mash of grain, but how they're distilled is what causes them to taste different. Unlike vodka, which is distilled at a high proof (190 or above) and processed to remove all the flavor, whiskey is distilled at a low proof that allows it to retain its flavor. It is also aged in wood, which vodka is not.

Whiskeys are produced in four countries—the United States, Canada, Scotland, and Ireland—and with the exception of American whiskey, take on the name of their countries. And as with wine, whiskeys produced in other countries, even though they may taste similar, cannot legally be called Canadian, Irish, or Scotch.

Whiskeys vary in alcoholic strength, from 110 proof American bottled in bond whiskey, to 70 proof Canadian whiskys, sold only in Canada. Most whiskeys sold in the United States are either 86 or 80 proof, depending on the distiller and brand. Federal law requires that the label on each bottle be plainly marked with the proof of the liquor.

Bartender Knowledge

The term "proof" came out of the pioneering era of distillation. To determine the strength of liquors, distillers would mix equal quantities of the spirit and gunpowder and then apply a flame to the mixture. If the gunpowder failed to burn, the spirit was too weak; if it burned too brightly, it was too strong; and if it burned evenly, it was proven.

Rigidly defined by law, American whiskeys include bourbon, corn, sour mash, Tennessee, blended, straight, bottled in bond, and rye whiskeys.

Canadian whisky is made under government supervision in accordance with the regulations governing the manufacture of whisky in Canada. Blended whiskys are a mix of grain whisky with malt or bourbon or rye according to the country of origin. In Canada, approximately 9 percent of the blend may be whiskys from other countries, or even distilled fruit juices. This gives Canadian whisky its distinguishing characteristic of being light body.

Scotch whisky is made in Scotland. There are two types: blended and single malt. Blended scotch whisky is just as the name implies, a blend of whiskys, and in this case, it is a blend of malt and grain whisky. Irish whiskey is the same except that it is made in Ireland.

Single malt scotch comes from one distillery and is made from only one malted barley. The taste of the scotch depends on the distillery. The traditional distillery regions for scotch whisky are Highland, Lowland, Islay, and Campbeltown. Each distillery produces a malt that has its own unique personality because of its location, its climate, the area's wild yeasts, its source of water, the shape of the still used, and any specific

malting requirements it may have. All of these factors have an effect on the individual character and flavor of a single malt scotch.

Whiskeys, like wine, have many nuances. If you think that your clientele will be big whiskey drinkers, we suggest that you work with your liquor purveyor or subscribe to a magazine, such as *Whisky*, to educate yourself on the complexities of this spirit.

What to Pour

When setting up your bar, you need to think about your patrons and what they might drink. For instance, if you're opening a neighborhood bar in a mostly blue-collar area, most likely you won't be serving up Evan Williams 23 Year Old Bourbon whiskey, which is about $140 per bottle. But you may serve a less costly cousin, Evan Williams Kentucky Straight Bourbon whiskey. Using the information about who your customer is from Chapter 3 will help guide you to what your bar should serve.

Well Brands

Well liquor is the "default liquor" used to make a drink. If your patron asks for a drink without calling the brand of liquor she wants poured, you'll make the drink with you well liquor. Your bar's drink menu will determine what will make up your speed rack but a typical well has brandy, gin, rum, tequila, scotch, vodka, and whiskey so that your bartender can make any drink quickly.

When setting up your well brands, talk to your liquor distributor, as he may have gain brands or specials on brands that you can use for your well. Depending on your area, possible brands that you can use as your well liquors are:

♦ For bourbon/whiskey: Jim Beam, Early Times

♦ For brandy: E&J, Fleichmann's/Barton, Raynal, Salignac (Cognac), Kel (Cognac)

♦ For gin: Seagram's, Gordon's, McCormick, Boodles

♦ For rum: Bacardi, El Dorado, Appleton Estate, Ron Castillo

♦ For scotch whisky: Ballantine, Cluny, Clan McGregor, Grantt's, Mc

♦ For tequila: Baja, Herradura, Montezuma, Sauza Blanco

♦ For vodka: Gordon's, Fleichmann's/Barton, Luksusowa, Olifant, Smirnoff

Call Brands

Patrons have their favorites—their favorite drink made with their favorite brand of liquor. Numerous brands of liquor exist, and hoping to have all on hand is daunting, not to mention expensive. Following you will find some popular brands of spirits that you may want to consider when stocking your bar. Start with a bottle and see whether your patrons order it.

Liquor	Brand
Brandy	Asbach Urait, Christian Brothers, Cornet, Calvados, Cardinal Mendoza, Korbel
Cognac	Courvoisier, Delamin, Hennessey V.S., Martell V.S.O.P., Remy Martin V.S.O.P.
Gin	Beefeaters, Bombay, Damak, Hendricks, Tanqueray
Rum	Bacardi Dark, Captain Morgan, Cruzan, 10 Cane Rum, Goslings, Malibu, Parrot Bay, Whaler's
Tequila	Cabo Wabo, Don Julio, El Jimador, Jose Cuervo (Especial and Tradicional), Patron Silver, Sauza Commemorativo
Vodka	Absolut, Armdale, Clear Heart, Finlandia, Fris, Ketel One, Sky, Stolichnaya, Tanqueray Silver, Vox
Whiskey/Bourbon	Blanton's, Booker's, Maker's Mark, Old Grand Dad, Rip Van Winkle, Wild Turkey, Woodford Reserve
Whisky/Canadian	Canadian Club, Canadian Mist, Crown Royal, Seagram's V.O.
Whiskey/Irish	Bushmill's, Jameson
Whisky/Scotch	
Blended	Ballantine's, Chivas Regal, Cutty Sark, Dewar's, Drambuie, Johnny Walker Red
Single Malt	Cragganmore, Glenfiddich, Glenlivet, Macallan
Whiskey/Tennessee	Gentleman Jack, Jack Daniels

Premium Brands

Imagine a call spirit but better and more expensive—to you and to your guest. That is what a premium brand is. These are the high-end cognacs, and the gin, rum, tequila, and vodka that should be sipped and not added to a cocktail. Here are a few suggestions to have on hand depending on your clientele.

Liquor	Brand
Brandy/Cognac	Hennessey Paradis and Richard, Martell Cordon Bleu, Remy Martin Louis XII
Gin	Bombay Sapphire, Junipero, Tanqueray 10
Rum	Bacardi Gold, Bacardi 8, Gosling's Black Seal
Tequila	Jose Cuervo 1800, Patron Gold and Anejo, Tres Generaciones
Vodka	Belevedere, Bong Vodka, Chopin, Ciroc, Cristall, Grey Goose, HanAsia, Jewel of Russia, Mor, Pearl, Turi, Trump, Zyr
Whiskey/Bourbon	Basil Hayden's, Evan Williams Vintage Kentucky Straight, Knob Creek, Woodford Reserve Distiller's Select
Whisky/Canadian	Canadian Club, Canadian Mist, Crown Royal, Seagram's V.O.
Whisky/Scotch	
Blended	Dewar's Reserve, Johnny Walker Black, Blue, Gold and Green, Royal Suite
Single Malt	Cragganmore 12-year-old, Glenfiddich 12-year-old, Glenlivet 12-year-old, Macallan 12-year-old
Whiskey/Tennessee	Jack Daniel's Single Barrel

Storing

Spirits are quite resistant to spoilage because of their high alcohol levels. But with most of your product, you will want your storage area in a cool, dry place. Remember that you don't want to hold on to anything too long. Inventory is money, and if it isn't moving then you're not making money.

Serve It Up

In the movie *Cocktail*, Tom Cruise was a bartender who used showmanship when pouring drinks for his patrons. And you can find bartenders today that inspired the movie or were inspired by it. However, in the real world of barkeeping, flying alcohol could mean profits that are poured away. And no one, especially you, wants that.

Perfect the Pour, Protect the Profit

Measuring the amount of alcohol that is in each drink ensures that your profits don't go down the drain. Each bottle should contain about 10 servings of alcohol. If you get less than that, you lose money. There are two ways to measure the amount of alcohol you are serving up:

1. Use a shot glass or a *jigger*.

2. Use a metered pour spout or other liquor control system.

def•i•ni•tion

A **jigger** is a two-sided metal shot glass with one side measuring a half ounce and the other measuring 2 ounces.

The shot glass method, where you pour the liquid into the shot glass before the glass, can be slow. Most bartenders would prefer to straight pour, where 2 counts = 2 seconds = approximately 1 ounce. This is just another way to overpour. To achieve the best of both worlds, you may want to opt for metered pour spouts that fit right into your bottles or a liquor control system that automatically dispenses alcohol while charging the guest at the same time. These make sure that you're dispensing an ounce and a half of alcohol each time.

Create a Signature Cocktail

Creating a signature drink is just another way to draw people to your establishment. It could be an improvement on an old favorite, just as the owner of the Blue Coyote did. The Blue Coyote in downtown Palm Springs was a good Mexican restaurant but it wasn't until the owner created the Blue Coyote margarita that his business grew and he had to expand the walls of his building. Or you could create an entirely new drink. Either way, if it's awesome, word will get around.

If you decide to create your own cocktail, know that most contain three different ingredients. The first is the base: vodka, gin, whiskey, or tequila. The second ingredient brings the main flavor to the drink. For instance, vermouth is the main flavoring of a martini, and cranberry juice is the main flavoring of a Cape Cod. The third ingredient is a special flavoring to enhance the taste of the base and add color. Examples include grenadine and blue curaçao. Finally, you cannot forget the garnish—fruit slices, orange peels, mint twigs, lemon twists— that decorates the glass.

Beer Goggles

Measuring drinks too carefully will slow your bartenders down and possibly elicit groans from your customers who want more. Try to disarm them by making yourself available and working your magic. If you don't, you may not have an establishment.

Another thing to remember when playing mixologist is the weight of the ingredients you're using, as some may be heavier than others. You will want to pour the heaviest liquor into the glass first and then layer the lighter ones on top. Pour the lightest liquor in last.

The Least You Need to Know

- Flavored liquors, such as rum and vodka, are big sellers, about 15 percent of distributors' sales.

- Bourbon, scotch, and whisky are all whiskeys, just produced in different countries.

- Look to your theme and your customers to determine what to pour.

- Liquor is resistant to spoilage.

- A lot of spillage can mean an end to profits; measure your pours.

- A signature drink can be a draw to your establishment.

Suds 101

In This Chapter

- Become the brew master
- Figure out how many types of beers to carry
- Avoid a mug of suds
- Serve up the perfect bottle
- Learn how to store beer

Beer is the oldest and most popular alcoholic beverage. In 2006, 186 billion gallons were sold, according to the Brewer's Association. Says a lot, doesn't it? If you were considering not selling beer, you may want to reconsider.

Some bars focus their theme on beer. For instance, the Yard House boasts that each location has a keg room that contains 600 barrels, some 1,000 gallons of beer, and anywhere between 130 to 250 beers to choose from. This popular alcoholic drink can be served in almost any type of bar. The secret is to understand the different types and how each fits into your bar menu. This chapter will introduce you to the vast and adventurous world of beer and how it can be a popular character in your bar. Bottoms up!

The Wide World of Beer

Beer is produced all over the world. And if you travel a lot, you might find that beer makes the world seem small. But what is this nectar that makes a hot summer day seem cooler and a bad day at work okay? This drink is fermented sugars that come from a starch (mostly commonly malted barley, but also wheat, corn, and rice).

Usually beer is made with malted barley, hops, water, and yeast. Ingredients, production methods, and traditions vary when it comes to beer. These variables help determine whether the beer is a lager, ale, or hefeweizen. But no matter what, beer is brewed, going through five stages: mashing, sparging, boiling, fermenting, and finally packaging.

Bartender Knowledge

Just like scotch whisky, the water used in beer determines its taste since it comes from a local source. The minerals in the water are important to beer because they influence the beer's character. Different regions have different water. As a result, different regions are better suited to making certain types of beer. For example, Dublin has hard water well suited to making stout, and Pilzen has soft water well suited to making pilsner, but water from these cities could not be used to make the other's style of beer.

Mashing manipulates the temperature of the water and starch mixture so that the starch converts to a fermentable sugar. The mixture is brought up to the desired temperature and held there for an amount of time to allow the enzymes in the starch to produce the compounds needed for fermentation. Then, the fermentable liquid known as wort is extracted and rinsed. This process is known as sparging. The wort is then boiled, which increases its sugar concentration. Hops are added during boiling to extract bitterness, as well as strong flavors and aromas from the wort. During fermentation, the wort becomes beer. Using yeast to turn the sugars in the wort to alcohol and carbon dioxide, the fermentation process can take a week or months depending on the yeast and the strength of the beer. Once this is done, the beer will be packaged in a keg, cask, can, or bottle.

Tip Jar

When choosing beers for your bar, make sure you select ones with a range of bitterness, which is measured on the International Bitterness Units scale.

Domestic vs. Import

Countries like Austria, Britain, Belgium, Czech Republic, Denmark, Germany, Ireland, and the Netherlands have created styles of beer based on the water and starch. United States brewers, and even Canadian brewers, have adapted the styles from the above countries to create their own indigenous types.

Microbrews vs. Mass Breweries

Microbreweries are beers that are brewed regionally. The difference between microbrews and mass breweries is output. Microbrews produce only 15,000 barrels a year. Each year microbrew sales increase approximately 40 percent. This growth trend has spurned mass breweries to buy shares of microbreweries.

Ales

Ales are defined by the strain of yeast used and the fermenting temperature. The yeast is top-fermenting and is fermented at high temperatures, which speeds the process along. These temperatures also cause the yeast to produce significant flavor and aromatic products that make the beer have a sweeter and slightly fruity taste that resembles apple, banana, pear, pineapple, plum, or prune. Examples include Samuel Adams' Summer Ale, Samichlaus Ale, and Bass Ale.

Dark Beers

Dark beers are usually brewed from a pale malt base with a small proportion of darker malt added to achieve the desired shade. Other colorants—such as caramel—are also widely used to darken beers. Very dark beers, such as stout, use dark or patent malts. These have been roasted longer. The most famous example of a dark beer is Guinness.

Lager

Lagers are the most consumed beer in the world. Their yeast is bottom-fermenting and typically undergoes a primary fermentation and then is given a long secondary fermentation. It is during this secondary stage that the lager clears and mellows, resulting in a crisper-tasting beer. This stage of the production also helps the lager distinguish itself as a cleaner, dryer, and lighter-tasting beer than ale. Popular examples of this type of beer include Harbin Lager from China, Kirin Ichiban from Japan, Molson Canadian from Canada, and Tecate from Mexico.

Light

Beer on a diet is light beer. It has less calories and less alcohol. To produce light beer, the brewing process is manipulated at each stage. The mashing technique is tweaked, and the fermentation process occurs at a higher temperature. The bottom line is that most light beers have less alcohol and half the carbohydrates of regular beer. Some beers have a light version, such as Miller Lite, Bud Light, and Samuel Adams Light.

Pale

Produced using pale malts, the most common color of beer is a pale amber. Pale lager is a term used for beers made from malt dried with coke. In fact, most of today's beer is based on the pale lager brewed in 1842 in Pilsen, Czech Republic—light in color and high in carbonation, with a strong hop flavor and an alcohol by volume content of around 5 percent. Examples of pale lagers are the import brands Pilsner Urquell and Heineken, and the American brands Budweiser, Coors, and Miller.

Hefeweizen

Hefeweizen means "wheat beer" in German. It is an unfiltered wheat beer that has yeast in it. The difference between wheat beer and the other varieties presented here is that it is brewed with both malted wheat, about 65 percent, and malted barley, about 35 percent. Regular beer is only brewed with malted barley. The result is a beer that has a lighter flavor and paler color than other barley-brewed ales. These beers also tend to be highly carbonated and will look cloudy when poured into a glass that is traditionally garnished with a lemon slice. Examples of hefeweizen brands are Pyramid, Widmer Brothers, and Red Hook.

Specialty Brews

It's the season for Pumpkin Ale, Octoberfest Ale, Summer Ale, or any one of the hundreds of varieties that breweries come up with during different times of the year. These special brews are marketing tools for the breweries, but they are also well-crafted beers.

How Many Types of Beers Should You Carry?

Beer brands and styles are so numerous that it would be impossible to carry them all and make money. Now certain beers are more popular than others. Marketing helps that. Having these more popular brands will help you make money. But owning a bar means that you create an experience for your patrons. And depending on the theme and the price point of your bar, the array of beers that you carry can add to that experience. Why should your customer face the same old beer selection that every other bar in town sells?

Make beer a part of the experience by putting some thought into your selections. Think about balance between the big breweries and the small breweries, between import and domestic, and between all the beer styles.

When balancing your beer selections, remember this: for every mass-brewed beer, a smaller-crafted beer exists that tastes better and costs more. Introducing your patron to a new and better beer may enhance their experience and have them coming back to find that brew or to find another great beer.

Tip Jar _____

Your beer distributor can work for you by offsetting the costs of table tents (promotional materials that sit on your table) and menus.

Depending on the theme and the capacity of your bar, you can start with a beer list that has four domestic brews, two imports, three imported crafted beers, and three domestic microbrews. If your bar and theme is more beer-heavy, then you need more than this. Let your theme be your guide.

It's easy to get bored with your offerings. Feel free to rotate your selection to keep things interesting. Sure, you'll have some selections that will be constant, but you can bring in local brews or imported crafted beers. Another way to do this is to create a list of specials. This will help to create a buzz and a base of beer-loving regulars who will do plenty of word-of-mouth marketing on your behalf.

If you have a bar that can sustain having a large beer selection, like the Yard House that we mentioned earlier in this chapter, then you may want to consider having a beer menu. Just like a proper wine menu, your beer menu would list the brewery, origin, beer style, and perhaps a brief description. This educates your customer and satisfies them because they have a choice. And satisfied, happy patrons can mean repeat customers and dollars in the till. But if you go to all this trouble (and even if you don't), train your staff about beer. They should be able to help your guest navigate your beer selections.

Again, we cannot stress enough that you should let the ambience, theme, and customer determine the number of beers you have on hand and the types of beers you offer.

Serving It Up

All it takes to serve beer is to pour from a tap into a glass or pull out a bottle and a frosty mug, right? Well, yes and no. True beer connoisseurs know that temperature, glassware, and how it is poured—whether it comes from a tap or a bottle—figure into the taste of the beer.

Temperature

Get the temperature right and you have significantly influenced your beer drinker's experience for the better. Get it wrong and he may go elsewhere. For instance, colder temperatures accent the crispness of beers such as pale lagers; warmer temperatures allow the more rounded flavors of an ale or a stout to be perceived.

To be more specific, acclaimed beer writer Michael Jackson proposes a five-level scale for serving temperatures:

- Well Chilled (7°C/45°F) for light beers or American and Australian lagers

- Chilled (8°C/47°F) for Berliner Weisse, a dry wheat and barley beer made in Berlin

- Lightly Chilled (9°C/48°F) for European lagers, all dark lagers, and German wheat beers

- Cellar Temperature (13°C/55°F) for regular British ale, stout, and most Belgian specialties

- Room Temperature (15.5°C/60°F) for strong dark ales

Depending on your space and setup, you will probably not be able to keep the perfect temperature for all your beer selections if you run the gamut. So keep serving temperatures in mind when creating your beer menu.

Glassware

It's easy to think that all beer should be drunk out of a pint glass, and for your bar that may be the case. But if you are considering a bar with a theme that lends itself to an extensive beer selection, then you may need a variety of glasses, as many consider the glass as part of their enjoyment of the brew. Invest in the proper glassware for each beer style, if your bar warrants it, or grab as many free offerings as you can from brewery reps. For example, pouring Duvel into its tulip-like glass will create a meringuelike head and will allow the nuances in aroma and taste to emerge.

No matter what their shape, the cleanliness of your glassware can have a significant effect on the taste of the beer you are serving. Truly clean glassware will ensure the best presentation for beer because detergent residue will immediately kill head retention, and dirty glasses can cause excessive foaming and overflow of draft beer. That's why it is so important to not only clean your glasses but choose the right detergents. Bleach or iodine-based ones will be smelled by your customers and oil-based detergents will affect head retention.

Bartender Knowledge

Prevent soggy cocktail napkins by sprinkling a bit of salt on them. Or, better yet, ditch the salt and use coasters instead, which are usually free from brewery reps; or print your own and double them as business cards or promotional pieces.

Another reason to have your glasses pour-perfect is because your glass can tell you a lot about your pour.

The Pour

Pouring beer is an art form. Just as opening a bottle of wine is a presentation that adds to the experience of the drinker, beer pouring also adds to the taste of the beer.

Many factors affect the pour: rate of flow from the tap or the bottle, tilt of the glass, and position of the pour (in the center or down the side) into the glass. These things influence head retention, *lacing*, and turbulence of the beer and its release of carbonation.

How do you make sure you're pouring perfectly? Follow these steps:

1. Grab a clean glass. Depending on the beer that you're serving, it can be a clean, frosted one.

2. Hold your glass at a 45-degree angle. Pour the beer, targeting the middle of the slope of the glass. Don't be afraid to pour hard or add some air between the bottle and glass.

3. At the halfway point, bring the glass at a 90-degree angle and continue to pour into the middle of the glass. This will create the perfect head—this is a good

def•i•ni•tion

Lacing is the ring left by the head as it moves down the glass as the beer is drunk. As the beer nears its end, a series of rings should be present on the glass wall.

thing because it releases the beer aroma. Adding distance between the glass and the source as you pour will also make a good head—the ideal being ½ inch if you are using a pint glass up to 1½ inches for other glassware.

Beer Goggles

Watch for the overpour—it can send beer and profits down the drain. The anatomy of an overpour is this: the bartender pulls the tap head, tips the glass deep, and allows the beer to flow over until the desired level is reached (usually it is with a minimum amount of head). Up to a half pint of beer is wasted.

At this point, your glass can tell you a lot about your pour. The perfect pour creates a head that is around 1 inch and remains for the beer's entire consumption. No bubbles should be present; if there are, it means that there is a film in the glass. Also, your perfect pour should inspire lacing.

Draft

If you were to travel the globe tasting beer, you would find that most beer is served from a pressurized keg. This is what's called draft or draught beer, and it is the most common way to dispense beer. How does it work? A metal keg is pressurized with carbon dioxide gas that drives the beer to the dispensing tap or faucet. Some beers, notably stouts, such as Guinness and Boddingtons, may be served with a nitrogen/carbon dioxide mixture. Nitrogen produces fine bubbles, resulting in a dense head and a creamy mouthfeel.

Bartender Knowledge

In an attempt to take the draft beer experience to-go, Guinness introduced, in the 1980s, the beer widget, a nitrogen pressurized ball inside a can which creates a foamy head. Now canned and bottled beers containing a beer widget may sport the words "draft" and "draught" on their labels. Brilliant!

One of the most important things to remember about serving draft beer is that your tap lines need to be maintained on a regular basis. If they are not cleaned, or if you have kegs on for more than 30 days, the result can be funky-tasting beer and wasted beer. Perfect pours don't waste a drop of beer, unless there is a keg or tap line issue. Learning how to care for this beer system is a profitable thing to do.

Bottles

Beers are typically filtered before bottling; however, more and more bottled beer is *bottle conditioned*. When this is the case, pour the beer slowly, leaving any yeast sediment at the bottom of the bottle. Unless, that is, you're pouring a wheat beer, in which case the practice is to pour in the yeast. For example, if you're pouring a hefe-weizen, pour 90 percent of the contents and then swirl the remaining 10 percent in the bottle to suspend the sediment before pouring the rest into the glass.

def•i•ni•tion _____

Bottle conditioned beers are unfiltered and unpasteurized.

Storing

Just as the pour can influence the beer-drinking experience, so can how you store the beer prior to serving it.

The first rule of thumb is that beer should never come into contact with heat or light, because both can destroy the beer and turn it into a skunk.

Store your beer in a cool area, away from direct light, sources of heat, and in a constant temperature environment. Beer benefits from cool constant temperatures; usually around 50–55°F is ideal for most beers. Higher temperatures and you'll risk shortening the life span of your beer; lower and you'll induce cloudiness. A good rule of thumb: the higher the alcohol, the higher the temperature; the lower the alcohol, the lower the temperature.

A beer's transformation into a skunk happens usually when the beer has been light-struck—when the beer has been exposed to sunlight for a period of time. When this happens, the hop molecules are torn apart and left to bind with sulfur atoms, hence the skunk smell. Bottle color, such as green or clear, is usually blamed, but brown bottles may not prevent this from happening.

The take-home: be diligent in the way that you store your beer. Bottled beer can become light-struck in less than one minute in bright sun, after a few hours in diffuse daylight, and in a few days under normal fluorescent lighting.

The Least You Need to Know

◆ Beers have types that reflect their processing.

◆ Think of your beer selections as a wine list—there should be a variety that satisfies your patrons.

◆ Know how to truly pour beer to minimize waste and maximize flavor.

◆ Clean glasses make all the difference.

◆ Be diligent about how you store beer to maintain quality.

Chapter 14

Grape-ology Explained

In This Chapter

- ◆ Winemaking 101
- ◆ All about white wines
- ◆ The allure of red
- ◆ Deciding what to offer
- ◆ Educating the staff
- ◆ Knowing how to store the bottles

Have you seen the 2004 movie *Sideways?* Two men go up to California's Santa Ynez Valley to go wine tasting as a bachelor party. The best man, Miles, is a wine snob. Snubbing his nose at the wine-to-drink-at-the-moment merlot, his favorite is the complicated pinot noir. If you don't know much about or have a small appreciation for wine, you may want to rent it. As one friend told us, he learned a lot in the two hours he spent watching this film.

Besides highlighting the fanatic behavior that wine can inspire, *Sideways* also reveals that wine drinking, despite the amount of science and creativity that goes into making the beverage, can be reduced to a trend. As a bar owner, you need to discern what is popular and what is good. It's the casual wine drinker who uses trends to decide what she'll be drinking. If you don't know what's hot and what's not, you may not have stocked enough. On the other hand, you may have clientele that are knowledgeable about wine. In that case, you better know your stuff and have the wine selection to prove it. In this chapter, we prime you on winemaking, the styles of wine, storage, and deciding what to serve.

Just Because You Saw *Sideways* Doesn't Mean You Know Wine

Francis Ford Coppola once said that making films and wine—he's also a winemaker—are almost the same: each depends on the source material and takes a lot of time to perfect.

Making wine is a science and an art form. There are wine lovers, wine drinkers, and wine wannabes. And as you'll probably get at least one of all these wine types in your establishment, you should have some knowledge of this great grape elixir. Here's a crash course in winemaking, the accelerated version.

Beginning in the vineyard, grapevines are planted in a location where they can get adequate water and have access to sunlight. When grapes first appear on the vine, their sugar levels are low and they're acidic. The longer they stay on the vine, the sweeter they become.

Once the grapes fully ripen, they are harvested either by hand or by machine—usually between February and April, depending on the climate of the region and the variety of the grape. The winemaking process begins almost immediately after the grapes are harvested. The first step is tipping the fruit into the crusher. Just as the name implies, this machine crushes the grapes and releases the juice. Don't worry; the stems, the skins, and other items that are not grapes get separated.

Bartender Knowledge

Grape juice is clear whether it comes from a red grape or a white grape. The color of finished wine comes from the skins. Therefore, to make red wine, the juice is in contact with grape skins. Juice for white wine is not.

Now the fermentation process begins. This is the process whereby the grape sugars convert into alcohol with the addition of yeast to the juice. The yeast consumes all the juice's sugar to produce alcohol and carbon dioxide. If white wine is being made, fermentation probably takes place in stainless steel tanks; however, the more full-bodied varieties may be fermented in oak barrels. This gives the wine greater flavor and *complexity*. The type of red wine being made determines the vessel that the juice ferments in—stainless-steel tanks, oak barrels, or open concrete fermenters. The bolder the red wine being made, the longer the juice ferments with the grape skins. The result is more flavor and deeper color. During this time, the temperature is controlled to ensure that organisms don't appear and that the yeast can function. If the juice is exposed to oxygen during this process, it is damaged.

Once the yeast cells' job is done they die, falling to the bottom of the container. The result is wine, which gets transferred to a container to age before it is bottled.

def•i•ni•tion

An essential element in great wines is **complexity,** which is a combination of richness, depth of flavor, intensity, balance, harmony, and finesse.

Now that it is bottled, it is sitting around waiting for consumption. The more you know about each wine, the more you sell. Time to learn more about your chardonnay, merlot, sparkling wine, and, oh, we wouldn't forget pinot noir.

White Wines

White wines get a bum wrap. Those who think they are in the know turn their noses up at them. They believe that white wines are the lesser-flavored and bodied wine and that red wines are more complex, but guess what? They're wrong. White wines can be aromatic and complex and satisfying if you know what you're looking for. Here we introduce you to two of the most popular white wines—chardonnay and sauvignon blanc.

Chardonnay

Favored by college co-eds attempting to look sophisticated, chardonnay is the training wheels of the wine world. And, honestly, we don't know why. Chardonnay is a versatile grape that grows in a variety of climates and, as a result, comes in many different styles. Perhaps these styles lend themselves to understanding the complexities of other wines. They have enough variety that the immature taster may not know what they are getting themselves into.

Nonetheless, chardonnay is popular and the world produces enough to fill the demand and allow for discovery. Like many wines, chardonnay was primarily produced in France, or more specifically, in the Burgundy region. These wines are known as White Burgundy; other French wines made with chardonnay grapes are Meursault,

Montrachet, Bourgogne or Montagny or Maconnais, and Chablis. In addition to French White Burgundy, other countries are making their name producing chardonnay—Chile, Australia, New Zealand, South Africa, Argentina, and the United States (specifically California).

In fact, California chardonnay became popular in the 1970s. Regions influenced by a cool maritime climate, such as Anderson Valley, Carneros, Monterey, Russian River, Santa Barbara, and Santa Maria Valley, produce wines that have placed California on the map for chardonnay.

When well made, chardonnay offers bold, ripe, rich, and intense fruit flavors of apple, fig, melon, pear, peach, pineapple, lemon, and grapefruit, along with spice, honey, butter, butterscotch, and hazelnut flavors.

These countries not only provide the different climates in which the grape is grown but also the different techniques that are employed by the winemakers. Since this is an easy-to-manipulate grape, winemakers get creative building more complexity using techniques such as barrel fermentation, sur lie aging (a process in which the wine is left in its natural sediment), and malolactic fermentation (a process that converts tart malic acid to softer lactic acid). No other white table wine benefits as much from oak aging or barrel fermentation. Chardonnay grapes have a fairly neutral flavor, and because they are usually crushed or pressed and not fermented with their skins the way red wines are, whatever flavors emerge from the grape are extracted almost instantly after crushing.

As a result, chardonnay can be described as a particular style. In general, most chardonnays can be categorized as one of these four types: crisp, fruit-driven, rich and complex, and dessert.

- ◆ Crisp chardonnays are usually grown and produced in cooler climates and tend to reflect flavors such as citrus, apple, smoke, and mineral-like. As a result, they are the driest of the chardonnays. Wines that fall into this category are Chablis, Pouilly-Fuisse, and other White Burgundy.

- ◆ Fruit-driven chardonnays tend to be grown and produced in warmer climates and tend to have distinctive fruit flavors such as apple, pear, and lemon. As a result, they are a little sweeter because of a hint of residual sugar. Wines that fall into this category are often a bit more commercial (think of a grown-up wine cooler) and will appeal to the white zinfandel convert or the just-turned-21 co-ed.

- ◆ Rich and complex chardonnays are bolder wines that vary significantly because they are based on the vintner's design. Usually these wines have been barrel aged and therefore have distinctive flavors such as butterscotch, vanilla, or nutmeg.

They're also buttery and dark in color. Many of your pricier wines fall into this category.

◆ Dessert chardonnays are your sweet wines, and they are not easy to find. As the name implies, they tend to pair nicely with dessert.

Sauvignon Blanc

Sauvignon blanc is a white grape that is native to the Loire and Bordeaux (where it is usually blended with semillon, another grape). It's widely planted in the western United States, South America, Australia, and New Zealand. In fact, it put California on the wine map, where it is often known and labeled fumé blanc. While the chardonnay's styles are based on the taste, sauvignon blanc's styles depend on how much the grapes are shaded and whether it is aged in oak.

The *varietal* identity of sauvignon blanc is typically similar to grass, bell pepper, or grapefruit. However, often it picks up an aggressive "catbox" or "gym sock" odor when the grapes lack sun exposure or are harvested too soon.

Barrel fermentation and blending it with other grape varieties, such as semillon, can also modify the sauvignon blanc aroma and complexity. Blending adds richness and an extra element to the aroma, and softens the sometimes abrasive or aggressive character of sauvignon blanc. But it is this character that makes it a distinctive wine. Here are the most common smell and/or flavor characteristics found in sauvignon blanc–based wines:

◆ Herbal, such as grass, weeds, lemongrass, and gooseberry

◆ Wood, such as vanilla, and sweet wood

◆ Vegetal, such as bell pepper, green olive, asparagus, and chili pepper

◆ Creamy, such as butter

> **Bartender Knowledge**
>
> Shaded grapes tend to produce a wine that is slightly green tinged with a grassy flavor, while grapes that have been exposed to sunlight have a citrus flavor and melonlike aroma.

> **def•i•ni•tion**
>
> **Varietals** are the different types of wine that receive their name from the grapes that wines are made from. By law, the wine must contain 75 percent of that grape.

- Fruity, such as grapefruit, lime, and melon

- Mineral, such as oak, smoke, toast, and flint

- Aggressive, such as cat litter and gym socks

When it comes to versatility and pairing with food, a dry sauvignon blanc is your best choice. Its high acidity allows it to accompany the most pungent foods—cilantro, raw garlic, smoked cheeses—that would otherwise overpower other white wines.

Red Wines

Ah, the wine color of the moment, red. Deep in hues and supposedly rich in complexity, red wines are what people who consider themselves "wine drinkers" consume. Never mind that the two most recent hip varietals were red—merlot and pinot noir (the latter due to the success of the movie *Sideways*). People who drink red wines only drink red wines. Here's what you should know about the most popular of the red grape bunch.

> **Bartender Knowledge**
>
> Cabernet sauvignon, merlot, and pinot noir are types of grapes that lend their names to varieties of red wine. In the United States, wines are typically named after the grape that produces them. In contrast, Europeans usually refer to wines by the location where they are grown.

Cabernet

Cabernet sauvignon is king of the red grapes because it's mainly used for wine production and is one of the most widely planted grape varieties, along with chardonnay. It is the principal grape in many Bordeaux wines. Its thick skin produces wine that can be high in *tannin*, which affects its taste.

def•i•ni•tion

> **Tannins** are the astringent compounds found in grape skins, seeds, and stems that make your mouth pucker and feel dry when you drink red wine.

The best cabernets start out dark purple to ruby in color, with firm acidity, a full body, great intensity, and concentrated flavors—currant, plum, black cherry, and spice, as well as herb, olive, mint, tobacco, cedar, and anise. This wine has an affinity for oak and usually spends 15 to 30 months in barrels, a process that imparts a woody, toasty cedar, or vanilla flavor.

Merlot

Merlot is a red wine grape used as both a blending grape and for varietal wines. These wines usually have medium body with hints of berry, plum, and currant. Its softness and fleshiness, combined with its earlier ripening, makes merlot an ideal grape to blend with the stronger, later-ripening cabernet sauvignon.

Tip Jar _____

The best cabernet sauvignon is made with 100 percent of the grape.

Merlot is produced primarily in France, Italy, Romania, and California, and on a lesser scale in Australia, Argentina, Canada's Niagara Peninsula, Chile, New Zealand, South Africa, Switzerland, Croatia, Hungary, Slovenia, and other parts of the United States such as Washington State and Long Island. It grows in many regions that also grow cabernet sauvignon but tends to be cultivated in the cooler portions of those areas.

Because of the soft and fruity nature of the merlot grape—sweeter, smoother, and lower in tannins—it blends well with other grapes. In fact, it accounts for an average of 25 percent of the blends. Despite its versatility, merlot that isn't blended is a popular choice of American red wine drinkers.

Pinot Noir

And here is the Hollywood superstar, the romantic, the diva of the wine world, pinot noir! Grown in diverse locations around the world, pinot noir may produce some of the finest wines. This may be because it is a difficult grape to cultivate and transform into wine; thus, there's more care in the winemaking.

Pinot noir thrives in France's Burgundy region and is also planted in Australia, Canada, Chile, Germany, New Zealand, Switzerland, and South Africa. But lately it is the United States that has increasingly become a major producer of this varietal. Some of the best pinot noir comes from California's Sonoma County's Russian River, and the Central Coast's Santa Lucia Highlands; and from Oregon's Willamette Valley. In the vineyard, the grape is sensitive to light exposure, soil types, and pruning techniques, and is prone to bunch rot and other fungal diseases. During the winemaking process, it's sensitive to the fermentation method and yeast strains. Ah, the challenge.

Despite these complications, pinot noir wines are among the most popular in the world and draw accolades comparing the wine to falling in love and sex. Its range of flavors, bouquets, textures, and impressions may be the reason. Pinot noir is of light to medium body with hints of black cherry, raspberry, or currant. We think Miles from *Sideways* summed it up best, when he described pinot noir:

"It's a hard grape to grow … it's thin-skinned, temperamental, ripens early … it's not a survivor like cabernet, which can just grow anywhere and thrive even when it's neglected. No, pinot needs constant care and attention … it can only grow in these really specific, little, tucked-away corners of the world. And only the most patient and nurturing of growers can do it, really. Only somebody who really takes the time to understand pinot's potential can then coax it into its fullest expression. Then, oh, its flavors, they're just the most haunting and brilliant and thrilling and subtle and ancient on the planet."

Zinfandel

Commonly referred to as "Zin," zinfandel is the mostly widely planted red grape in California. Much of it is made into white zinfandel, a blush-colored, slightly sweet wine. Real zinfandel, the red wine, is the quintessential California wine.

Versatile in nature, zinfandel can be blended with other grapes, such as cabernet sauvignon and petite syrah; it can be made in a claret style, with berry and cherry flavors, mild tannins and oak shadings; and it can be made into late-harvest and port-style wines that feature very ripe raisin flavors, chewy tannins, and alcohol above 15 percent. One of the most popular alter-egos of zinfandel is white zinfandel, which tends to be sweet. It's a sharp contrast to the grape's zesty, spicy pepper, raspberry, cherry, wild berry, and plum flavors, and its complex range of tar, earth, and leather notes.

Despite its many uses, zinfandel is a challenging grape to grow because its berry size varies significantly within a bunch, which leads to uneven ripening. As a result, zinfandel often needs to hang on the vine longer. Closer attention to viticulture and an appreciation for older vines, which tend to produce smaller crops of uniformly higher quality, account for better-balanced wines. These are sometimes denoted on the label as "ancient vines."

What Kind of Wine?

Most likely in your bar, you will serve the more popular varieties discussed above. But here are some lesser-known wines that can possibly round out your wine offerings, depending on your theme, your customer, and your storage space:

 ◆ Chianti (Red) [Key-AUN-ti] is a wine-growing area within Italy that produces some exceptional red wines. This area hosts seven subregions: Rufina, Colline

Pisane, Montalbano, Classico, Colli Aretini, Colli Fiorentini, and Colli Senesi. The differences in style of Chianti between these regions are immense, and even within a region, Chianti can vary greatly from one winery to the next. It is the Classico region that is most popular.

◆ Gewürztraminer (White) [geh-VERTS-trah-mee-ner] is a floral, crisp, and refreshing wine that pairs well with spicy dishes. If the grape is harvested late, it becomes rich and complex, a perfect dessert wine.

◆ Petite syrah (Red) [peh-TEET sih-RAH] is known for its dark hue and firm tannins. It has an intense peppery flavor.

◆ Pinot grigio (White) [PEE-no GREE-zho] is soft, gently perfumed, and has more color than most whites.

◆ Riesling (White) [REES-ling] has a tendency to produce dry or just off-dry wine. Its high acidity and distinctive floral, citrus, peach, and mineral accents pair well with food. It can be found under synonyms such as White Riesling, Rhine Riesling, or Johannesburg Riesling.

◆ Sparkling wines are any wine that has been allowed to complete the final phase of its fermentation in the bottle so that the carbon dioxide produced is trapped. Sometimes labeled as champagne, it comes in categories that reflect the wine's sugar levels: extra brut, brut, extra dry, sec, and demi-sec. An extra brut champagne will be very dry, while a demi-sec is sweet. Brut (dry), extra dry, and sec lie in the middle of the continuum with off-dry to semi-sweet offerings.

◆ Syrah or Shiraz (Red) [sih-RAH or shih-RAHZ] is a red wine that is rich, complex, and distinctive with pronounced pepper, spice, black cherry, tar, leather, and roasted nut flavors.

Beer Goggles

Sparkling wines not produced in the Champagne region of France can be labeled as "champagne," but a U.S. regulation requires that it can be used only if the actual place of origin appears next to the name. Don't confuse your customers: sparkling wine is sparkling wine.

Assembling Your Selection

If you decide to offer wine at your establishment for a reasonable price, people will come to you. Usually, you will want to make a profit of about 20 percent on your wine sales, but don't get too greedy. Mark your wines up too much and your guests will scoff and feel taken advantage of.

When you assemble your wine list and wines-by-the-glass offerings, keep these things in mind:

- **Theme.** This is the guiding principle of every decision you make. If you're running a neighborhood bar in a college town, a high-priced wine selection most likely won't fly. Instead, you'll want to stock a lot of chardonnay and white zin, thanks to those co-eds.

- **Storage.** Doesn't it always come down to space? For the most part you want to store wine bottles in a cool, dark place. When we say dark, we mean away from sunlight. In your stock room, the bottles should be stored on their side rather than upright. This will keep the cork moist and airtight. Place white wines or sparkling wines in the refrigerator the night before to make sure they're chilled by opening the following night. Otherwise, you don't want to store them in there long term.

- **Variety.** A red isn't just a red. When creating your wine list, think about the fickle tastes of your guests. Your wine list should be as eclectic as they are. If you're lucky enough to be located near local wineries, you should feature them. Make sure you have a good balance of reds and whites and enough different varietals to give your guests a choice. But variety doesn't just refer to the types of wine you serve. It refers to the various ways you serve your wine: full bottles, half bottles or splits, and by the glass. It also refers to price points: a range of expensive, mid-priced, and inexpensive.

Training Your Staff

Again, depending on your bar, you want your staff informed about your offerings. To do this, hold regular tastings, paired with menu items and other foods that lend themselves to the wine's flavors.

An easy way to do this is to read the wine's label. For example, Cambria pinot noir's label boasts of hints of blackberries and cherries. Now sit down with a glass of wine and the hints of wood or fruit it refers to (in our example, blackberries and cherries). Smell these aspects and then smell the wine. Does your nose recognize them in the wine's bouquet? Now sip the wine—do you taste them in the wine? Eat a berry, then take a sip. Do you taste it now? Do the tastes complement each other?

This allows your staff to speak knowledgably about the wine selection and help your customer find the offering that suits their wants. Your wine distributor or a winemaker can be helpful in conducting these seminars. Many have tastings for their clients.

Tip Jar _____

Be a stealth educator. Post articles from magazines like *Wine Spectator* or *Food & Wine* in the back of the house.

The Least You Need to Know

♦ Varietals in the United States are named after the grape.

♦ Red wine and white wine are made almost the same way, with the main difference being how long the skin has contact with the juice.

♦ All wines have certain characteristics.

♦ Lesser-known varietals can round out your offerings.

♦ Consider your theme and the amount of storage you have, then make sure you provide variety when choosing what wines to serve.

♦ Training your staff to appreciate wine and present it correctly will help you sell more.

Menu Matters

In This Chapter

- ◆ Just drinks?
- ◆ Tummies drive business
- ◆ Keep it flowing
- ◆ Make taste buds happy
- ◆ Half-price eats

Food. It can drive people to your place when the live entertainment isn't there, or there's no sports event on television, or the promotion is no longer working.

Think about your own dining-out habits. Do you crave certain items from different establishments? We bet when you can't stop thinking about an item, you head to the place that serves it to pick it up. Your menu can bring patrons in the door for those great nachos, a juicy burger, or even a stellar salad.

This chapter will help you decide whether to serve food; if you decide to do so, it will also help you determine how to set up your menu and use it to bring business into your establishment.

To Serve Food or Not

When it comes to deciding whether to serve food, consider these three things: your licensing, your space, and your drive.

The licensing use is probably the most important. If you have a food and beverage license, you must serve food. If you have a straight-up bar license, as in alcohol only and 21 and over, you're not required to serve food.

In the case of the former, the law and the ABC require that a certain percentage of your sales come from food. It rarely comes out that way, but that's what they require and they can enforce it if they want to at any time. With a food and beverage license, you must have a menu that is put together to meet at least the bylaws of your local ABC (each local ABC differs in what is considered a menu or any laws regarding alcohol). For instance, your menu could offer three entrée choices, a salad, and a dessert—this might be enough to comply with the law for that particular license.

But if you have a food and beverage license, and you have more of a bar and are not selling food, then you're skating the issue of what that license is meant to be. It might violate your zoning or the stature of your license. Then the city can enforce the food issue and the percentage of sales to make sure what you have is also a restaurant and not just a bar. For instance, if you are having troubles with the city, they can come in with the ABC and audit your sales to check that they match your food and liquor license. The percentages differ from city to city, but let's say that at least 60 percent of your sales should come from food and the other 40 percent (maximum) can come from liquor. If you are not selling that much food, the city and the ABC can make you re-establish your business as a bar only and your license as a liquor license only.

"What's the big deal?" you say. Well, then the city will say that since you're a bar and not a restaurant and bar, which is what your license may be, some things need to be re-evaluated. For instance, fire permits and capacity issues might come into play. They might lower your capacity to match bar/nightclub guidelines. Any employees under 21 years of age can no longer work for you because the establishment is now 21 and over. You may even lose a portion of your business since families will never be able to come in. That's why licensing is so important when deciding whether you want to serve food or not.

Bartender Knowledge

The body burns alcohol at a regular rate of roughly 30 ml. (1 oz.) an hour.

A lot of different considerations come into play when you serve food—different health codes; hiring a cook, which is another labor expense; not to mention it's another thing to think about. Be sure to consider all these aspects in determining whether to serve food.

Now if you just want to open a bar, the thought of expanding your vision to include food can seem a bit daunting. But there are compelling reasons to do so.

It's good to offer food in this day and age because it makes your establishment more user-friendly. Communities perceive restaurants with bars more favorably than bars that don't serve food. Food consumption delays the effects of alcohol as well, which makes law enforcement look upon you more favorably, since your customers have the option to eat something before they drive away from your establishment.

Tip Jar

Create a signature food item that makes people think of your establishment when they think of that food. For example, serve stellar turkey burgers and you may have a full house every night.

Another reason to make a move toward the kitchen is that food can help grow your business. When running a bar or a nightclub, you schedule *promotions* that help draw people in on a nightly basis. (We discuss these more in Chapter 22.) A promotion can be something as simple as live entertainment, a jukebox, a drink special, or a happy hour. If you become stale—you know, turning your promotion over and over, until it has run itself into the ground—you need something else to attract people to your establishment.

That something else can be food. Ron Newman, the owner of the former Red Onion chain, offered what we think is very clever and educational advice for bar owners: you can have a promotion and it can run its course, or you might not have a promotion or a drink special for many weeks. But until you think of something, the food will always be the spark to the next level. That next level could be just keeping your business afloat. If there's nothing on the television, there are no sports, there's no band, there's no dancing, and it's just the DJ, the bar, you, and the customer, what's left? Nothing. But if you have food, it sparks the promotion—the reason they can keep coming back. And it buys you time to find another way or come up with another draw (which is what a promotion is).

Food keeps people coming back. People can drink anywhere. And a drink pretty much tastes the same anywhere. What's going to make your place stand out more than the other? Food may be one of those things. A friendly bartender or cocktail waitress can help, but a good juicy burger, or chili cheese fries, or whatever it is, will bring the customer in. You want the customer to say, "Mmmm, I come here for these."

def•i•ni•tion

A **promotion** is an aspect of marketing that is meant to drive business. It is supported by advertising, publicity, and public relations. A successful promotion increases sales.

Bartender Knowledge

Snacks that are a mixture of fats and carbohydrates are a good choice as they will help lessen the absorption of alcohol. Examples include bread with olive oil, peanut butter–filled pretzels, and cheese and crackers.

If you decide not to serve food, at least have peanuts, popcorn, or something similar on hand. These snacks do pose a bit of a catch-22. Because they are salty, they entice the drinker to drink more even though they help soak up the alcohol. We recommend you have some food, based on your clientele, somewhere in your establishment. It's just a good thing all the way around—especially when it comes to alcohol and driving. You don't want your customers to get into trouble; you want them to have a good time and be happy, so they can return safely the next time.

Let Your Vision Lead You

As with everything else, design your menu around your theme. For example, if you have a beautiful Hawaiian-themed bar, serve chicken teriyaki with pineapple. That type of food with that type of theme can be a culinary experience because it has a culture behind it. It won't make sense to serve hamburgers, something completely opposite from the theme.

Sports bars and pubs usually serve comfort food: meat and starch, such as burgers and fries, bangers and mash, fried zucchini, poppers, and all that grease. Meatloaf can be considered a comfort food and so can steak and potatoes.

Remember that menus can be changed and adapted as you go. Always. If something isn't selling well, get rid of it. Or if you put a special out there and people gravitate toward it, saying that they wish it was on the regular menu, then maybe it is worth it—if it is profitable and isn't a loss leader. To be able to put it on the menu, it's got to be profitable.

Tip Jar

Small plate items are a bit bigger than an appetizer but not the size of a full entrée. They're fun because the customer can order one, and then another, and then another …

Try to keep it simple. If one of your partners is a great chef, use his expertise and offer a really great menu. Say your place is open from 5 P.M. until 2 A.M., and you're paying money for that lease. Maximize your efforts during your business hours. By using your partner's culinary expertise, create a menu that can be served the entire time or create various menus for specific times. An example is a late-night menu that may be served from 11 P.M. until 2 A.M. only. You might be surprised. Who knows, people may start coming for the food.

In a small neighborhood bar, if you stick with comfort foods, it may be easier to tap into your customers' tastes. You can create a menu that has a variety of old standbys, such as burger and fries or macaroni and cheese, or you can play up one particular comfort food. For example, in west Los Angeles, one sports bar serves four different types of cheese-steak sandwiches along with french fries. The bar is simple: a bar and about ten tables. It is staffed with a bartender and a cook, though on weekends it may have a cocktail waitress. The menu reflects the simplicity of this operation. Another example is the Burger Bar in Las Vegas. Everything there is a burger, including the dessert. As a customer, you choose the bun, the patty, and the condiments. Sticking with these comfort foods that people tend to love helps them come in the door, even when there isn't a big game on.

If something is requested a lot and is cost-effective, go ahead and put it on the menu. Don't be afraid to try new things, especially when it comes to food. But never sacrifice quality. Some restaurants change the menu on a monthly or quarterly basis just to be different—but they keep the standards in place.

Know Your Potential Patrons' Taste

When you started this process, you took a long hard look at whom your potential patron would be. Now it's time to entice potential taste buds and their perceptions of value.

First, consider your bar. Is it high, medium, or low end? Price your menu items accordingly. For instance, if you want people to stop by when they get off work and see their friends, then price point comes into play. If you have done your job, your atmosphere will help people want to come to your place. Ultimately you want them to come more often. That means that your prices need to be reasonable if you want them to come to your place, rather than grab something from somewhere that's closer to their work and that's cheaper than your place. They want to go somewhere they enjoy and get a beer and a burger without breaking the bank.

Or let's say you're a high-end bar with a late-night menu. Then you want to structure your late-night menu accordingly. Your patron may be someone who works late and comes in after work. They can choose between you and maybe Carrows or Denny's, and you want them to choose you.

Bartender Knowledge

If you're running a large place like a nightclub, you can serve your regular menu until a certain point. Afterward, dwindle your kitchen staff down to one or two people—a cook who knows how to make those four or five items that make up a late-night menu.

No matter what, you want to think about how your clientele will come to your place and how they will eat. If you're a pub, having comfort food available late at night might be appreciated. Or you can offer a limited menu if you are expecting a late-night crowd. But it always should be reasonably priced and the food should be of good quality.

So how do ensure that your food is competitive to anyone down the street or around the corner? One factor is the recipes that make up your menu. Your food will rely partially on your cook or chef. We don't think you're going to wear the hat of the chef if you are the bar owner. But you could. You could hire someone to run the bar if your expertise is in the kitchen.

Beer Goggles

Don't try to serve everything to everyone. Keep your theme in mind when choosing menu items based on your research.

To come up with your menu, do your research. You could go to several different restaurants and wish that you could have a great turkey burger, slab of ribs, or whatever it is that you want. You will be designing as you go. But then when you decide what's missing from your town and what you want to serve, you can get recipes from the Internet, other friends, other chefs, and other establishments far away. Say that you are based in Colorado and you have a great dinner while on vacation in Florida. You might ask the owner for the recipe; after all, you're on the other side of the country. He might give it to you. And there you go—you have a recipe.

Or you can design your own recipe or have a chef design it. If the latter, have a sampling with that chef and choose from there, based on taste and price points of the items. You can also order premade items from vendors. Sometimes these items are frozen and just need to be heated up. Or sometimes, depending on the item—usually desserts—they are delivered ready to serve daily. There is nothing wrong with these options. In fact, they tend to be a win-win. Your customer gets fed and you have saved time and money preparing him good food.

Establishing Your Happy Hour

Happy hours help a restaurant create a bar business—especially if the place doesn't have a strong bar business. It also allows customers who are not familiar with your food to sample it. If you are a bar, a happy hour does the same thing. In fact, a happy hour does something else very important: it creates a nucleus.

In all bars, the nucleus brings people in early enough to make second or third turn-overs happen. If you have nothing going on early, then you may only have one turn-over. (A turnover is how many times a table is sat at and served.). This really isn't a money-making proposition. But if you're getting a nucleus in early, then you get some of those people to hang out for later and you get your normal crowd that comes in later.

A happy hour can be anything. It can offer half-price appetizers or drinks, or drink specials. Or you can get creative. Take, for instance, the owner of a bar called the 19th Hole. For happy hour on certain days, she will cook whatever she feels like—let's say meatloaf—and lay it on a chafing dish off to the side—for free. And the free food entices the happy hour drinkers to come in. It fills them up and makes them happy. That's why it's called a happy hour, right?

The normal happy hour is early—around 4 to 7 P.M. Sometimes it's good to schedule a late-night one if you see that your business is dying out. Create one or two happy hours if you have a big enough place. That late-night happy hour menu could reflect who your customer will be then.

If you're running a regular bar and trying to get people to come to your place after their shift is over, instead of the two or three other places they could go, think about what it's going to take to get them to choose your place to meet their friends and laugh and eat some food and have a good time.

The Least You Need to Know

- ◆ Your zoning and licensing may determine whether you must serve food.
- ◆ Food will always be the spark to your next promotion.
- ◆ Your food should be tied to your theme.
- ◆ Comfort foods are always popular.
- ◆ Think about how and why your customers will eat at your place when planning your menu.
- ◆ Happy hour can be whatever and whenever you want.

16

Choosing Your Suppliers

In This Chapter

- ◆ Finding your purveyors
- ◆ Contracts and credit reports
- ◆ Pricing and profits
- ◆ Don't be afraid of running out
- ◆ Hitting par
- ◆ What inventory really is

When you open a bar, it isn't just a public living room where the community can hang out. In order to make money, you need to sell something—specifically, alcohol. To get the liquor, beer, and wine you will sell, you need to order it from distributors. You can't go to the local Costco and buy it even if it is cheaper. Alcohol is a controlled substance and the government makes numerous laws regarding its sale.

If you are serving food, you will have to find suppliers that deliver the quality you want synonymous with your establishment, as well as the plates and utensils to serve it and the glassware to serve drinks. This may sound like a lot, but one of the easiest parts of starting your bar is finding your purveyors.

In this chapter, we discuss how to choose your suppliers and how to make sure you order enough to get your business started. And the nice part—it's easier than you think.

How to Handle Food, Liquor, and Wine Suppliers

Just as you are in the business to make money, so are purveyors of liquor, wine, and food. They will find you to introduce themselves and discuss what they can offer you. If you are starting a new business, word will get around. You'll have three vegetable guys and three meat guys and four alcohol guys hit you all at once, and usually they have territories.

Liquor and Wine Distributors

The number of companies that provide liquor and wine distribution is limited. In fact, there isn't much you can look for in a wine and liquor distributor because you will probably use all of the companies that distribute liquor in your area. One distributor will have an exclusive deal to carry certain brands, and another will carry other brands. So most likely you will have to deal with all of them.

Some purveyors have a division that sells wine and a separate division that sells liquor. One salesperson will sell you just the liquor and the mixes; the other will sell the wine.

Depending on where you live, you may buy wine from a distributor who works with local wineries or a specific wine distributor. In any case, many small and large distributors have wine tastings, so you can choose intelligently from their selections or experience a new product.

Beer Goggles

Liquor companies cannot pay promotional dollars to you as the bar owner; it's illegal and is considered a payoff. They have to pay a sponsor or a third party for an event. Mixes, such as Red Bull, Rockstar, and Coke, can pay promotional dollars, though, because they aren't a controlled substance.

Your liquor and wine distributor will try to work with you to save you money. For instance, a common occurrence is that your representative will offer you a less expensive alternative to a certain mix, but which tastes nearly the same. If you can save on your mix, then you are making a greater profit on each drink. If they can help you save a little bit in one area, then you might spend more in another. It is in their best interest for you to succeed. Finding new accounts is no fun.

Food Distributors

Food distributors will be knocking at your door left and right to get your account, especially if you are just opening up. Even if you're open, they'll still be trying to get your business. Don't worry about finding them, because they will come to you.

One thing you can do to help you choose is ask the manager of the closest restaurant to you who their purveyors are—who supplies their meat, vegetables, seafood, and so on. If you hire an obscure purveyor who might be able to deliver only once a week, for example, you may not be able to maintain the food quality that you want or may run out of supplies more quickly. Another reason for asking your neighbor is that if you run short of curly fries, for example, and they serve the same ones down the street, you can ask to borrow some with the promise that you can replenish their supply during your next delivery or with your next order. Either one of you could get a run on an item and might not get a delivery that night, so you can usually borrow from each other. It's great to have that option at your fingertips—that is, as long as you have a good rapport with your neighbor.

You also want to pick your purveyors based on the quality and the standard that you want to create with your food. Food comes in A-, B-, C- and D-grade. (Many times these are listed in your order catalogs.) What's going to be the appropriate level for your establishment? What kind of quality—A-quality, B-quality, C-quality, or D-quality—do you want to serve at your place? We always say, personally, never skimp on quality. If you need to charge a quarter more, it's worth it, because if you're serving quality beef and chicken, for example, then people are going to walk away happy.

As far as vegetables go, you could get everything from one purveyor, but we recommend against it. Quality of vegetables differs more between vendors than meat does. Meat vendors can be more consistent with their product. Produce is a more delicate product. Of two vendors that carry strawberries at the peak of the season, usually one will have better berries at a better price than the other. But that other vendor may offer better raspberries. Quality controls are different between the produce and meat vendors as well. Even the seafood vendors work differently than meat vendors. You would rather have different choices so you can look at the price point per pound and compare.

Keep in mind what a distributor's pricing can do to your food costs. Know the price points of their food to make sure your food costs stay in line. What is that plate going to cost? What is your profit margin going to be when building a menu? What is your

Bartender Knowledge

Food prices are like the stock market—they go up and down.

cost to produce a meal? And to manufacture it, cook it, and bring it out to the customer? How much can you waver on those prices and still make a profit?

You have to be constantly vigilant about your food prices. Produce prices can get out of control depending on the weather; for example, a harsh winter freeze may have destroyed crops. Salmon might cost more at a different time of year. You might have to get the more expensive Alaskan salmon. It's important that you are able to buy from two or three different purveyors to keep your menu price at a certain level. If there's a great buy today on the grade of beef that you want, but next week it promises to go up, you need the option to buy from a different distributor. It is very important to shop around so you can control your food costs. That's the only way to make money in the food business.

Remember that food spoils, so not only do you have to worry about buying it at a price that allows you to make a profit, you have to worry about spoilage. Liquor can sit on the shelf for a long time. But when it comes to food, it's on a time clock that is constantly ticking. If you have a lot of lobster that is nearing its expiration point, you might need to get creative and incorporate it into different things: a lunch item, an appetizer, as part of another dish. You are basically making it a special so that you don't have any spoilage.

Tip Jar

Having a chef on staff or as a partner is great for keeping your food spoilage low, because part of their education is proper purchasing and the creativity to develop special recipes.

Quality is everything. Some people think they can serve grade-C food and that their customers won't know the difference. We don't believe that. We believe that the customer knows where the best hamburger and the best steak are. If you have a bar and are going to serve food, serve quality food. Serve the grade-A, the grade-B. Pay a little more and you can charge a little more. People don't mind paying a bit more for quality. And we are strong believers in that, because we have seen owners change the quality of their food, only to have customers notice and take their business elsewhere. It's the management thinking, "Okay, how am I going to cut costs so I can make more profit? How can we squeeze the penny?" Well, that's where they go wrong. A penny wise is a dollar foolish.

Negotiating Contracts

Your suppliers may try to have you sign a contract for a year, in return for which they might to offer you a better price point. But the only thing that they always ask you for

is a filled-out credit application. They want
to make sure that you buy food on credit
instead of *COD*, and for that a credit application is needed. That's so you can call in your
orders and get a monthly bill, bimonthly bill,
or whatever they allow.

def•i•ni•tion

COD means cash on delivery, or
pay on receipt of merchandise.

Any contract that you sign will be a contract that outlines your terms of payment. The
credit application will determine how long you'll be allowed to hold a balance or to
pay a bill. They don't say you have to do business with them for a certain time. They
just wouldn't deliver if you didn't pay. The contract is all on their terms: you receive
product and you will pay for it in a certain amount of time.

The reason you don't want to sign a contract is so you can keep your options open
with regard to finding different distributors for better pricing when you need it.

If you do decide to sign a contract, do a corporation guarantee, not a personal one.
That way, if your business fails or you can't pay for any reason, they can't come after
you. They will go after the corporation. The bar business is full of newcomers, so
companies want to do a personal guarantee.

Purchasing Supplies

When it comes to buying glassware, paper supplies, and other nonconsumables,
everything can be ordered from a supply giant, such as Sysco. But because it is a big
umbrella company, you can shop around and possibly get a better deal from a local
supplier. If you get it from a supply giant, you will probably pay a premium because
they bring it to your door.

Triple L is one of the largest purveyors for restaurant equipment. And Temper glass,
a manufacturer, is a division of Triple L. It can be cheaper to go to the manufacturer.
This way you are eliminating the middleman who will jack up the price. Breakage is
a big deal in the industry. It's easier to look around for your nonconsumable items
to find the best price. You could order it from a supply giant who carries everything
under the sun, but you will spend a little more money because they deliver it with
your normal order. To save some money, you can go to different vendors. There are
places where you can get paper; there are places where you can get glassware; there
are places where you can get certain types of mixes.

Purchasing Place Settings and Glassware

When placing your first orders for plates and utensils, order three times your occupancy, which means one setting per person plus another two settings in reserve.

For glassware, order one-and-a-half times your occupancy, because the variety of glassware can be a little trickier. Stackable glasses are the way to go behind the bar. Order more stackable glasses and fewer martini and margarita glasses, which don't stack. And of course, you will have some of all types of glasses in storage. But it depends on how many people you can serve in the building and at the tables; usually it is one and a half. For example, if your capacity is 100, you should consider getting 150 glasses.

Keep in mind that you can use universal glassware for different drinks. Rocks glasses, for example, can be used across the board for mixed drinks and pint glasses can be used for beer and sodas. Once you see exactly what your clients order, you can buy more of your specialized glasses. If you are a fancier place, however, don't serve a margarita in a tall glass—serve it in a margarita glass. Presentation is everything.

Be smart about who your customer is and what she will drink. There is a neighborhood bar in Palm Desert, California, called the Red Barn. Steve recently went in there with a couple of friends who ordered martinis. The drinks were served in martini glasses. But when Steve went up to the bar to order another round, the bartender kindly asked him to bring the glasses back so he could wash them and serve the drinks properly. You see, the Red Barn doesn't get many martini drinkers and these were the only martini glasses they had. The owner knows his clientele's taste and orders glassware accordingly.

Beer Goggles

Only order what you need. Inventory is like cash. The more you have in your stockroom, the higher your cost of doing business.

Size is another factor to consider. You don't want to get too big of a rocks glass because you will pour more mix. Larger glassware can throw your costs out of line.

Ordering Liquor and Wine

When it comes to your first order of liquor and wine, the purveyor will try to oversell you—especially items you don't need. Does a sports bar need a single malt scotch? We don't think so. They'll also offer you a special that requires you to order 10 cases to get a certain price. Just order the minimum when starting out. You don't want to overstock, because it will sit on the shelf and take up your inventory; your cost of goods will be stagnant because it's not moving. You want to keep products that you move in your inventory so you are replenishing it dollar-wise. You'll find out what your place requires after multiple reorders are established.

You don't know what your volume will be, so you don't want to overstock because that stock is going to sit on the shelf. Remember you are going to order twice a week, so if you see an influx or you are running low, don't worry that you aren't going to be able to get it the next day.

Do your initial minimum order unless it's a popular well liquor, such as vodka—then you'll want to order a case and a half. You'll pour your well liquor often so you'll want to have a case on hand. One bottle isn't going to be enough on a busy night. Depending on the size of your bar, you can go through 10 bottles of well vodka. Everything else, your call liquors and premium liquors, should only be ordered at the minimum until you know what your clientele is drinking. After you know that, your ordering will become more staggered. This means that you will have more of your well liquor, you will have a bit less of your call brands, and you will have the minimum order amount of your premiums. It's a three-two-one ratio—three bottles for well, two bottles for call, and one bottle for premium liquors. You can always set up your liquor room and then set up a *par sheet* and say, "Wow! We sold a lot of premium" or "We sold a lot of tequila." Then you can adjust your orders and your par sheet to match your sales. But until then, stick to the minimum order.

Your par sheet helps you keep track of your inventory and allotment—what you started with and what you don't have at the end of the night. Keep your par sheet in the liquor room and update it at end of the night. It should be compared to your breakage sheet. The breakage sheet lists what was requisitioned out, and who requisitioned it to whom (the barback, well 1 or 2, etc.) at what day and time during the course of the evening. Looking at that sheet can tell you what you sold during the week at a glance.

> **def•i•ni•tion**
>
> A **par sheet** keeps track of what you have on hand and compares it to what you need to have to determine what needs to be ordered.

Your par sheet can tell you what isn't being sold as well. Stuff that isn't being used is affecting your bottom line because it's sitting in dead storage. It's like buying a piece of kitchen equipment that you never use.

Just get the basics and you can go from there. If you need something you can order it the next day. Simplify your ordering to maximize your profit.

The Least You Need to Know

◆ Order one-and-a-half times your occupancy for glassware and three times your occupancy for place settings.

◆ Consider paying for your deliveries by cash only.

◆ Order the minimum amounts of alcohol for your first order.

◆ Use multiple food purveyors to keep your food cost low.

◆ Inventory is the same as cash.

◆ Never sacrifice quality.

Chapter 17

Determining Your Prices

In This Chapter

- Price point defined
- Controlling the market
- Competitive pricing
- Covering the costs
- No short selling allowed

The bar business is supposed to be a money-making enterprise. To make money, you have to charge for the party in progress. This isn't like having friends over at your house, where they come in and you pour them a drink. In your bar, you need to set a price for that drink. What will it be?

This chapter will help you determine how much to charge while keeping your bottom line and your competition in mind. At the end of the week, ultimately you want to see a black number, not a red one, staring back at you.

Factors to Consider

When you start off, how you set your prices depends on what kind of bar you are, where you are located, and what you're trying to accomplish financially. If you are an ultra-lounge or a themed bar on a main throughway, you will structure your prices differently than if you are a drive-up destination. You don't want to structure your prices too high or too low for your location.

Tip Jar _____

If you have a high-end bar, then you need to position it to command that higher price at the bar. You can charge a premium for a drink because you are commanding the atmosphere around you to be able to charge that price.

Check Out the Competition

The best way to get the price quote that you want to put into your well, call, and premium liquors, as well as your beer and wine, is to check your competitor's prices, as we discussed in Chapter 3.

When you first open your place, you want to set your pricing so you hit the marks that you set and incorporated in your pro forma. To do this you will have to put a value on the drink by determining what it's worth combined with the atmosphere. You don't want to go too low if your atmosphere creates a demand for a higher-priced drink, because you have a higher overhead and labor cost. The product that you sell (hopefully at a volume status) should create a profit margin in the end.

Get a range of prices in your area, from the high-priced hotel bar or five-star restaurant to a more urban or down-to-earth bar. Now you know what the highest and lowest prices are that you can charge. Evaluate your lease and compare it to your competitors as far as what they serve and what kind of atmosphere they create to command that price. Then you will have an idea of what you can and can't charge.

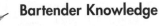

Bartender Knowledge _____

A lot of people have happy hours, where they charge lower prices but make up for it in volume to get the profit. Less profit and more volume are still better when achieving your goal.

People notice whether a drink is 50 cents more or 50 cents less. It means a lot. When they buy two margaritas for $14, they lay out that $20 and get $6 in change. If they can go down the street and get a similar-tasting margarita for $6 each, they'll get $8 change for the same purchase. They'll notice how much they put back in their pocket and how much they'll have for a tip.

Determine how much you can charge costwise to make a profit while paying for your business on a daily basis, weekly basis, and monthly basis. What do you need to do to keep minimum cost per day to make a profit and stay in business? Be sure to factor in your lease, your insurance, your product cost, and your labor cost. You should know that if you serve 100 drinks on a Sunday afternoon and make $7 per drink, you will make $700. Out of that $700, what is your takeaway profit?

You can break it down even further. Let's say that the cost of a well drink is 32 cents. Now you have to consider that it has to be manufactured. What is it going to cost to manufacture that drink for an hourly bartender to be paid? Is it another 20 cents to manufacture it? The juice that might go into it is another 10 cents, so now you're up to 62 cents. Now you know what your bare minimum is on that one product. From that point on you determine how much you want to make on that well drink.

Then you can evaluate it. Is it as much as your competitor charges? He's getting basically the same cost breakdown on his liquor, but what does he have that allows him to charge more? A better atmosphere? Patio? Ambience? Theme? What do you have? Something similar? A good patio in a better location in town? Then you can command a better price for your drink.

Another price that you may need is a *cover charge*. From the very beginning of your operation, you have to choose whether you have a cover charge or not. If not, you are going to let people in free of charge to enjoy the night's featured entertainment. So if you don't charge a cover and your house band is performing, you have to incorporate the cost somewhere—the drink price or the food price must cover the entertainment cost. If not, you can hope that your advertising and promotion will bring in enough business to make a profit.

Basically, you want to decide how to pay for the entertainment without dipping into the bar receipts. If the band costs $700 and you charge a $10 cover and your place holds 100 people, a hundred people will pay for the band and make you a $300 profit.

Tip Jar

Look at your competitors' cover charge and set it from there. Steve chooses to go higher than his competitors so he can attract a better crowd (and a better-dressed crowd) and provide a better ambience on the inside.

Check Out the Competition Again

After you set your prices, always go back out and compare yourself to your competition. Eventually you should try to establish relationships with other local bar managers. It makes research much easier. All you have to do is make a phone call to find out what they're charging. It is almost like controlling the marketplace.

It's like gas stations on the same street that change their prices as their competition does. You have to price yourself properly. Unlike gas stations, though, you try to set your course and hold to it.

Bartender Knowledge

You may find out that your competitors raised their prices. Find out why, because it may affect you. Did the cost factor for that product go up? Did distillers make it go up? Did their rent go up?

If your competitor is savvy, they'll want to know what the other places are charging to see if they're above or below you. Your competition is a great barometer. But at the same time if you're new and you want to entice people to come in, then you might want to charge a quarter less for your drinks. It could be part of your marketing plan to charge a little less at the beginning and after a year kick it up a quarter. But only do this if you have enough profit built into your planning to afford it.

How (Not) to Sell Yourself Short

Always factor in what you absolutely need to make. Keep this in mind before you get caught up in what your competitors are charging. Ultimately, you first have to look within yourself and see what your scenario means to you and what you need to charge. This applies to food as well.

Each place is different because of square footage, lease cost factors, product cost factors, and its personal scenario. Places might be similar, but each and every place has a different scenario for pricing.

The Least You Need to Know

◆ Let your scenario set your prices.

◆ Cover charges can pay for entertainment.

◆ Visiting all the competition, from the highest-price place to the lowest, is a good method for determining what you can charge for your well, call, and premium liquors.

◆ After you set your prices, always go back out and compare yourself to your competition.

◆ Pricing can be a marketing tool.

◆ No matter what your competition is doing, don't sell yourself short. Be true to what you need to make.

Part 5

Back-of-the-Bar Business

Do you know that song that begins, "One hundred bottles of beer on the wall"? A barkeep must have come up with it while he was counting inventory or on a night when he was selling a lot of beer.

The back of your bar is where all the business happens. While the front of the house is having a dandy time, the back of the house is tracking sales, expenses, and inventory; handling risky situations; and cleaning. The back of the bar keeps it real so the party guests can continue having a good time.

Did we mention that you would need to do math? More specifically, you should like to count: "Ninety-nine bottles of beer on the wall ..."

Chapter 18

Money Matters

In This Chapter

- ◆ Didn't think you were in sales?
- ◆ Profit is the name of the game
- ◆ Making yourself accountable
- ◆ Point of sale
- ◆ Calling security
- ◆ Hello, Mr. Taxman

The bar business is a lot of fun, but ultimately it's the money that counts. Sure, you could say it's the energy and the excitement that drew you toward the service industry, but you won't be in it long if you don't pay attention to the money side of it.

It's the money side that makes this a risky business and can get the best intentioned into trouble—lots of it. And with the government to boot! This chapter is your heads up. It will discuss what matters in the bar business: sales, expenses, and inventory, and how to not hemorrhage money or get into a mess with your favorite government agency, the Internal Revenue Service.

Tracking Sales, Expenses, and Inventory

That bottle of vodka, keg of beer, case of wine, and so on are all gold—at least to you, the bar owner. It's your expense, it's your inventory, and ultimately, it's what you sell and the heart of what you do.

By keeping your inventory in check, meeting sales goals, and minimizing expenses, you should be a profitable operation. The first step is to pull out that pro forma you did in Chapter 4.

Setting Sales Goals

Remember all those numbers that you projected and forecasted when you were doing your business plan? Now it's time to make them happen. If you accurately did your homework these numbers shouldn't terrify you.

When you forecasted your sales by calendar months and made seasonal adjustments according to any influx that your town or city gets, you set your sales goals. After you've been in business for a few months, you may want to adjust them to better reflect what is going on in your business. At that time, you will have a better understanding of the average check amount for each guest.

Maintaining Profitability

Now that you're living your pro forma, it's time to make sure that the number at the bottom of the profit and loss statement is black.

Usually your expenses derive from your rent and your basics, such as your utilities and insurance. You have to forecast your expenses on a monthly, bimonthly, and quarterly status. Your ad budget is another necessity that you want to project out. If you're opening a business, you include your grand opening budget. If you have an existing business, you want to put 4 to 5 percent of your gross toward your advertising.

Tip Jar

Money spent on promotions and advertising affect your bottom line the most. It is this expenditure that brings sales to you.

A lot of people make the mistake of not accounting for advertising costs until it's too late. Then they throw a bunch of money into it, which doesn't work because they haven't taken the time or given the money beforehand to find the advertising structure that works best for them and their business. That's why it is a necessity to use your advertising budget.

On your pro forma, you projected your cost of goods to be about 25 percent of gross sales. Your cost of goods should go up 3 percent as most costs would per year. And then 5 percent of your sales increase each year, which is a conservative outlook. Your labor costs should also be on the conservative side because you don't want your labor cost to be a higher percentage than your liquor or food costs. Your labor will be determined by the size of the place and the number of people you need to run it.

Your sales should increase 5 percent conservatively if you're doing well or 15 percent if you're doing phenomenally. But make sure that your cost breakdowns are proper so you do show a profit at the bottom—that beautiful black number that most of us hold our breath for at the end of the month even though we're doing everything right. It's even all right if it's a black zero—at least you're balanced.

As we discussed in Chapter 16, always pay for supplies COD. When your liquor inventory comes in, pay for it right there, whether it's a check or cash. You don't want to get caught up in a 30-day, 60-day, or 90-day credit line. Pay your bills COD and then it's done—it's out of the way. And you own everything that's in that building. It's always nice to have that credit if you need it to get

Beer Goggles

If your costs are through the roof one month, and your sales are down but labor costs are the same, you know someone is stealing from you.

through a tough month or something, but save it for the tough times. Try not to start out that way. Only use the credit when you need to; otherwise, pay cash. This will also help you with cash flow.

Choosing and Using Accounting Systems

Finding the right system to keep track of your sales, expenses, and inventory will help you find the right pro forma formula that will work. You can build a lot of this into a point of sale system.

Accounting or financial software programs, such as Microsoft Money or QuickBooks or Quicken, let you build forecasts and projections of your monthly inventory, costs, labor costs, and everything else. They help break all of this down for you on a monthly, bimonthly, quarterly, and yearly basis. This way you can find out the direction your business is going.

Choosing Cash Register vs. Point of Sale

In creating your processes and procedures, you have probably looked at getting a point of sale system. These all-in-one computer tools can make life very easy. The size of your place determines whether you should invest in one.

If you have a bigger place, you'd use a POS system that you can input everything into—down to the percentages each day, inventory, labor costs, everything. Usually, even though you have this incredible POS system, you have manual systems to double-check your numbers, or you can use a second software program like Quicken to double-check your books and make sure everything is correct with your labor costs. It is incredibly important that your costs don't get out of hand.

But in a small place, if you don't have a POS system, it isn't a big deal. You can use regular computerized cash registers from Costco or an office supply store. Because it's a smaller operation, one or two registers will do. If this is the case, you input all of your inventory costs into a program like Quicken to cross reference.

And don't think that there's anything wrong with running your business on less technologically advanced systems. The old way makes you work a little bit harder but the return is that you will appreciate how to track things: your inventory, your food costs, your labor costs, and so on. In addition, you'll be especially attuned to how these costs can get out of line quickly.

> **Bartender Knowledge**
>
> A lot of places don't have POS systems, so don't think you need one just because everyone is doing it. These bars use the old guard of ledger systems for no rhyme or reason. It's not better than the POS, it's just time-consuming.

Even though you're running a small operation, you may still opt to use a POS system. The system's coming down in price because it's no longer a novelty. For larger houses, however, it's becoming a necessity because it tracks everything that would take you hours and hours of work time to do. When you input your liquor into the computer, the POS system itemizes everything down to the penny and the percentage. If you use it to your advantage, you're going to be way ahead of the game.

If you do opt for the POS system, you need to learn your POS inside and out. Otherwise, it will become a PITA (pain in the ass). A lot of people don't take the time or don't have the time when they're building a place to learn the POS. They usually have to be educated by the regional representative for that system, and that can be costly because after a couple of times he comes down, the representative gets too stretched out and you don't see him for a month or two. This is terrible if you need a menu change or a price change.

Buyer beware. When you buy one, make sure that their support team is good because you don't want to be stuck with something that is high tech that you don't know how to use. A lot of POS people come out and want to sell you the system and make money, but that's it—you never see them again. They want to make a quick buck and sell you the system, but when it breaks down or you need training on it, you may be on your own.

If you're buying into a place, you can buy their existing POS, including the existing leasing program. But make sure that when you take over the POS system, a) it is paid for and see if you need to reinstall it as a new end user, b) there is proper support available so you can learn how to use it properly, and c) the company that makes it is still in business. Why would you want a system that nobody knows how to run? Maybe they don't know how to use it because the company has invented new software. Believe it or not, that happens a lot in this industry.

It's great to have a POS system when it is up and running, as long as you have good support and you buy it at the right price. And if you go with a common register and a software program, then at least you know where to get another one if it breaks down. You have a number to call so someone can walk you through it.

Beer Goggles

If you buy into a place that has the POS system already, make sure the previous owners weren't leasing to buy and that the system is up-to-date; otherwise you're stuck with it.

Managing Shrinkage

You almost have to look at the product you are selling—food and liquor—as cash. So every time you go to the liquor room, that's like your safe. And every time you go to the safe, you're taking money out.

Well liquor is included in your inventory and goes into the front end of the bar, so you have to treat it like gold. Keeping your PC (pours consumed) in check is important so you don't have a high number on your inventory costs.

If you have a bar manager, you need to put your trust and faith in him. If you're the bar manager who's in charge of all that, then you have to keep a check on your inventory. Unfortunately, you have to watch every person that works for you like a hawk, especially if that person is doing a lot of business for you. He's manufacturing those drinks for a profit, but you have to make sure that he's putting that cash in the register and not in the tip jar—just giving the customer the drink and taking that money, stealing from you by not ringing it into the register. Watching the bar to make sure this isn't being done is all you can do.

def•i•ni•tion

Spotters are people who pose as customers to make sure no one is stealing from you and to make sure that you give great customer service. They're like secret shoppers.

Another way is to hire *spotters*. Spotters come in on a quarterly or monthly basis, whatever you hire them for. They see if your bartenders and waitresses are charging the right prices across the board. So if you have two bars and someone orders a well drink, is it going to be the same price at both bars? Is this bartender going to charge a little bit more or is he going to put the money in the till? After they've been to your place, they give you an itemized report. They send it to you and let you know what their experience was from the curb up, from the bathrooms to the mirrors to whether they were greeted at the door. Was the bartender friendly? Did he manufacture the drink properly? Did he overpour the drink? Did he give you the right change back? Did he run a tab?

It's always nice to have a spotter come in and give you an evaluation. You might think that you're on top of things but at the same time you might find out things that could be improved on. You can then share it with your crew and tell them what was actually done.

It's worth every penny to hire a spotter. If you want them to concentrate on one person or an area they will do that. The ability to have them come back the following weekend is even better because once you alert your crew that you had spotters come in last weekend, then the employees think that you aren't going to have them in again soon, so the employee that they didn't catch stealing will start stealing again. Stack them two days, two weekends apart. It has to be confidential between your manager and yourself, or you don't even have to tell the manager.

Bartender Knowledge

If someone is stealing, the spotter will actually go to court with you.

Other things can help you minimize shrinkage and cost. Cameras are good. Place them at your back door, at the liquor entry, or over the trash. This way you can tell when someone is going through the back door and throwing stuff in the garbage trying to disguise how they're going to steal your meat, your poultry, or your beef. A lot of places don't know what's going through the back door.

Keep everything under lock and key. The manager is responsible for everything on that inventory sheet. Your inventory sheet or par sheet is a requisition of that inventory taken out of the cooler or that liquor room and signed off by the person issuing each item out of that liquor room, usually a bar manager or a manager. This establishes checks and balances for the people who work for you. Having checks and balances in place prevents money from walking out the door.

If you find that your costs are high, consider doing inventories more than once a month. You could do them weekly or biweekly. This is good if you know that something is going on but you can't put your finger on it. You can even consider doing it daily. That's the great thing about the POS system. Compare your requisition sheets in your liquor room against your POS system. If you see that you entered in four bottles of Smirnoff vodka and you have four broken in the back and your sells are not showing that many vodka drinks being sold, then you know that someone is overpouring or they're giving the drink away and the money is being put in their pocket—or it's going out the back door.

Tip Jar

Put cameras where your employees can see them. It will make them think twice before walking out with a bottle of champagne in their backpack.

Keeping the Taxman Happy

You will be responsible for paying quarterly taxes, monthly sales tax, workman's comp, and payroll taxes. You should plot out in your calendar when they are due. You have to work out your dates with your accountant and your bookkeeper and make sure that everyone is on the same page. You as the owner know how much you made each month. Don't forget that you have to pay taxes on that income. Remember to incorporate those tax dates into that formula.

Here's a good example of what can happen when you're not diligent about paying your taxes. There's a cute little bar called Main Street Bar. It's been open three years and has been through the rough start-up years. It's up for sale and the new people must inherit the losses of the old owners, which is $200,000 in back taxes. The business is sold for $145,000. To buy the business, it's $345,000, because you have to assume the back taxes—otherwise they're going to take the liquor license away. In other words, you would have to make an agreement that you will buy the business for X amount of dollars and agree to pay off the taxes for the old owner.

The taxes can run away from you, so if you don't pay your taxes the government will get you one way or another. Just another reason to have an accountant around. If you keep operating in the negative like that you'll get off on the wrong foot. You may not have things in place like your formulas to pay all your expenses, including your taxes. They can build up. What the government can do is enforce a lien against your property, your equipment, and your liquor license. When you start getting behind like that, you're just going to end up losing the business or selling it for a ridiculously low price. For instance, when the Main Street Bar was for sale previously, they wanted $795,000 for it. Look what happened because the owners didn't pay the taxman.

To avoid spending the money that should be going to your taxes, you should pay them monthly. If they are not due monthly, you should put that money aside monthly. Make sure you pay and wash your hands of it, because there are a lot of people who have lost their bar because of taxes. Then there are people who have paid their taxes, made a lot of money on their bar for a couple of years, and then sold it for more than it was worth because everything was paid up.

The Least You Need to Know

- Your inventory is money spent. When it's wasted or stolen, so is your money.

- Paying for your inventory by COD is a good method to keep you profitable.

- Remember that your pro forma is a living document. Update it when necessary to make it accurate.

- The size of your place will determine whether you should invest in a POS system right away.

- Old-school accounting systems can make you more aware of tracking your inventory and help you notice when things are going astray.

- Keep up on your taxes. They can get away from you quickly and land you in a bad spot.

Chapter 19

Risk Management

In This Chapter

- ◆ Flirting isn't harmless
- ◆ Stealing 101
- ◆ Compliments of the bartender
- ◆ You're drunk
- ◆ Being neighborly

When you throw a party at your home, you worry that your guests may drink too much and embarrass themselves, that something might get broken, or that your neighbors will complain about the noise. (If you're smart, you've invited your neighbors.)

When running a bar, you worry about all of those things and a few others on a grander scale. There are more guests and you have to make sure they don't drink too much because you don't want them to get in their cars and drive. Instead of worrying about stuff being broken, you worry that someone is stealing from you (not that it couldn't happen at a private party). And neighbors are neighbors and sound will always be an issue.

This chapter will take a look at the reasons why the bar business is a risky one. From dealing with your staff to the customers you serve to the neighbors you share the air with, running your bar will never be boring.

Staff

Working in a bar is fun. People who work in them usually are outgoing. And in many ways, when you go to work in a bar it's like going to a party. There's drinking (around you by customers), there's flirting, and there's joking. Just like that neighborhood party. But here's the thing: it isn't a party, it's a business.

That harmless joking and flirting can be seen as *sexual harassment*. If you get busy and forget to write down that drink you served, it isn't being a good host, it's stealing. This is the serious side of the party.

Sexual Harassment

In the past, bars have always been a very flirtatious work environment that spawned many romantic relationships, as well as fun and friendly ones. Now sexual harassment is very much a part of the collective consciousness.

def•i•ni•tion

Sexual harassment is sexual behavior that is deliberate, uninvited, unwelcome, and usually repeated, and that is perceived by the recipient to be embarrassing, offensive, demeaning, or compromising.

It's a very touchy subject, and a manager or an owner should protect himself in a number of ways. One is to have all employees sign off on a sexual harassment policy. This policy outlines the do's and don'ts of behavior that may be seen as sexual harassment. It can also state that sexual harassment suits cannot be filed unless the harassed notifies the harasser that his or her actions are inappropriate, thus placing the responsibility on the person who is feeling uncomfortable to say so.

Unfortunately, some people file sexual harassment suits for a living. A worker can pinpoint the owner or manager as the person they want to trap in a sexual harassment case, get them in a sexual position somewhere in the bar, and then accuse them of sexual harassment.

Bartender Knowledge

If you are worried about you or any of your managers being accused of sexual harassment, you can carry extra insurance that can help protect you and them from having to personally pay out of pocket to settle or fight these suits. An extra $4,000 per year may help buy piece of mind and might be worth every penny.

In an environment where men and women flirt, however, things happen. People are only human. But sometimes after a liaison that was consented to by both parties, one of them goes after the other maliciously. It happens all the time.

In this day and age, you must be careful. You probably shouldn't date someone from your work establishment unless one of you leaves and no longer works at the bar. Still, you can't control when people start dating, and it will happen.

Even if you brush up against someone nowadays it can be considered sexual harassment, and that's difficult not to do in a crowded bar. Bars in general are a hotbed of sexuality, from scantily clad waitresses to hunky bartenders. It would be nice to be able to tell who should and shouldn't work in this type of charged atmosphere, but you can't. You can only be careful. People come to bars to celebrate all things and go there for all reasons, and not always the right reasons.

You can be set up and sued for sexual harassment. It is an easy suit, and most of the time, it's settled out of court. Unfortunately, a lot of people out there are vindictive and looking for a lawsuit.

Stealing

Most bar owners could write a book about the millions of ways that people have stolen from them. Just when you think that you have figured out all of the tricks, people find another way to take your profits.

People say the quick sleight of hand is how to steal. In a crowded and busy bar, where drinks and money are moving around at the speed of light, the hand can be very sly and go unnoticed. The biggest temptation to steal is in the cash business.

When bartenders are holding tabs in a busy place and they are manufacturing drinks, they don't always go right back to the cash register. They may have a regular seated down at the end of the bar who has started a tab. They make a drink but they don't write the drink down for the credit card. A lot of bartenders and waitresses can be the most honest kids in town, but because they have so many tabs going with credit cards they forget to write things down and things slip through the cracks. They may have six people at a table ordering rounds and maybe one of the rounds doesn't get rung up because the waitress or the bartender just forgot because they got busy. It happens all the time. And if the spotter is in that night, it looks like the bartender is stealing.

 Beer Goggles

Be vigilant about thieves on the busiest nights. Those are the times when the most cash can be taken.

On the other side of the coin, a lot of bartenders are thieves that bounce around and prey on new places. They do this because they know that there will be a new influx of people who they'll be able to sell their charm to. They'll tell you how good they're going to be and how they came from another place that was busier with a great reputation. But a lot of thief bartenders prey on new establishments that they know will be busy because of the people behind it, or the ambience of it, or they know that everyone will flock to it. That's what a thief takes advantage of.

A thief relies on the fact that most new businesses are not ready to handle the influx of people they will get. And so the owners will depend on their employees in good faith. They prey on the new person on the block, knowing that she doesn't know what the old person knows.

These people see each new establishment as their new lion's den, where they can work the house and put money in their pockets—maybe more than at their last den. They can ring up a lot and make the house happy, but at the same time get away pocketing 10 percent or 20 percent more that should be going to the house. For example, instead of $1,200, they rang $1,000. Where does the extra $200 go?

If your thief is working side-by-side with another bartender at the same register, then he'll blame it on him. Or if you have a line of bartenders where everyone has his own register, he can grab another bartender's bowl. Thieves always try all these tricks to stay one step ahead of you.

Bartender Knowledge

Some bar owners would rather train a new person with their system because they can catch the person stealing quicker than someone who has been in the business longer.

Tip Jar

Charge your complimentary drinks to the promotions area of the P&L, then you've only lost the cost of the drink. These can be managed with the Complimentary Drink Log in Appendix D.

When you have that great bartender who has been around for years, the only reason he is still there is because he has a great personality, he knows what he's doing, and everyone loves him. He will make good money because the customers are going to tip him big.

If you work with your bartenders and give them a little bit of slack and a little bit of room to buy someone a drink, you may be able to limit the illegal profit-sharing that your bartenders may be participating in. You can do this by being straight with them. Tell them, "Here's the deal. You don't steal from me; I won't steal from you. You'll last a long time and make a lot of money here with me. I know the temptation there is to buy someone a drink or buy them a second drink. I will give you the opportunity to buy someone a drink who is buying a lot of drinks from us."

At this point, you can handle it a couple of ways. You can give them a set number of drinks that they can comp a night or have them pull you aside or send a waitress over to get you if they want to buy someone a drink.

Now you have accomplished a few things: you may have curbed the stealing that the bartender may do, you allow him to look like a great guy to the customer, you made the customer happy because he got a free drink, and you may have fostered a camaraderie between the bartender and the customer. Ultimately, the customer will want to come back and spend some of his good money. You make the bartender happy because he will get more cash from the customer. A comp drink is easy to do as long as you are in control of it. And you control it by setting limits with your bartenders and waitresses.

Smart, thieving bartenders will be on the money at the end of the night because they know how to adjust their bank. So they will know how to balance it out using their tip jar. The only way that you can really catch this is to have them close out their bank for a few minutes and take a break while you count their bank and see if they balance. If they don't, you know that they have been stealing along the way. It's like a spot check. It's important to tell your bartenders when you hire them that you will do this.

Beer Goggles

Just because someone is over on his bank doesn't mean you're safe. Being over is just as incriminating as being short.

Constant monitoring coupled with many defense mechanisms will make it easier for you to trust the people who work for you. If you put the security cameras in, put the right point of sale system in, bring the spotters in on an occasional basis, and do your spot checks and keep control of the liquor room and keep controls in place, then you have a better chance of keeping on top of theft.

And just when you thought you have heard it all: some bartenders will try to replace a bottle of liquor, let's say vodka, that they have been pouring a lot of because they know that the tickets or POS system will show that not a lot of vodka was poured, especially if they have been pocketing tickets. So they will pay for that $20 bottle of vodka (when they have probably made about $200) and *marry* the bottle to where the level should be. Or they front-load it and just add it to the inventory so you'll never know. The only way that you will know is if you check that label (which would cause a lot of problems on your end) and see if the bar code matches up with the bar codes of what you bought form your purveyors.

def•i•ni•tion

To **marry** the bottle means to mix alcohol from two bottles into one. It's an illegal practice.

Customers

Believe it or not, your customers can be difficult for various reasons, but mostly because they are drinking alcohol.

Intoxication

You are in the business of selling alcohol to customers, but that does not mean that you can allow them to get drunk. Don't be afraid to cut people off if they seem to be reaching their limit. Speak to them privately and professionally; you don't want to embarrass them. Doing so reduces your liability and is just good business.

Why? Because the person legally responsible for the intoxicated individual is "the hand that served the drink," meaning your bar and your bartenders. If one of your guests leaves your establishment legally intoxicated and gets in an accident, you are liable. And let me tell you, if he was already drunk before he arrived to your place of business, he is still your problem.

The best way to protect yourself legally is to educate your staff about blood-alcohol by using some of the charts that are available from many states' Department of Motor Vehicles. Educate your staff about how not to overserve a guest. Teach your bartenders not to overpour since this could push even the most well-meaning guest into legal intoxication limits.

It sounds like a daunting task, doesn't it? But it isn't. Usually you can talk the keys away from anybody, but you have to be persuasive. The first thing you tell an intoxicated customer is that they've had too much to drink and that you can no longer serve them. Usually they get angry. If you have valets, you want to alert them of the situation. If the patron tries to get his car keys from them, have them run the keys to you so you can handle it by sending him home in a cab, and most of the time that's it.

If the person does get upset, alert him that, unless someone in his party is sober enough to drive, then you are not going to let him drive. You may need to call the police. The police respect you for doing that. The police officer can help you by intervening. He tends to be more persuasive—giving them the choice between a cab or jail.

Tip Jar

It's a good idea to have security or bouncers on busy nights to handle unruly and aggressive customers.

Usually when a customer has had too much, she may want to fight. You might have a problem because she bugs other customers, or she's doing something that's inappropriate and you tell her to stop. When the person becomes completely belligerent, you have to have her escorted out, sometimes with force. You don't want to hurt the customer, but you want to restrain her until the police get there because sometimes the person is violent.

Transportation

You want to post a policy in place about what to do in case of an intoxicated guest. Part of the policy is that you will always call the person a cab.

Another thing you want is a designated driver program. The designated driver program is one in which a customer who functions as the designated driver for his group gets free sodas and coffee for the night. You can also let him know that other nonalcoholic offerings are for sale.

Tip Jar

Before a major holiday you can provide transportation to customers as a promotion to get media attention. It allows the community to know that you are aware that more drinking goes on during that time of year.

Neighbors

Most of the time if you know your parameters, and you know that you are zoned properly, then your sound issues are not sound issues. You can usually defuse a bad situation with those who live around you. Unfortunately, anyone can make a sound issue.

Sometimes these people buy a home near a property zoned for a bar, and because they haven't done their homework, they make it an issue. Some people take up missions, and sometimes those missions are against you.

To protect yourself against these problems make sure that when you are zoned, whether it is grandfathered or not, it is not a conditional permit. If you are zoned for live entertainment, make sure you have the correct permits—a cabaret and a dance permit—and plenty of parking. As long as you're doing all the proper things with the city or town, you should be okay. But if you still have extruding sound, you may have to *mitigate.*

For example, a very popular Mexican restaurant in downtown Palm Springs had an awful problem with sound on their patio. The music of the live mariachi band traveled down the street. They have an open patio,

def•i•ni•tion

To **mitigate** is to try to alleviate a possible leakage of sound. Though sound travels, you will be asked to lessen its volume; you can do this by adding barriers, like walls, to muffle it.

so they put in glass shutters, which was a step to mitigating. The reality is the sound still traveled up, but it was enough to make the city happy.

Sound does travel, but it travels in different ways. Some people can measure the sound for you. Legally your decibels have to be below a certain level before and after certain times. Each municipality is different, and industrial and residential areas are different. Your decibels go up and down throughout the evening depending on the noise and even on the song that is playing.

So if you have someone attacking you and you have all the proper stuff from the city and you know that you are right, or even if you know you are right and you still mitigate the sound, the best thing that you can do is sue the person for interfering in your business so they will take up another hobby, like shopping.

Liability Insurance

You can be sued for the right reasons and for the wrong reasons. That is just part of doing business. Therefore, you need liability insurance for your establishment and worker's comp for the people who work for you.

Someone can slip and fall in your place. If someone leaves your establishment intoxicated and they get killed or kill someone, then the family can sue the person who hit them and the place where the person got intoxicated.

Anything can happen. Anything that happens on your property is a liability. Even after someone has left the building, if something happened while on your property you are liable even if you are not responsible for what happened. So liability insurance for the bar business is a must.

The Least You Need to Know

- Be aware of potential sexual harassment issues.
- Constant monitoring and many defense procedures can lessen theft.
- Beware of the bartender, because he has a lot of opportunity to steal from you.
- When cutting off someone, treat them courteously.
- Have a plan in place for dealing with intoxicated customers and post it for all employees to see.
- Sometimes you want to work with the neighbor and the city to accomplish things, but sometimes that doesn't work.
- You must have liability insurance for your bar.

Chapter 20

Keep It Clean

In This Chapter

◆ More than a cleaning crew

◆ Which areas need the most attention

◆ Keeping a schedule

◆ Maintenance affects cleanliness

Sticky and smelly, with a swarm of fruit flies. Sounds like the telltale signs of a dirty bar—something you don't want. In Chapter 11, we discussed the importance of hiring a fabulous cleaning crew. But they aren't the only ones who will keep your bar stink-free and the health department happy. Your staff and your procedures will add to the work of a good cleaning crew.

Consider this chapter your clean-freak friend. You know, the one whose house is guest-ready at a moment's notice. We'll tell you what needs to be cleaned when and how often, how to make sure fruit flies don't set up camp in your speed rack, the importance of maintenance, and those all-important bathrooms.

Setting Up a Cleaning Schedule

Market research companies have done surveys and found, virtually without exception, that the cleanliness of an establishment is important to customers deciding whether to return to a bar or restaurant. What a sad state of affairs if you have great food, great atmosphere, and a bit of magic, but dirty glasses or messy bathrooms. Cleanliness doesn't drive growth, but it can sure kill it.

A good cleaning crew makes sure that the floors are clean, the hood and the grill are clean, and the bar is scoured, but their job is easier if you and your staff take a bit of pride and pick up a mop and a scrub brush on a regular basis. By setting up a cleaning schedule for different areas of the bar, you can ensure that all areas get the white glove treatment.

What Customers Should (and Shouldn't) See

If you serve food, it's obvious that your kitchen needs to be clean, but customers don't see the kitchen. They decide how clean your place is by what they do see, mostly in *high-impression areas.* They also make a lot of assumptions; more specifically, if what they see looks bad, they don't want to think about what they can't see.

def•i•ni•tion

High-impression areas are places or people that the guest can't help but notice. These include the outside and entrance, the bathrooms, the floors, the tables and chairs, the glassware, and your employees.

For a customer, your place can never be too clean. In fact, a customer is more inclined to notice when things are dirty or messy. Rose-colored glasses are not your patrons' accessory of choice. When it comes to cleanliness, it's their inner Ebert & Roeper that rules: you either get a thumbs up or thumbs down. Don't believe us? Ask them.

Remember, you only get one chance to make a first impression. Make sure it's a good one by making the following high-impression areas a priority when setting up your cleaning schedule.

The Exterior

In Chapter 8, we discussed the importance of curb appeal and making the experience inside translate to the outside. The same thing goes for cleanliness. If your parking lot is littered with empty bottles and napkins, or your landscaping is overgrown, a potential patron may question how tidy the inside is. Walk around your establishment and pick up any trash you see. If lights are burned out and it's dark, potential patrons may also question your commitment to their safety.

The Entrance

Besides being free of trash, what do your doors look like? Are the doors full of cracks, chipped paint, and scratches? There shouldn't be any taped-up fliers, memos, help-wanted signs, or any other generally tacky pieces. (You will, however, need to make sure that state-governed signage is clearly and neatly displayed.) Watch the entrance area for mud being carried in from outside and dirty carpets or throw rugs. Carpets or throw rugs are fine, but keep them clean. Finally, watch for cigarette butts and gum being disposed in this area.

The Bathrooms

On busy nights, the restrooms are the unruliest areas of your bar. They're frequented as much as the bar itself. They're also the most scrutinized area of your establishment. In many customers' eyes, the restrooms are a window into how clean the kitchen could be (or not). Your guests want bathrooms that are clean, well lit, stocked, and free from graffiti, debris, and odor. Depending on your establishment, a bathroom attendant can help keep this area in order no matter how busy the bar gets. (We discussed bathroom attendants in Chapter 11.)

The Floors

Even in the darkness of a nightclub, a dirty floor gets noticed. Whether there is food on it or a guest steps in something sticky, the floor is the last thing that most employees look at. They're concentrating on the guest, not looking down. Also, they're familiar with the place, so they tend to look up and out. Your customer isn't familiar with your layout and tends to look where she is walking by peering straight down at her feet.

Beer Goggles

Don't forget to check the undersides of the tables and chairs for gum. Clean it up quick, because the next customer will not think that this is a free breath mint or that it's a new decoration for their pants or purse. Yuck!

Underneath the customer's feet, you want them to see perfectly clean floors and floorboards. Stash hand vacuums and mops in easy-to-get-to areas for periodic cleaning by your staff throughout the night.

The Tables and Chairs

We're sure that you have sat down at tables that still have the previous occupants' drink glasses on it or have witnessed the cursory wipe-down as you were sitting at a table, hoping that nothing was getting pushed onto your lap. Keep the tables and chairs clean. You should use one sponge or towel to wipe off the tabletops and a totally different-looking one for the seats of chairs. If you have a booming bar business and it's difficult to have the cocktail waitresses clean their station, consider hiring a busser to do the job.

The Glasses (and Plates and Utensils)

Water spots or mishandling of glasses and utensils are bigger issues than the occasional dirty knife because they make the customer think these things are dirty. Customer perception is reality. That's why it is important to teach your staff to examine carefully all serving vessels—glasses, plates, and utensils. It's also important to make sure that these things are washed and stored properly: face down or handle up and without touching the working end.

Tip Jar

Ban your staff from touching the top 2 inches of any glass. This is an unsanitary practice. Instead, train them to hold the base of stemware and the bottom of bucket glasses. This keeps fingerprints away from the drinking area of the glasses.

The Employees

Clean uniforms, clean-cut appearance, and clean hands send the message that the employees have pride in their job, the service they provide, and the business. Such an appearance also gives customers confidence in your business—that it takes pride in its professionalism, cleanliness, and atmosphere. Have your employees wash their hands multiple, bordering on excessive, times throughout every shift. Teach them to keep their hands away from their hair, nose, and eyes and tell them that each violation of this rule results in another thorough hand washing. Finally, be sure to follow your local health department's guidelines for all cleanliness and sanitation procedures.

Daily, Weekly, Monthly

Your bar should have a cleaning schedule broken down into what needs to be cleaned, how often, by whom, and how it should be done. If this seems like a daunting task, it is. This kind of planning, however, is as important as your business plan. If carried out diligently and properly, it can win you accolades from the health department. Think about it: if you live in a city where the local news loves to expose establishments that fail health inspections, wouldn't you rather end up on the list of the cleanest rather than the dirtiest? Of course you would!

How do you create your schedule? In the words of *American Idol* judge Randy Jackson: "Let's break it down, dawg." First, take a look around your establishment and list all the areas—bar, cocktail stations, service station, host desk, bathrooms, and so on. Then write down all the equipment in those areas. For instance, in the case of the bar, you would list: reach-in refrigerators, speed rack, ice bin, service sink, washing station, back of bar, soda guns, well guns, cutting boards, garnish rack, and so on. Then, refer to what your health department looks for when doing inspections. These areas should be addressed daily if not weekly. An exception to this would be cleaning the grease trap if you serve food. This should be done on a weekly basis. But knowing what your health inspector is looking for helps provide the basic knowledge of must-have cleanliness. Now to determine what needs to be done in each area, consider these seven steps when making up your cleaning schedule:

1. Determine what should be cleaned. Honestly, everything should be cleaned, but you should pay special attention to surfaces that are prone to contamination and consider less obvious areas such as door seals to refrigerators. This should be the first thing that you do for each area, as mentioned above.

2. Consider what needs to be cleaned and how often. The nature of the item or the surface will determine when and how frequently it will be cleaned. For instance, if the item comes into direct contact with food or if it is a surface that is prone to any kind of contamination, you want it cleaned after each time it is used. If it is difficult to get to or needs special equipment or tools to clean it, however, this piece of equipment (such as draft lines) may only need to be cleaned monthly.

3. Identify how these things need to be cleaned and if any precautions need to be taken. Here is where you would specify what chemicals and materials are used for each particular area or piece. This should include the type of cleaning equipment (e.g., scrub brush, dishcloth, mop) and the detergents and/or disinfectants to be used. It should also explain how to dismantle equipment to be cleaned and precautions to take, such as "unplug machine" or "wear protective gear" like rubber gloves.

4. Assign each cleaning task or area to a person or position. In the draft lines example, you may assign that task to the bar manager or the lead bartender. When talking about the grease trap or the hood, this is a job for your cleaning crew. Daily cleaning tasks can be closing duties for bartenders, cocktail waitresses, cooks, and barbacks.

5. Identify who will be responsible for ensuring that the cleaning tasks have been completed. Most likely, this person will be you or a manager.

6. List where the cleaning materials are kept and who to report to when stocks are running low.

7. Review your schedule periodically for adequacy, and when you bring in new equipment or work processes have changed.

Once you've completed these steps, you have your schedule for each area of your bar, and you can create area-specific cleaning checklists. These help your staff remember what needs to be done and when, and they help you know what has been completed.

Besides having this more structured cleaning regimen, instill two other principles with your employees: "Clean as you go" and "A little goes a long way." In the clean-as-you-go philosophy, you basically clean up any mess you see. When everyone on staff follows this philosophy, the bar is a much cleaner place. Any time you serve liquids or foods, messes happen. But cleaning as you go helps take care of any such overflow mess. This rule means that you clean up after yourself and any others who forgot to clean up after themselves as you go about your other duties.

This falls in line with the little-goes-a-long-way school of thought. If everyone is cleaning up around them, these little tasks add up to make a greater impact; in this case, a really clean establishment. You can formalize this a bit by assigning each staff member two or three small tasks that they do throughout their shift. These tasks can include cutting garnishes as needed, wiping down chairs and tables, restocking napkins, and so on.

Cleaning the Bar

Your bar is the center of your business. The last thing you want is for it to smell like fermented alcohol. Each day, all areas should be cleaned and the floors should be scoured. While you focus on making sure that the entire bar area is clean, pay particular attention to the following areas:

◆ **Condiment containers.** Fruit flies love to make these home when they become sticky. Clean thoroughly each night.

◆ **Coolers.** Glasses sometimes break inside there. If this happens, empty the entire cooler and clean.

◆ **Floors and bar mats.** These get sticky quickly, so clean nightly. If you don't, the fermented smell will come along with the pests.

◆ **Guns, soda or otherwise.** Mold can grow in the holsters, so clean and sanitize these nightly.

◆ **Hand sinks.** These should be used for washing hands only. Make sure they are stocked with paper towels and soap.

◆ **Ice bins.** Keep ice scoops out of bins and the holders clean and free of standing water or debris.

◆ **Shelves.** Areas where liquor bottles and glassware are kept should be washed twice weekly.

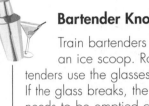

Bartender Knowledge

Train bartenders to use an ice scoop. Rookie bartenders use the glasses instead. If the glass breaks, the ice bin needs to be emptied completely and immediately.

Maintaining the Equipment

Customers usually consider upkeep and cleanliness as the same. So if something is broken, the patron will perceive it as ugly and dirty, even if it is sparkling clean. The other thing is that if your establishment has all sorts of maintenance issues, then most likely it is dirty, too. If you aren't willing to take care of simple upkeep on equipment, then you're probably not taking the time needed to clean thoroughly.

Therefore, maintenance plays a significant role in the overall perception your customers have about the cleanliness of your restaurant. Broken-down equipment, heating and cooling system problems, cracked glass and mirrors, overgrown or long-gone landscaping, wobbly tables and chairs, and dripping faucets all send a poor message to your customer about the upkeep of your establishment.

Another aspect of maintenance is pest control, which should be done monthly (and even sometimes weekly). Even if your restaurant doesn't have pests (as far as you know), you can't afford to risk getting them. You're running a business that serves consumables—drink and possibly food. One missed visit from your pest control company can turn ugly quickly. Contracting a pest control company can be done reasonably and in some states may even be required legally. Check with your local health department to see what is required.

Cleaning the Bathrooms

We keep harping on the restrooms because they are so important in your guests' perception of the cleanliness of your establishment. In the bar business, this area can get gross fast. How many times have you gone into a beautiful place only to go into the bathroom and find papers on the floor, an empty soap dispenser, and no more towels? Well, that's a bad experience.

As we have discussed before, bathroom attendants help prevent a dirty experience on busy nights. But if you have a neighborhood bar, this may be out of place. You need to determine this based on your business. If your bar is standing room only on Friday and Saturday nights, having a cocktail waitress or a bartender straighten out the restrooms may not be an option. At that point, it's nice to have an attendant to just organize chaos within the bathroom. When everything is working up front, you also want the bathrooms to be nice and beautifully designed and clean. But to keep that cleanliness up, those bathroom attendants make sure that the towels and toiletries are stocked, and take care of anything else that might come up (people do get sick) to make the experience a nice one.

During the off hours, take the time to have the cleaning crew remove any graffiti that may appear in the stalls and really scrub the grout in the tile. This is a high-traffic area, and the grout gets gross and black easily—the tiles get embedded with dirt. Try to have the floors steam cleaned monthly, if not weekly. Also, repair any discoloration in the sinks and toilet bowls. While this may come about because of age, it looks dirty because it hasn't been maintained. At some point, you may need to replace the toilets, which isn't a bad investment when you consider that the bathroom is a high-traffic and high-impression area. Remember, all in the name of cleanliness.

Cleanliness is next to godliness in the service industry. Most start out with the best intentions, only to get lazy and complacent until the whole thing is out of control. Successful owners stay on their game. They look at the business from the perspective of a new customer. They also realize that daily, weekly, and monthly preventive maintenance schedules and calendars are crucial.

We all know how important first impressions are. A first-impression approach to cleanliness is the only way to keep the highest standards. If you think about the first impression of a potential customer for life, your place will always look brand new.

The Least You Need to Know

◆ Your bar's cleanliness is an important factor when your customers decide whether they want to come back or not.

◆ Set up a cleaning schedule to ensure that all areas of your bar are getting the white glove treatment.

◆ Teach your staff to examine all glasses, plates, and silverware before using them or serving a customer.

◆ Be sure to follow your local health department's guidelines.

◆ Make sure that your employees clean as they go so messes are not left for others to deal with.

◆ When something is broken, customers perceive it as dirty. Keep all maintenance current.

Part 6

Opening the Doors and Beyond

You have to get the party started somehow. Throwing a huge party in your honor to celebrate all the hard work you've done to this point seems like an awesome idea. But that first party is just the start of the party in progress that is your bar. You need to keep the word out that it's more fun and exciting at your establishment than the guy's down the street or the girl's place opening a few blocks over.

In fact, your opening night is just the beginning of convincing others to join you in your place to watch the game, escape from their spouse, meet old and new friends, or just to relax. Welcome to the party.

Chapter **21**

The First Impression

In This Chapter

- ◆ Make some grand plans
- ◆ Don't be soft
- ◆ Invite everyone
- ◆ Set the date
- ◆ Budget for success
- ◆ Take the time to train

You only get one chance to make a first impression. We've said it throughout this book and we'll say it some more in this chapter. And if we don't drill it into your head by the end, then maybe this isn't the business for you. Why? Because in many instances, the bar business is one of appearances.

The night you open begins the excitement of your place. It should tantalize the public by stimulating all of their senses. The night you open starts the word-of-mouth that will fill your barstools on the next night and many nights after. And most importantly, this is the night that begins the fun that will be synonymous with your establishment.

This chapter will discuss what you need to do to start your business with a bang—the date, the budget, the marketing, and the training. Now get ready to get this party started!

Impressing Joe Public

Grand openings are exciting, especially when they're for bars. We discussed how this business is a party in progress, and opening night is just the beginning. So you want to plan it well and make sure that everything goes off without a hitch.

When planning for your big entrance into the nightlife of your area, keep in mind that you want the whole evening charged with excitement. You want every sense that your customer has to come alive. The experience starts from the curb up.

Bartender Knowledge

If you would like to provide free libations during the VIP party before you open the door to the public, consider having a third-party sponsor, like a radio station, co-host the event. This way the champagne will be complimentary of that company because they paid for it. It makes them liable but it makes it legal because ABC looks down upon serving alcohol for free.

Think about the ways that you can create that experience. For example, searchlights help build excitement as guests drive up to the building. Once they arrive, visually, the red carpet is out front with the host greeting everyone; the special foods you serve play on the guests' sense of smell; and the drinks play on the guests' sense of taste.

Pay attention to every detail—whether it's a decorative ice sculpture in front of the bar to a chocolate fountain to whatever you want to do that's exciting—but remember that it may cost a little bit more money.

Preparing for Your Grand Opening

When it comes to planning for your grand opening, the most important thing to keep in mind is timing. Everything must be done by the day you want to fling your doors open and invite the public to party with you. This is especially true if you build your place from the ground up.

Tip Jar

Pick the date that you think you can open and add two weeks to it. This will be the night to hold your grand opening.

You have to make sure that you dot your i's and cross your t's. All agencies involved must have signed off for permit reasons. Nothing is worse than picking a date, advertising it, and then realizing that you won't be ready for business because the health inspection or the fire inspection hasn't been done.

You don't want to scramble at the last minute to get everything finalized. You want to have a two-week period prior to your opening date to know that all legalities are in place and signed off. This way if something doesn't happen (you are dealing with government agencies), you have a window. When the date comes, if you do it this way, you should be good to go.

Here's the laundry list of agencies that must sign off for you to open:

♦ **Fire department.** Fire codes should be met and occupancy levels should be determined.

♦ **Health department.** Second inspection completed that checks establishment in ready-to-operate condition. You probably had your first inspection done when you leased or bought the space or during construction.

♦ **ABC.** Period of waiting is over.

♦ **Building inspection.** If you built out some things or had to make additions to meet current codes, this inspection needs to be completed.

♦ **City permits.** Even though you may not have dancing or entertainment, have the necessary permits that your city requires for you to offer these things. These permits can be known as dance, cabaret, or live entertainment permits. As we have discussed before, having them before you open allows you to expand your business and not be held back by the whims of government.

♦ **Licenses.** Business and liquor licenses and any government warnings should be displayed in the right place.

The importance of picking and sticking to your date is knowing that you have enough of a grace period to clear all the leaps and hurdles of your licensing. Use the extra two weeks to get the staff training done, make sure your uniforms are in, and so on.

If all goes well, you'll have the greatest opening that you can have with your business. As we said, you only get one chance to make a first impression. (We warned you that you would be hearing this again!) If you have all the senses and the elements in place, you are off to a phenomenal start.

The Invitation List

You also want to have a two-week lead-in to get your invitations to the big night ready to go and handed out in the community. You can start counting your RSVPs so you know how many people will come. Ultimately, though, you should just plan on the maximum number of people that you can hold for your establishment with food and liquor on that opening night.

Your grand opening isn't just to make a first impression on the public; it also gives you an opportunity to thank those who have helped you get this far and introduce your business to community leaders. This is why your invitation list is so important. Who do you want to come to the party?

Make your list and check it twice. You don't want to forget someone who will be important in the future and who would be offended by not being invited to your grand opening; from the mayor to the city planners that helped get you through, invite all the people that worked on your building. You want friendships with everybody in all those agencies so there is no hidden agenda and everyone knows what is going on in your establishment. You are inviting everybody, and there is always someone in government who should be invited. Most bars would rather keep, for instance, the police chief away. We say invite the chief. It is always better to take a pro-choice stance; by that we mean invite everyone you can and allow him or her to make the choice on whether they will come.

Set the Date

Steve used to say years ago, "Open on a Thursday night," but in the last 10 years he has changed his mind for this simple reason: a lot of people can't go out on a Thursday night. They have to work the next morning. Plan your grand opening for a Friday night. Then Saturday will be just as strong if people hear about it and word rings loud throughout the community about how good of a time they had on Friday night. In fact, they might return on Saturday night and bring friends.

Bartender Knowledge _____

A lot of people do a "soft" opening or have a party two or three nights for their grand opening. *No.* Go for the gusto—don't hold back on your first night. Remember, you're creating your first impression.

Setting Up a Budget

What you will do for a grand opening is more than you would do for marketing as your business continues (we discuss this in detail in Chapter 22). For your grand opening, you want to cover all the bases, so create a special grand opening budget that is above and beyond your normal marketing budget.

You will have expenditures that you normally don't have:

- **A publicist.** You can write about it yourself, but it's good to have a publicist. When you send out a press release on a place and it's your place, you're being biased. But when you have it written by a third person and it's about you, people take it more seriously. It's an extra fee for that publicist, but it's well worth it. Not only will they write the press release, they will send it out to the media and handle any requests that the press has.

- **Printing.** This cost will be above and beyond what you normally spend because you will be spending money on invitations. Make a spectacular invitation that will catch the eye of those you are inviting to your grand opening. Make sure it represents your bar's theme.

- **Advertising.** You will go above and beyond your advertising dollar for your grand opening because you're branding a name. You therefore want to test the waters and get the word out about this special event to as many people as possible.

- **A VIP party.** This is where the invitations come in. Before you open the doors to the public, you will have a VIP party from 8 P.M. to 10 P.M. You will then open to the general public at 10.

- **Food costs.** If you serve food at your VIP party, the cost is part of your grand opening budget. Usually, you won't charge food to your promotional budget.

- **Liquor costs.** Just like food, if you serve drinks to your VIPs or charge a discounted rate, this will also become part of the grand opening budget.

- **Entertainment.** You may want to bring in that special band that will cost an extra grand or two for the evening to really spice up things.

- **Security.** You may need extra security on hand in your parking lot just to be on the safe side.

These are some of the important ingredients of a grand opening that most people seem to do along the way instead of having ready on opening night. These expenditures are necessities in your opening budget that you would not normally do on a regular advertising budget for your monthly expenditures like your food, your invitations for your VIPs, your advertising above and beyond your normal advertising budget whether it be used for television or radio or print, and searchlights.

The Importance of Training

Sure, two weeks before your grand opening you make sure that all your permits and licenses are in place, but two weeks before that (one month out) you make sure that you have the staff you want—interviews are taken care of and processed and everyone is on board that will work for you. Start training them at least three weeks before the grand opening.

While more time to train is always better, it doesn't turn out that way for several reasons. When you hire someone, and many people forget this, most of the time they won't be starting for a few weeks or sometimes a month. So you want to make the possible starting date very clear and suggest that if they have another job to keep it until training begins or after training is done, depending on the number of hours you have set aside to get it done. Some people need immediate work and live paycheck to paycheck. You need to give these people enough notice to when you are going to open, because in many cases they cannot wait for you to open. That's why it's so important to have an opening day. You don't want to hold someone up from making a living. A lot of bar owners don't do this, and they end up losing that great waitress to someone else because she needed the job right then and there.

When it comes to training your employees, it will be a bit different than after you open the bar. For one, you won't have any shadowing going on. All of your training will be done in a closed establishment with the only interaction being between you and your employees.

By this time, most of your establishment should be built out, especially the bar. Therefore, you can hold your training sessions there. You will go over the drinks that you'll serve and have the trainees study from a manual that you put together as you go along. You should have your sections in place and your stations in place. This can be done once you have established the bar's floor plan—where you are going to put your tables and chairs and the buddy bars and the actual bars themselves.

You must train your staff about the drinks that you serve. You need to know how your drinks are classified from a well to a call to a premium to a soft drink. And you need to know how to call it out to the bartender. That's the thing that's very important. There is a procedure in place that most old-school bars use so the bartender knows in what order to manufacture the drink. But if it's coming through a computer, the bartender sees it and manufactures the drink.

And then of course, there's knowing what is on your premium liquor list; what the house wine is; what kind of well liquor is served; what kind of call liquor is served; what kind of draft beer is served; what kind of premium beer is served; what kind of wine, domestic and imported, is offered; and what the price structure is for all of these things. This information should be included in your manual, along with all recipes, food and drink. The manual should also include using the point of sale (POS) system: how to key in orders, and cash versus credit card. Those are all trained procedures that you need to walk through and learn so they don't get buried the night that you open.

When training your employees, instill your philosophy on customer service in them. For instance, the house is always right; the customer is always wrong. We're kidding, but the bottom line is that the customer is always right to a point, but you can't be taken advantage of.

For example, when Carey waited tables a large family would always come into the restaurant where she worked. This particular chain had a "customer is always right" mentality. This family of 12 seemed to always know when a new manager started. They would drink a lot of premium alcohol and eat nearly all of their meals but would complain bitterly that everything was horrible. Even the small children nagged. All of the servers saw this family the moment they came in and would pray they wouldn't get seated in their section. They would warn the new manager and sure enough when the family made a stink, the new manager would end up comping the entire meal, and the server would be out of a tip. This family took advantage of a restaurant's policy to always do right by their guests. This might be one of the reasons why the chain isn't as successful as it once was. When faced with situations like these, and you will be (especially if you serve food), you have to go with your gut. You'll be able to tell when the situation is suspect.

You want to make that customer happy. Anticipate his every need. And what we mean by that is: if you serve cocktails and you see a drink that is nearing halfway, that is when you approach the table and say, "Do you need another martini?" (or whatever he is drinking). Let them know that you have one coming for them. Don't wait for them to ask you. If you serve food and you have already given them their order, and the condiments they might need are not on the table, get them on the table. Don't make them ask you for something while the food sits cooling. Anticipating the customer's needs up front is what makes for good service.

To make sure that customer service isn't an issue on opening night, have some private practice sessions. This is when staff friends, family, the workers on the building, and anyone else who helped get you to this point are invited to have some drinks and food and basically be guinea pigs a couple of nights prior to opening. It allows you to walk through and reenact what a night of business would feel like. Since you have only one chance to make a first impression, don't make this a *soft opening*. This should be a private session.

def•i•ni•tion

A **soft opening** is when you quietly open your doors to the public and run the business hoping to get the kinks out before your grand opening.

Some people believe in soft openings, but we don't when it comes to a bar. We believe that you get one chance to make a first impression, so fill the bar to the top. And that's what people like. If there aren't that many people there, guests are going to say, "Oh, that was okay." But if it's jam-packed, people will talk about how it was so fun, and that they barely got in, and they ran into people that they hadn't seen forever. That's a success story.

These private practice sessions are the only way that your employees get to run through the POS with real customers. It allows you to get the kinks out, with live transactions taking place, but without money being exchanged. Or if it is a smaller place, you can work on procedures about how you are going to work from your kitchen to your runners to your servers to your bartenders.

You and your managers should be watching to make sure that everything is working well and talking to the "customers" for feedback. See if your staff is serving the customer, see how quick things are coming out of the kitchen and the bar, and make sure things are running smoothly. You also want to see how they react to things on the second and third round. Afterward meet with your staff and discuss what went right and what didn't. Training is a hands-on experience.

Even if you have a small place, it's a good idea to bring in friends and people who worked on the place to work through the system. The manager gets to close out the night and see how it will work on a larger basis. We don't care if it's a place that only holds 25 people and is 1,000 square feet or less—it's good to practice before you open. Practice makes perfect.

The Least You Need to Know

- You only get one chance to make a first impression; make sure it's fantastic.

- Have a separate budget for your grand opening; it will be larger than your normal promotional budget.

- Don't open your doors to the public unless it is your grand opening; don't have a soft opening.

- Hold private practice sessions for your staff to iron out the kinks prior to opening night.

Chapter 22

Marketing on a Shoestring

In This Chapter

- ◆ Promote, promote, promote
- ◆ Look beyond the walls
- ◆ Big business boom
- ◆ Assembling your arsenal
- ◆ Take to cyberspace

Sure, you can open the doors to your bar, sit back, and wait for the customers to pour in. But we wouldn't bet that you'd be open a year from now. If it were that simple, there would be a greater number of successful bars, and as we've discussed before, only 3 out of 10 bars succeed.

To guarantee that you are among those three, you need to generate ways to market your bar and bring in the customers. In the bar business, these ideas are called promotions, and in this chapter, we will discuss the different types of promotions you can do and help you figure out which will work for your establishment.

As we've stated, the bar business is a party in progress. Here's how to keep it going and make money in the process.

Successful Marketing Starts In-House: Promotions

The primary goal of promotions is to move your business forward by attracting your target clientele and adding to your vision. You are not supposed to expand your business to be something for everyone. It is important that you understand that the promotions you run can control the destiny of your bar: they determine clientele and atmosphere. That's why you should keep on track with your clientele base and keep in mind the image of the bar that you are creating.

Design promotions that either support or are supported by your original theme. You can tailor your promotion toward the group of people you want to attract or clientele you want to create. By creating more promotion, you stay on track with what you're doing already. The tough part is drumming up and creating promotions that work for you way in advance.

If you don't know anybody and you don't have a consultant or a public relations firm that can help dream up something within the boundaries of your theme, then you can consider hiring someone to do so. But if your budget is low, you must educate yourself. One way to do that is to surf the Internet for and go to different clubs and bar sites that are similar to what your theme might be. You may remember seeing a promotion that happened on the other side of the country and think that there might be a way to translate it so it can work for your bar. Look at what everyone else in the world is doing (isn't the Internet great for research?), not just in the United States, for promotional nights to help them create clientele. Another way to educate yourself is to see what everyone else around you has created, because you don't want to offer what your competition does.

Beer Goggles

Don't get greedy when expanding your clientele. You are playing with the devil if you think you can have it all. You might just scare away your loyal customers.

Now a lot of times, you can control your internal promotions by hooking up with a radio station or a television station. They may even come to you with an idea. For example, they may propose a 1980s-themed party, or a Boogie Nights party hosted by whatever radio station is in your area. They will sell you a package (the DJ, the promotion on-air), and you will provide the drink specials. They might do this party once a week or twice a week for X number of weeks. On-air, they will tell the people to come on down and enjoy the festivities and their favorite DJ. People will reach out to you in many ways, but you still need to control your own destiny.

Using a Promoter

Many ideas are built on borrowed concepts. They didn't come out of thin air. People see it somewhere and they want to do it for their clientele. But if those things don't work, you can hire a *promoter*.

Some promoters take over a venue and at times change its name for the night. A good example is one that Steve went to at the Venetian Hotel and Casino in Las Vegas. The promoter, out of Los Angeles, transformed the club into Candyland and gave the club a new title, "Candyland at the Venetian." Inside the club were girls dressed in red and white candy cane–striped dresses, handing out candy canes to all the customers. Candy canes were everywhere. On stage, swing sets with candy stripes were set up for the girls to swing on, while there was a huge white wizard that walked on stilts on stage. The DJ played pumping music. And periodically throughout the evening, it would snow. So cool!

def•i•ni•tion

Promoters take over a venue and sometimes change its name for the night. When you use a promoter you reap the benefits of selling your product, and in return you pay them a promotional fee or they may earn whatever the cover charge is for the night. They are not allowed to share in the alcohol sales; it's against the law.

While the wow-factor was high in that example, not all promoters help business. In fact, one way to get off track is to let the wrong promoter come in. He can bring in a group that normally doesn't patronize your place, which can be good or bad. If bad, your clientele base will run the other way. They may not say the crowd is one they don't want to be around; they will just stop showing up. Because you were too greedy, you will lose your good clientele base for the ones that you invited to the special promotion. It all pertains to how you control your promotional nights.

We don't like dealing with a promoter unless we know everything they will try to accomplish under our roof. You are the king of your own domain; don't let a promoter try to take that from you. Good promoters have great reputations, so know whom you are dealing with. Everybody says they are a promoter, but are they really? What are their intentions? Are they doing it for ego reasons or are they trying to be someone they are not? A lot of people go into the promotion business with the wrong perception of what a promoter should be trying to do.

Even with good promoters, you must know their background; you have to know what they are all about and what they want to accomplish. You have to know what they are doing in print with your logo, because the logo represents you and your establishment, and they are only representing themselves (and it happens to be at your place). Never give in to a promoter who wants to use and abuse you. You set the bar for what your establishment will provide and what kind of clientele base you want. Once you compromise with a promoter, you compromise your ability to keep your theme in place.

Tip Jar

Make sure you get to approve whatever the promoter will put your logo on before it goes into mass production. Otherwise, it can make you liable for something you would never do, such as offer an open bar to the public beyond the legal time.

Promoters will also help you with official event parties. The promoter can help you invite VIPs to the party, after which you open your bar up to the public.

The mileage that you'll get out of this type of party is considerable. You'll make money that night because the public will enjoy peeking and eyeing the people in that special area, especially if celebrities attend. That kind of word-of-mouth is phenomenal, so that promotional fee that you may have to pay out, or the expenses of the food or the searchlight, is worth it. Doing these types of parties brings miles and miles of promotion and repeat customers and gives your place a higher status. Also, having celebrities enjoying themselves in your establishment goes a long way in publicity.

But know this: official-event party promoters pick you; you don't pick them. They pick you because of your establishment and your reputation. You can try to court event party planners, but most of the time they know what type of establishment they want to host their "official" party.

Coming Up with Your Own Promotions

Ultimately, we believe in promoting from within yourself: coming up with your own promotions and adding sponsors to your own promotion. If you build your own internal promotion, you don't need promoters.

You can incorporate all types of promotional nights into a week. For example, you can host a service industry night. You pass out special service industry cards that allow special drink prices and certain people in. You can host a contest, such as a Go-Go-a-Rama dance competition or a bikini contest. Get sponsors for prizes. All of this is building your promotion for the night; get the word out by radio, e-mail newsletters, and flyers. Just identify a customer base and promote to it through advertising, which we discuss more in Chapter 23.

The theme of your bar, as well as the size of it, will come into play when identifying good promotions for you. Consider your location when deciding your promotions. Having a special band on a particular day may attract customers. For instance, having a nine-piece reggae band on a Sunday afternoon may appeal to people who are in the mood to chill and relax and have a drink before the workweek begins.

Tip Jar

For a contest, six is a good number of contestants. If you have more, it's a measure that your promotion works.

Friday and Saturday nights can be normal nights. You can center a promotion around a particular act or type of music. For instance, the House of Blues in the Mandalay Bay Resort in Las Vegas hosts a gospel brunch on Sundays. While their clientele is always changing, the gospel music fits into the Southern theme of the bar and restaurant.

You'll also use all that research you did when you were opening your bar. Identify groups that would mesh well with your core clientele and then plan promotions for less busy times to bring those people in. You always want to use your promotional nights to attract a customer base and give them a reason to come out and have a fun time in your establishment. In this day and age, people need something to get them in to have fun. Examples of promotions are Monday Night Football or any other popular sporting event, such as a pay-per-view fight where you have drink and food specials during the game or event.

Each promotion you build needs to be calculated. You should forecast it all the way through and when one ends, such as Monday Night Football, you need another one in place so you don't miss a beat. That is the key to a successful place. You must keep things exciting for your customers so they don't get bored and you don't become stale.

Corporate Functions

Just because you run a bar doesn't mean that you can't take advantage of meeting-planning dollars—the money that companies spend on parties, conventions, and annual meetings. In fact, depending on where you are, the convention trade is a great group to target, especially if you can work with them in advance.

It is the responsibility of you or anyone who may help you market your business to contact corporations that will be coming to your city for their annual meetings or conventions. Most cities make this list available. Your convention and visitor's bureau has it. Some of these companies can be contacted while others request not to be.

def•i•ni•tion

An **off-property night** is a night when a convention spends money to line up an event at a venue other than the hotel or convention center. These events can bring in lots of money—usually enough for you to close your establishment to the public.

If you are creative, you get a hold of the planner six to eight months in advance and find out if they have picked an *off-property night* location.

Corporate money is great. It is one of the biggest hidden treasures when owning a bar, because their events are usually on off nights when you don't have a lot of business. No matter what the size of the corporations, they are good contacts because they are unfound revenue bases, not to mention they usually are fun people, too.

Getting the Word Out

You can have a beautiful establishment with no one in it because you haven't promoted outside your four walls. You have to go out and get the business; don't wait for the business to come to you.

Now that you have the promotional pieces in your hand—the one-time VIP passes, the guest passes for free admission before a certain time (see "VIP Cards and Passes" later in this chapter), the flyers—train your staff to hit hotels and their staff. They should talk to everyone: the concierge, bellmen, front desk staff, managers, sales manager, pool attendants, servers, even guests at the pool if the management will allow it.

Flyers

When you think about flyers, you might think of the guys on the Las Vegas Boulevard, shoving flyers toward people strolling the Strip. Flyers can be effective marketing tools when used correctly. You want to distribute them in a controlled area, unlike on a main strip in Vegas, where people are moving. During the latter, you repeat yourself; you repeat yourself; and, oh, did we mention you repeat yourself? Does it show in numbers? Yeah, maybe you get 5 percent of those people to react to it.

Five percent isn't a great return for the amount of work that entails. That's why we prefer going into controlled environments. For instance, leave the promotional item—the flier, pass, VIP card, and/or business card—at stores up and down your main boulevard. To do so, introduce yourself, explain where you are from, give the business owner or manager the promotional material, and explain that they are for their customers to put in their bag as a bonus.

It makes you look good, it makes them look good, and it gives their customers a place to go out and wear that beautiful dress they just bought (and saves them money). The store owner can put the flyer up on the counter, and it's a conversation piece. It isn't a loss leader; it doesn't cost them anything and it's a tangible item right at point of sale. You could even have stands made if you'd like.

When Steve did this in Palm Springs, he would have salespeople and store owners trained to call him when they needed more passes. And he'd deliver immediately, replenishing their supply. When this happens, what do you have? You have a bunch of stores working for you by handing promotional materials out and calling you when they need more. Imagine people who own their own shops working for you. It allows them to give something to their customers and help their customers.

Eventually everyone throughout the city becomes a concierge in one fashion or another. Everyone will be asked, "Where should I go for this?" It's just a question that gets asked and everyone has a favorite destination because they go there themselves. So if you get the locals on your side, they become your promotional people above and beyond what you do.

Tip Jar _____

You can work with owners of restaurants, hotels, and even hair salons to display your promotional items. Think outside of the box.

Website

We believe that a website is a necessity these days. The Internet has changed everyone's life in one fashion or another. Remember the days when we actually sat down and wrote a letter and put a stamp on it? We don't mail letters anymore; we e-mail them. We feel that having a website that you can update is a better way to communicate with the masses. You can reach people one-on-one in your city and make sure that everyone knows what's going on.

You may also want to offer a website where people can interact with others, whether it's other people or other businesses. This is a great tool for the future. It means a little more time and money, but the effort goes a long way. And the best way to find out if it works for you is to put your website address on any piece of promotional material that you put together—a flier, a pass, and so on. You will be surprised how many people visit your site. You can record the number of visitors by having either a counter on your website or just using software that records the impressions for you that you can check on.

This is also a good tool for people planning a visit to your area who are booking a hotel room. It's always good to have your website linked to any hotel sites in your area, because it helps promote your establishment to the planning tourist.

You can either take the time to develop your own website or you can pay a web developer to do so. The best way to find a good developer is to ask friends or family or business colleagues who have websites if they have worked with someone they like. It's our experience that referrals are the easiest way to find someone. Check out some of the other work that the person or firm has done. If you like what you see, talk to them. Most can help you secure a domain name and design your site to meet your needs.

Mailing Lists and Newsletters

Any time you collect information in this day and age, ask for all the vitals (except Social Security number). But more importantly, ask for their e-mail address, so if you want to send out a massive e-mail, you can. And if you have all the other pertinent information like sex, age, occupation, and so on, you can target it. The result is that you can target your mass e-mails and promotional messages to specific demographics. You can still use a standard promotion flyer or card advertising for that night, but you can also separate your collected e-mail addresses into groups and write specifically to that group, urging them to come to your place.

Your e-mail list, which you have garnered from all around town, from the hotels to the shop owners to the food servers—from all of those people who have been working for you—has turned into gold. You have successfully advertised beyond your four walls by getting out there and making connections. Now that you have them, you have to maintain them.

VIP Cards and Passes

VIP cards are mainly used in nightclubs. VIPs are basically members of the club. For a fee or dues, they enjoy certain benefits, such as getting themselves and a guest in for free, getting in at any time without waiting in line, and receiving a discount for some special events. VIPs beat the cover charge, which in turn makes them feel like they are a part of the club.

You choose the price of membership, let's say $250. It expires after a year, and the reason it expires is to get them back into the club and have them to spend more money.

Ninety percent of the time you give them out as complimentary to certain people. Specifically you give them to industry folks, from sales managers who would send you groups to the general manager or the bellman who sends you business—anyone you think deserves a VIP card.

It is a good tool to use for locals who come to you often and send you a lot of business. It may cost you 50 cents to produce the actual card, but it will bring you thousands of dollars in return. It is one of the best tools you can have.

Now, unlike the VIP passes, the guest pass is a one-time pass that gets the holder in free before a certain time. Those guest passes are to get a nucleus into the bar or club before 9:30 P.M., after which the passes expire. If someone with a guest pass comes a minute later, they have to pay the cover. Distribute these passes to hotel employees and others who can send business your way. When handing out guest passes, it's important to make it very clear to the people who will be handing them out that there is an expiration time. Otherwise, they may overpromise what the pass can do and end up looking like a fool to the person they gave it to when it doesn't deliver. You don't want that to happen, because it can weaken your relationship with that hotel employee or shop owner.

Sponsorships

Sponsors can help you pull off the promotions that you dream up. You can hook up with your liquor salesman to do a tasting of a wine. You could hook up with a liquor sponsor as well. For example, Heineken may want to come in and do a promotion with you around a holiday, like Memorial Day, or a special event that might be happening in your city, for which you might host the official welcome party.

Which leads us to point out the importance of knowing what's going on in the community. For example, if you live in Los Angeles, there could be a runway show down the street, and it's a big production with sponsors. You, as the hot bar, can host the after-party and get your name out as a sponsor. You can either rent out the place for two hours for revenue or instead the use of the venue to hold the after-party might be your sponsorship. The runway show designer would have to find someone to sponsor or pay for the liquor if you will give it away.

Ultimately, once you get people coming to your bar, successful marketing happens inside of it—if they have a good experience, they'll tell someone who will then tell someone else.

Beer Goggles _____

You cannot give liquor away, nor can you be paid by a liquor company to do so. The exception is a private party at which they pay for the liquor and food for those invited guests only. If it isn't open to the public, it's okay.

The Least You Need to Know

- If you want to grow your business, you need to look outside of your four walls.

- It's never too soon to start promoting your bar.

- Remember that you are the king of your kingdom—you decide what promotions are right for your business and clientele.

- Corporate dollars and e-mail addresses are untapped gold.

- Being the location of official event parties can garner good publicity.

- Get the locals to work for you; word-of-mouth is powerful.

Chapter 23

For the Advertising Amateur

In This Chapter

- Advertising 101
- Five percent of gross
- Print, radio, TV
- The savvy buyer
- Hit the target
- Match the promotion

We mentioned in Chapter 22 that you can't just sit back waiting for the phone to ring and the customers to come. You need to develop promotions that will build interest so people come into your business. But once you've developed the promotion, how is anyone to know about it? That's where advertising comes in. Advertising introduces these promotional nights to the masses.

But advertising isn't just buying a commercial on the radio; it's being strategic in how you spend your money, who you want to target, and how you want to communicate with them. Depending on your location, traditional advertising venues may be cost-preventative. In that case, look to Chapter 22 for the guerilla marketing tactics that can be effective. But even if you don't think you can afford to advertise, read on about how you can and should.

Figuring Out How Much to Spend

We believe that marketing and promotion go hand-in-hand. A lot of people make the mistake of not advertising until the middle of their bar's life span or until the end of it. At that point, they throw lots of money at it and wonder why they spent all that money on *advertising* that didn't work. We'll tell you why it didn't: because people had already experienced the place, and because you didn't advertise, it was slow and wasn't "happening." And guess what? You didn't make a good first impression.

def•i•ni•tion

Advertising is considered a paid promotion of goods, services, establishment, or an idea that is part of an overall marketing strategy that includes public relations.

From the moment you open your doors to the public, consistency in marketing and advertising is of the utmost importance. You must advertise and promote beyond your four walls (which we discussed in Chapter 22). You must do it from the beginning to make that first impression work. You can have all the advertising money out there and not have a single person come in if it isn't done properly by choosing what's best for you.

When deciding how much money to spend on advertising, plan on at least 5 percent of your *desired* gross revenue. It's important to use your *potential* gross revenue because that's how you grow your business. What you gross right now might be a low number because you didn't advertise effectively in the first place. Using your potential gross also helps you achieve consistency in advertising, because you have to project and forecast what you are going to buy, such as package deals for advertising for a consistent amount of time. If you budget according to your fluctuating monthly gross, 5 percent of each month's gross will be a varying number.

Say you are currently grossing $30,000 a month, but you know the potential (based on what you believe each person will spend and your maximum occupancy) is $50,000 or $60,000. You need to create a marketing and promotional plan that will get you to that number. And the only way to get to that number is to project out on a quarterly basis, trying to determine what will work for your business—radio, television, and/or print (see the following section).

Tip Jar

Determine what your potential gross is by looking at what you believe each person will spend and your maximum occupancy. That is your maximum gross income. Any more may be unrealistic.

For example, if you want your gross to be $100,000 a month, 5 percent of that should go toward advertising, which would be $5,000 a month. Now you have a number that you want to create—$5,000 a month with a goal of $100,000 gross. Therefore, in the first quarter you will spend $15,000 in advertising.

Debating the Ad Options

Now that we have decided how much money to spend, we are going to ask, "What can I do to get the best bang for my buck? What am I going to spend my advertising budget on?"

Print, radio, and television are advertising venues. You need to pick whatever works best for you and the promotion you are running.

Print

Of course, advertising will be in print. Printing costs are part of the advertising budget. Technically promotional items like flyers are getting the word out.

At the same time, those printed items are great because you could leave them behind in places that your potential clientele may be. The print advertising could be drink table tents in your bar with promotional sides on them listing what promotions you are running during the week.

On the way out, you can hand out cards and such so customers can get it in their pocket and read about it later. But ultimately these in-house print promotions are not going to communicate to the numbers that you want so you can grow your business and make it wildly successful.

Tip Jar

When you collect data for VIP cards, ask your customers what kind of local media they enjoy—radio stations, newspapers, television stations. This gives you an idea of the best way to target them.

Print options like newspaper advertising fall into the advertising budget. Depending on where you live, however, your local newspaper may not be an option if it doesn't match the media habits of your target client or if it's cost-preventative. Your local alternative weekly or even the free newspaper in your area may be a better option.

If you're contemplating advertising in newspapers or newsletters, look at the circulation numbers and the distribution areas provided by the advertising salespeople. Make sure that the circulation is audited by an independent agency so you know what you are buying and who the reader is. If distribution is concentrated across town from where you're located, it might not be the best media buy for you. Only you will know that, though.

Radio

External advertising and promotion is a must, and the habits of your community will help determine what media to use. For instance, if you have a large car-commuting demographic, radio may be a good option. It puts your established brand name in the ear of the beholder. But like anything else, you have to keep consistent with it. One spot does not make a successful radio campaign.

Media outlets will help you create your ads, but you will come up with the key elements. While this is helpful, when it comes to radio, it can make your ad become white noise on the radio if all the ads are written by the same copywriters and voiced by the same popular DJs that the listener is tuning in to. Under this scenario, it's hard to imagine that your ad is having any impact on the listener. You may want to write your own ads and consider producing them out of town or hiring a company to produce the ad.

> **Bartender Knowledge**
>
> When you live in a media market that is very expensive, make the most of your in-house promotion. For example, if you have entertainment, such as a house band or DJ, they can tell people what's going on today and encourage them to come back for whatever promotion you have lined up the next night. This is especially good if you have a walk-up destination on a busy thoroughfare.

You could also send the ad out to an older DJ who used to be in the area and who has a distinctive voice. After it's produced, the radio station would put it in its lineup or queue according to the advertising you bought. You might pay more for the production and have fewer advertising spots in specific high-volume times, but at least you know that it won't fade into the background.

Television

Radio may be cost-effective in areas where print advertising is expensive. Depending on the climate, television advertising may also be cost-effective and draw numbers, especially during colder months, because more people stay home and are not in their cars as much.

Television may be particularly expensive because of the commercial production cost. Remember to consider what your promotion is and whether the boob tube will help create the excitement you need to drive customers into your establishment and make your gross sales goal.

Advertising and Promotions: Putting Them Together

Here's where the promotion works hand-in-hand with the advertising. Let's say you want to promote a Go-Go-a-Rama night that is also a service industry night. It includes drink specials plus a promotion that is fun and exciting to watch. Let's walk through the steps of building this promotion. You're going to find sponsors to provide prizes for first, second, and third places in the Go-Go-a-Rama dance contest, and you're going to have your drink specials for industry night.

A promotion like this calls for a medium that targets the local service industry and expresses the excitement and energy of the Go-Go dancing contest. In this example, radio may not be a bad idea. You can get your message about the night out to the masses and it will have a catchy promotional ad. But that's not all—you'll probably also do print by distributing flyers or cards that will inform people about what's going on that night. The third thing that you would do is put the flyer and the promotion information on your website so when you go out and promote it with your hand-to-hand public relations strategy, people have a place where they can reference the information you're talking about.

Now, if they didn't catch it on the radio and they didn't catch it in their hand with the print ad, they can look it up on the Internet even if they caught the tail end of the radio spot and heard nothing more than the name of your establishment. Having the ability for your potential customers to go to a website so they can look up that promotion and confirm it with their friends to make sure that they show up helps you drive business. And that is how you build your promotion using advertising each month.

Bartender Knowledge

Two reasons why customers come on a promotional night: a) for the product and the drink specials, and b) for the actual promotion, the fun contest or whatever it may be.

Let's say you designated $1,200 per month for radio advertising for 3 months for what will be a 3-month or 12-week promotion. After the promotion has ended, you evaluate the quarter. Did you get what you needed from your advertising and promotional dollars to get to your derived goal of your gross revenue of $100,000? Did you go below it? Did you go above it? Is your average where you want it to be? Did you do $90,000 the first month and $100,000 the second month? Did you meet your goal and then exceed your goal in the third month? You created your goal and now you either achieved it or not. If you didn't, you need to figure out why.

Ultimately, the type of advertising you choose will have a lot to do with the pricing. For example, in a metropolitan area, radio may be $250 a spot. If you have a gross revenue that is $100,000, 5 percent would be one week of advertising for that metropolitan area. You couldn't afford that radio station to help you draw in the masses.

Be a Smart Media Buyer

Just beware of one thing when buying advertising: someone trying to lock you into a package or one specific thing without allowing you to take the time and think about it. You are better at drawing your own picture instead of someone else drawing it for you.

Don't buy anything on a whim. Tell them you need time to think about it and have them leave their proposal behind. If they claim that they need to know now, apologize and say that you can't make a decision that quick, but maybe next time. This way, you're in control of your own destiny. They'll learn that you aren't some newbie who will jump on anything that sounds good. And it may sound good and creative, but it may not pan out for you—maybe for someone else, but not for you.

If you already know what's going to work for you, you'll get to pick or choose what will fit into your budget. But if buying advertising is Greek to you, here are some clues that you can use to figure it out.

Let's use a radio station as an example. What's going to make you want to advertise with a radio station? Knowing what kind of atmosphere is in your bar and what kind of image you want to create for your bar. If you're an Irish bar, you're not going to advertise on a hip-hop station. There are ratings for the station and age demographic; a radio station should show you an Arbitron or a Nielsen rating (any radio station will be a member of a rating system).

Beer Goggles

Do your own market research; ad sales reps have ways of showing you their market research that best matches your business.

Some people are skeptical of ratings and circulation numbers. You can choose to believe or not believe them, but do go through and see who their listeners are. Some stations' listeners may not be in tune to what your concept is. So if the radio station is country and you are running a trendy hip Euro-Asian flair bar, you're probably not going to advertise on that station. The demographics for the age bracket may work, but the rating organization will be able to break other things down for you.

Every market is different and every formula is different for your advertising, marketing, and promotion. It all depends on the area you're in.

Know Who Your Customer Is

Knowing who your target customer is will help you decide what media to use. For instance, if you create a high-end clientele base, then you are going to go after more high-end clients. To do that, you need to advertise in the media that they enjoy. Knowing those habits is very important. For instance, the teen Top 40 radio station may not be the best choice for advertising if you're trying to target college-educated professionals. Making contributions to your local National Public Radio station, however, might be just the ticket to reach them during their commute. Pull out the demographic research you did in Chapter 3 to better understand who your potential customers are and for clues as to the best ways to target them through advertising.

Most importantly, remember that advertising, guerrilla marketing, and promotions go hand-in-hand. You have the marketing, you have the promotions, you have the advertising. One has to work with the other. You just can't have a bunch of dollars going out to advertising and nobody promoting and nobody marketing. Externally and internally it all has to work in sync. Otherwise, your business will not grow and succeed.

The Least You Need to Know

- ♦ Advertising without promotion won't get you anywhere.
- ♦ Keep your gross income in mind, and spend advertising dollars accordingly.
- ♦ The cost of the media will be a large factor in choosing advertising.
- ♦ Don't make hasty media buys: read, digest, and determine if it's right for you.
- ♦ Your promotion will help lead you to a complementary advertising media that will match its excitement and energy.

Chapter 24

Planning for the Future

In This Chapter

- ◆ Playing with the menu
- ◆ Inflating prices
- ◆ Hiring a number two
- ◆ Passing on your dream
- ◆ Building your bar empire
- ◆ Deciding your future

Congratulations! You've done it—opened a bar and made it successful. Now what? Are you going to Disneyland?

Yes, a vacation is probably not a bad idea, but what about when you come back? Is it time to make some changes to your business? If you have been running your bar for a while, there might be some things that you feel you can improve upon. Maybe you have identified an element that is missing from your place and now would be a good time to add it: a manager, for instance.

It's even possible that you have enjoyed this journey so much that you want to keep going by either expanding this theme to another location or by opening another place that's completely different from the bar you have now. No matter how grandiose or minuscule your plans are for your business, this chapter will lead you in the right direction.

Adjusting the Menu

Now that you have been open for a while, you know your customer's habits. You know what they prefer to drink, you know what they prefer to eat. It's time to give them more of what they like.

What does that mean? You could create a signature drink featuring the liquors they prefer. You could create a different happy hour menu that features more of their favorite appetizers. Or you could even just change the food menu.

Tip Jar

Create the next drink sensation by doing some research. If your theme is based on a culture, see if there is a popular alcoholic drink in that country that you could serve. Who knows? You could create another mojito craze.

If you decide to do the latter, you want to keep the favorites and switch out what isn't. By looking at the items that work for you, you might identify some recipes that are similar that would be good candidates for the menu. You might also identify some holes; for instance, your menu may be sorely lacking a vegetarian dish.

After deciding on what items you would like to test, consider introducing each one separately at happy hour when you may have a large customer base. Depending on your food special at that time, you will be able to measure interest by how many orders you served and feedback from your guests.

Also look at your profit margin. You might have to update your menu prices. Every establishment must raise prices now and then. Inflation drives up the costs of products, services, utilities, and taxes, as well as increases wages and the expenses of employee benefits. To keep making a profit, you will need to raise your prices as your costs start to rise.

If your competitors are doing the same thing, it may be prudent for you to do so, too. Again, it's the perception to the guest, and if everyone's prices are comparable then he or she may not realize that you raised your prices.

Another thing to look at on your menu is your loss leader, if you have one. If you have a loss leader and you're not making a lot of money, the average check should go up if it's the sizzle that you are selling. The food is secondary and the percentage of liquor should be higher because that's what the customer is there for.

Last, if you are looking to change your menu to bring more dollars down to the bottom line, remember: never jeopardize the quality of your food. You're better off changing your menu or succumbing to charging more. You might lose a few pennies, but you gain a lot back on the average check for the liquor.

Hiring Other Managers

If you own a small bar and you get tired and want to see your family, you might consider hiring a manager or a shift person to come on board and relieve you. Before you do this, you have to feel comfortable with yourself and have enough of a profit margin to feel comfortable enough to afford a manager.

When hiring that person, it's always good to hire someone who mirrors yourself if you have a successful business. When we say that, we mean that person should mirror the procedures you want done and how you want things done consistently in the back and front of the house. Once you are able to teach someone exactly how you run your operation, then you have achieved even more success.

Beer Goggles _____

If you're having a hard time relinquishing trust to the manager you've hired, look at the bottom line and purchases. If they can follow your steps in terms of purchasing and accounting, you'll have an easier time trusting them.

Why? Because you could share you dream with someone else. They are living your dream and what you have created, and that is part of the magic, too. What's even better is now that person may be able to step away and do another place and leave other people behind that know how you want your place to run. Ultimately, you may be able to "cookie cutter" it someplace else or begin a franchise. You never know. That's how they start.

Expansion

Let's go back to downtown Palm Springs one last time. Near the heart of the main strip is a place called the Grill-A-Burger Bar and Grill. Its logo is a gorilla eating a hamburger, and the menu is simple, with burgers, sandwiches, salads, and fries. There is also a full bar. The owners have been pretty successful at this walk-up destination despite another extremely successful walk-up burger joint on the next block. Recently, they opened a second location in Palm Desert, California, about 30 minutes east of their original location.

This location is different from the first one. It's in a strip mall, which makes it a drive-up destination, and it's also a bit smaller in space. In their first week open, they had lines of people waiting to get in.

It just goes to show that when something is good, people know; when something is bad, they know even quicker. If you've been able to create a successful bar in your area, it's possible that you may be able to duplicate it in another area. But it isn't a given. Many factors come into play when trying to create a second bar.

One of the most important things to consider is whether you really want to expand and why. Once you know that, then you can begin to determine if this is something you should or shouldn't do. Writing pro-and-con lists has always worked for us because the lists allow you to look at the big picture—everything from commitment and drive to energy and support.

If expanding your business is something that you really want to do and you have the same energy and drive as you did when you opened your establishment, then you could possibly succeed in your second venture. But it won't be the same as opening your first place. This time you go into it knowing exactly what it takes to make an establishment successful—the hard work, the long hours, the public, and the employees.

Beer Goggles

If you didn't really enjoy opening your first bar or had a hard time with it, expansion isn't for you.

Know this: it will take more money, more people, more effort, and more focus. Think about the money you are making now. Do you have the financial resources to expand your business? How will adding another bar affect the bar you have now? Do you have the patience to repeat this process? Do you have the will? Answer yes to these things and you may be successful.

If you have a location in mind, make sure it's a location that is a sound business decision—not just because it's closer to your home or it's your favorite vacation spot. If you choose your next location as diligently as you did when choosing your first one, you'll have a better chance of success.

The simpler your theme is, the easier it will be to duplicate not just once but multiple times. Just look at the Grill-A-Burger Bar and Grill example. Keep your eye on the prize of opening one location at a time and allowing each one time to grow.

Opening another location requires an extreme amount of skill and patience. If you haven't been in business for a long time, then you might be growing too fast. While other establishments may have done this and been successful, many more of them have failed. That's why it's extremely important to analyze your situation and determine what's best for you. In the end, you might decide that owning one well-running, highly profitable bar is fine. Or you may decide that you still want to move forward and create your tiki bar, or whatever your dream theme is.

Things to Think About

Whatever you do, take the time to come to your conclusion. There is no time clock ticking and no stress about losing thousands of dollars if you don't decide. This decision is too big. Plus, you're running a successful bar now. While you're thinking about your next step, consider:

◆ **Recruiting, hiring, training, and retaining employees.** This becomes a priority and a concern the more locations you open. Maintaining staffing levels is more important when you have to be in more than one place at the same time.

◆ **Executing the theme.** Each bar needs to be the same. Think about the chain restaurants and bars that you have patronized. A Chili's in California is the same as a Chili's in Virginia.

◆ **Maintaining your vision for your bars.** Instead of you, the bar's visionary, always being present, you must instill what your expectations are for the bar in your many employees. That can be difficult when others are training. If you have any trust issues, this may be difficult for you to do.

Seven Principles of Expansion

After giving it much consideration, you are still bent on building your bar empire. Opening your second location is a bit different than starting your first place. Follow these principles to add another bar to your business:

◆ **Principle One:** Create a tactical action plan that is based on your first business plan but tweaked to address the demographics and the other characteristics of the second location. You want to be systematic each time you open a new location so you do not negatively affect your bar's brand.

◆ **Principle Two:** Hone your current operations into a well-oiled machine with systems that will be easy to duplicate as you open more locations.

◆ **Principle Three:** Make sure that your sales are moving upward. If your sales are increasing, it means that people are enjoying and liking what you're doing. If your bars' sales are declining, then you probably shouldn't open a new one.

- ◆ **Principle Four:** Have strong, effective financial control systems. If they are weak, that will only be magnified when you open multiple locations. Stabilize these processes before expanding your business.

- ◆ **Principle Five:** Re-evaluate your décor. Is it easy to recreate? Is it easy to maintain? Does it stand up to the test of time? This may mean remodeling the original location. Also remember that more locations mean you'll probably rely on others for maintenance.

- ◆ **Principle Six:** Have an effective and efficient marketing and advertising plan. Remember the 5 percent rule; when you apply it to each bar location, the cost becomes significantly more expensive. This means you should be very comfortable and confident that your marketing and advertising plan works.

- ◆ **Principle Seven:** Funnel your strong people to your new bar so you aren't starting from scratch. These people can help train new staff and ensure that each opening is a strong one.

Last, it is alright to just enjoy the business that you have just built. Or maybe you have decided after this journey that the bar business just isn't your thing. Plenty of people will buy a successful bar that has a proven record. Whatever you decide, we wish you much success.

The Least You Need to Know

- ◆ Changing your menu creates excitement for your customers.

- ◆ Menu price increases should be timed well.

- ◆ Purchasing is a great indicator of whether you can trust a manager.

- ◆ Follow the seven principles of expansion to ensure success.

Appendix A

Glossary

advertising   The paid promotion of goods, services, establishment, or an idea that is part of an overall marketing strategy that includes public relations.

Ansel System   The fire suppression system. Like the hood, it is located in the ceiling of the kitchen and stays with the building.

barback   The person who provides support to the bartenders by stocking and cleaning the bar area, as well as performing any other tasks that might arise behind the bar, such as cutting garnishes and taking drink orders.

beats per minute   Also known as bpm, it is a measure of music's tempo. The higher the number of beats, the faster the song is.

bottle conditioned   Describes beers that are unfiltered and unpasteurized.

break-even analysis   A common tool used to evaluate the economic feasibility of a new business. It is based on two types of costs: fixed and variable. It helps determine the point when the revenue is exactly even to the costs.

breakage   The number of empty bottles at the end of the night. Breakage can also refer to glassware that is broken or food that spoils.

buildouts   Construction needed to create a bar. These normally stay with a building, which is lucky, because building them yourself can be costly.

Caipirinha   A cocktail popular in Brazil made with lots of fresh limes and sugar cachaça (pronounced cah-SHAH-sah), a type of white rum distilled from sugar cane.

call drink   A liquor the customer calls for by name; for example, a Tanqueray Martini, a Captain and Coke, or a Patron Margarita. When someone doesn't call their liquor, the drink gets made with the well brand, or the liquor that is in the well.

chains   Bars owned and operated by one company, local individuals, or firms. They have centralized marketing and purchasing, which tends to mean lower costs and higher profits. Examples are Fado Irish Pub and John Harvard's Brew House.

chart of accounts   The list of general ledger account numbers that subdivide into associated titles using basic accounting equations.

COD   Cash on delivery, or pay on receipt of merchandise.

complexity   An essential element in great wines. Complexity is a combination of richness, depth of flavor, intensity, balance, harmony, and finesse.

curb appeal   The first impression that a building gives from the street.

distillation   The vaporization of an alcoholic liquid by heat; the condensation of its alcohol content is then collected and sometimes placed in oak barrels, pots, or columns.

egress   Denotes the ease of exit from an establishment.

high-impression areas   Places or people that the guest can't help but notice. These include the outside and entrance, the bathrooms, the floors, the tables and chairs, the glassware, and your employees.

hood   The ventilation system. Like the Ansel System, it is located in the ceiling of the kitchen and stays with the building.

ingress   Denotes the ease of entrance to an establishment.

jigger   A two-sided metal shot glass with one side measuring a half ounce and the other measuring 2 ounces.

lacing   The ring left by the head as it moves down the glass as the beer is drunk. As the beer nears its end, a series of rings should be present on the glass wall.

liquor license quotas   The number of licenses that are in effect in a community, based on population.

lounge   A luxurious, comfortable place to serve alcohol.

marry   To mix alcohol from two bottles into one. This is an illegal practice.

mitigate   To try to lessen a possible leakage of sound.

notice of allowance   A written communication from the U.S. Patent and Trademark Office indicating that a patent application has been allowed.

occupancy   The number of people that a building can hold safely.

off-property night   A night that a convention has money to line up an event at a venue other than a hotel. These can be events that bring in lots of money—enough for you to close your establishment.

par sheet   A sheet that helps you keep track of what you have on hand, compares it to what you need, and determines what you need to order.

promoters   Individuals who take over a venue and sometimes change its name for the night.

promotions   An aspect of marketing that is meant to drive business. It is supported by advertising, publicity, and public relations. A successful promotion increases sales.

proof   The amount of ethanol in an alcoholic beverage; it's usually twice the percentage of alcohol. Pure alcohol is 200 proof, being 100 percent alcohol. A combination of half alcohol and half water is scored as 100 proof or 50 percent alcohol. Proof is a measure of alcoholic strength, not necessarily of quality.

sexual harassment   Sexual behavior that is deliberate, uninvited, unwelcome, and usually repeated, and that is perceived by the recipient to be embarrassing, offensive, demeaning, or compromising.

soft opening   When you quietly open your doors to the public and run the business hoping to get the kinks out before the grand opening.

speed rack   A rack at thigh level where the most-used liquors are kept for quick access by the bartender.

spotters   People who pose as customers to make sure no one is stealing from you and to make sure that you give great customer service. They are like secret shoppers.

tannins   The astringent compounds found in grape skins, seeds, and stems that make your mouth pucker and feel dry when you drink red wine.

traffic counts   Exactly what it sounds like: the average daily number of cars or pedestrians passing a particular location within a 12- or 24-hour period. A traffic survey can be conducted by you, a real estate firm, a demographic firm, a planning commission, or the highway department to get this number.

varietal   Wine that receives its name from the type of grape that it's made from. By law, the wine must contain 75 percent of that grape.

well   Where bartenders make the cocktails. It is also the area where servers request drinks from the bartender and garnish the cocktails. Consists of the ice bin, speed rack, and three-sink area for washing glasses.

Additional Resources

Trade Associations

National Bar and Restaurant Management Association
www.bar-restaurant.com

National Restaurant Association
www.restaurant.org

Wine & Spirits Wholesalers of America
www.wswa.org

Government Agencies

Bureau of Alcohol, Tobacco, Firearms and Explosives
www.atf.treas.gov

Federal Trade Commission Guidelines on Franchising
www.ftc.gov/bcp/franchise/netrule.shtm

Internal Revenue Service Small Business Resource
www.irs.gov/businesses/small/index.html

United States Patent and Trademark Office
www.uspto.gov

Alcohol Beverage Control Boards for the United States, Canada, and Puerto Rico

Alabama (Control State)

Alabama Alcoholic Beverage Control Board
2715 Gunter Park Drive West
Montgomery, AL 36109
Phone: 334-271-3840
Fax: 334-277-2150

Alaska

Alaska Revenue Department
Alcoholic Beverage Control Board
5848 E. Tudor Road
Anchorage, AK 99507
Phone: 907-269-0350
Fax: 907-272-9412

Arizona

Arizona Department of Liquor Licenses and Control
800 W. Washington, 5th Floor
Phoenix, AZ 85007
Phone: 602-542-5141
Fax: 602-542-5707

and

400 W. Congress, #150
Tucson, AZ 85701
Phone: 520-628-6595
Fax: 520-628-6620

Arkansas

Alcohol Beverage Control
1515 W. Seventh Street, Room 503
Little Rock, AR 72201
Phone: 501-682-1105

California

California Department of Alcoholic Beverage Control
3927 Lennane Drive, Suite 100
Sacramento, CA 95834
Phone: 916-419-2500

California Board of Equalization
450 N. Street
Sacramento, CA 94279-0073
Phone: 916-445-6464

Colorado

Colorado Department of Revenue—Liquor
Enforcement Division
1881 Pierce #108A
Lakewood, CO 80214-1495
Mail: 1375 Sherman Street
Denver, CO 80261
Phone: 303-205-2300
Fax: 303-205-2341

Connecticut

Connecticut Department of Consumer Protection
Liquor Division
State Office Building
165 Capitol Avenue
Hartford, CT 06106
Phone: 860-713-6200
Fax: 860-713-7235

Delaware

Delaware Department of Public Services
Alcoholic Beverage Control Commission
Carvel State Office Building, 3rd Floor
820 N. French Street
Wilmington, DE 19801
Phone: 302-577-5210
Toll Free: 1-800-273-9500
Fax: 302-577-8141

District of Columbia

Alcoholic Beverage Regulation Administration
941 North Capitol Street, NE, Suite 7200
Washington, DC 20002
Phone: 202-442-4423
Fax: 202-442-4521

Florida

Florida Department of Professional Business Regulations
Division of Alcoholic Beverages
1940 N. Monroe
Tallahassee, FL 32399-0783
Phone: 850-488-3227
Fax: 850-922-5175

Georgia

Georgia Department of Revenue
Alcohol & Tobacco Tax Division
1800 Century Center Boulevard, N.E. Room 4235
Atlanta, GA 30345-3205
Mailing Address: PO Box 49728
Atlanta, GA 30359
Phone: 404-417-4900
Fax: 404-417-4901

Hawaii

Hawaii:
Department of Liquor Control
County of Hawaii
101 Aupuni Street, Suite 230
Hilo, HI 96766
Phone: East Hi: 961-8218
West Hi: 327-3549
Fax: East Hi: 961-8684
West Hi: 327-3550

Honolulu:
Liquor Commission City and County of Honolulu
Pacific Park Plaza
711 Kapiolani Boulevard, Suite 600
Honolulu, HI 96813
Phone: 808-523-4458
Toll-Free: 1-800-838-9976
Fax: 808-591-2700

Kauai:
Department of Liquor Control
County of Kauai
Lihue Civic Center
Mo'ikeha Building
4444 Rice Street, Suite 120
Kauai, HI 96766
Phone: 808-241-6580
Fax: 808-241-6585

Maui:
Department of Liquor Control
County of Maui
2145 Kaohu Street, Room 107
Wailuku, HI 96793
Phone: 808-243-7753
Fax: 808-243-7558

Idaho (Control State)

Idaho State Liquor Dispensary
Alcohol Beverage Control Bureau
Idaho State Police
PO Box 700
Meridian, ID 83680-0700
Phone: 208-884-7060

Illinois

Illinois Liquor Control Commission
100 West Randolph Street
Suite #5-300
Chicago, IL 60601
Phone: 312-814-2206
Fax: 312-814-2241

Springfield address:
101 West Jefferson Suite 3-525
Springfield, IL 62702
Phone: 217-782-2136
Fax: 217-524-1911

Indiana

Alcohol and Tobacco Commission
Indiana Government Center South
302 W. Washington Street, Room E-114
Indianapolis, IN 46204
Phone: 317-232-2430
Fax: 317-233-6114

Iowa (Control State)

Iowa Alcoholic Beverages Division
1918 S.E. Hulsizer Avenue
Ankeny, IA 50021
Phone: 515-281-7400
Toll-Free: 866-469-2223
Fax: 515-281-7385

Kansas

Kansas Department of Revenue Alcohol Beverage Control
Alcohol Beverage Control
915 SW Harrison Street, Room 214
Topeka, KS 66625-3512
Phone: 785-296-7015
Hearing Impaired TTY: 785-296-6117
Fax: 785-296-7185

Kentucky

Kentucky Alcoholic Beverage Control Department
1003 Twilight Trail, Suite A-2
Frankfort, KY 40601
Phone: 502-564-4850
Fax: 502-564-1442

Louisiana

Louisiana Department of Revenue
Alcohol and Tobacco Control Office
8549 United Plaza Boulevard, Suite 220
Baton Rouge, LA 70809
Phone: 225-925-4041
Fax: 225-925-3975

Maine (Control State)

Maine Department of Public Safety
(Liquor, Beer & Wine) Licensing
Liquor or Beer & Wine
164 State House Station
Augusta, ME 04333-0164
Phone: 207-624-7220
Fax: 207-287-3424

Maryland

Office of the Comptroller of the Treasury
Alcohol and Tobacco Tax Bureau
Louis L. Goldstein Treasury Building
PO Box 2999
Annapolis, MD 21404-0466
Phone: 410-260-7314
Fax: 410-974-3201

(Control State, Montgomery County only)
Montgomery County Dept. of Liquor Control
16650 Crabs Branch Way
Rockville, MD 20855
Phone: 240-777-1900

Worcester County Liquor Control Board
Worcester County
5363 Snow Hill Road
Snow Hill, MD—Worcester County 21863
Phone: 410-632-1250
Fax: 410-632-3010

Massachusetts

Alcoholic Beverages Control Commission
239 Causeway Street, 2nd Floor
Boston, MA 02114-2130
Phone: 617-727-3040
Fax: 617-727-1258

Michigan (Control State)

Michigan Liquor Control Commission
7150 Harris Drive
PO Box 30005
Lansing, MI 48909-7505
Phone: 517-322-1345
Fax: 517-322-5188

Minnesota

Minnesota Department of Public Safety
Liquor Control Division
Alcohol and Gambling and Enforcement Division
444 Cedar Street, Suite 133
St. Paul, MN 55101-5133
Phone: 651-296-6979
Fax: 651-297-5259
Hearing Impaired TTY: 651-282-6555

Mississippi (Control State)

Alcoholic Beverage Control Office
PO Box 540
Madison, MS 39110-0540
Phone: 601-856-1301
Fax: 601-856-1300

Missouri

Division of Alcohol and Tobacco Control
PO Box 837
Jefferson City, MO 65102
Phone: 573-751-2333
Fax: 573-751-5399

Montana (Control State)

Montana Liquor License Bureau
125 North Roberts
Helena, MT 59620
Phone: 406-444-0700 and 406-444-6900
Fax: 406-444-0750

Nebraska

Nebraska Liquor Control Commission
301 Centennial Mall South
PO Box 95046
Lincoln, NE 68509-5046
Phone: 402-471-2571
Fax: 402-471-2814

Nevada

Nevada Department of Taxation

(All beverage alcohol permits are regulated by each individual county.)

Carson City:
1550 E. College Parkway, Suite 115
Carson City, NV 89706
Phone: 775-687-4892
Fax: 775-687-5981

Elko:
850 Elm Street #2
PO Box 1750
Elko, NV 89803
Phone: 775-738-8461
Fax: 775-778-6814

Las Vegas:
Grant Sawyer Office Building
555 E. Washington Avenue, Suite 1300
Las Vegas, NV 89101
Phone: 702-486-2300
Fax: 702-486-2372

Reno:
4600 Kietzke Lane
Building O, Room 263
Reno, NV 89502
Phone: 775-688-1295
Fax: 775-688-1303

New Hampshire (Control State)

New Hampshire State Liquor Commission
Robert J. Hart Building
Storrs Street
PO Box 503
Concord, NH 03302-0503
Phone: 603-271-3134
Fax: 603-271-1107

New Jersey

New Jersey Department of Law and Public Safety
Division of Alcoholic Beverage Control
140 East Front Street
PO Box 087
Trenton, NJ 08625-0087
Phone: 609-984-2830
Fax: 609-633-6078

New Mexico

New Mexico Department of Public Safety
Special Investigations Division
6301 Indian School NE, Suite 310
Albuquerque, NM 87110
Main Office: 505-841-8053
Fax: 505-841-8062

New Mexico Regulation & Licensing Department
Alcohol and Gaming Division
725 St. Michael's Drive
PO Box 25101
Santa Fe, NM 87504-5101
Phone: 505-827-7066
Fax: 505-827-7168

New York

New York Division of Alcoholic Beverage Control
State Liquor Authority
84 Holland Avenue
Albany, NY 12208
Phone: 518-474-3114

New York City locations:

11 Park Place
New York, NY 10007
Phone: 212-417-4002
Fax: 212-417-4910

125 Main Street, Room 556
Buffalo, NY 14203
Phone: 716-847-3035
Fax: 716-847-3435

Syracuse district:
333 E. Washington Street, Room 205
Syracuse, NY 13202
Phone: 315-428-4198
Fax: 315-428-4201

North Carolina (Control State)

North Carolina Alcoholic Beverage Control Commission
3322 Garner Road
Raleigh, NC 27610-5632
Phone: 919-779-0700
Fax: 919-662-3583

North Dakota

North Dakota Office of the State Tax Commissioner
Alcohol Tax Section
600 East Boulevard Avenue
Bismarck, ND 58505-0599
Phone: 701-328-2702
Fax: 701-328-1283

Ohio (Control State)

Ohio Department of Commerce
Division of Liquor Control
6606 Tussing Road
Reynoldsburg, OH 43068-9005
Phone: 614-644-2411
Fax: 614-644-2513

Oklahoma

Alcoholic Beverage Law Enforcement Commission (ABLE)
4545 N. Lincoln Boulevard, Suite 270
Oklahoma City, OK 73105
Phone: 405-521-3484
Fax: 405-521-6578

Oregon (Control State)

Oregon Liquor Control Commission
9079 S.E. McLoughlin Boulevard
Milwaukie, OR 97222
Phone: 503-872-5000
Toll-Free: 1-800-452-6522
Licensing: 503-872-5124

Pennsylvania (Control State)

Pennsylvania Liquor Control Board
Commonwealth of Pennsylvania
Northwest Office Building
Harrisburg, PA 17124-0001
Phone: 717-783-9454
Fax: 717-787-8820

Rhode Island

Division of Commercial Licensing and Regulation
233 Richmond Street, Suite 230
Providence, RI 02903
Phone: 401-222-2416
Fax: 401-222-2417

Rhode Island Department of Business Regulation
Liquor Control Administration
233 Richmond Street, Suite 200
Providence, RI 02903-4213
Phone: 401-222-2562

South Carolina

South Carolina Department of Revenue & Taxation
Alcohol Beverage Licensing Section
301 Gervais Street
PO Box 125
Columbia, SC 29214-0137
Phone: 803-737-5000
Fax: 803-734-1401
Beverage Alcohol Licensing: 803-898-5864
(Phone numbers for South Carolina state government)

South Dakota

South Dakota Department of Revenue
Division of Special Taxes & Licensing
700 Governor's Drive
Pierre, SD 57501-2276
Phone: 605-773-3311
Fax: 605-773-6729

Tennessee

Tennessee Alcoholic Beverage Commission
226 Capitol Boulevard, Room 600
Nashville, TN 37219-0755
Phone: 615-741-1602
Fax: 615-741-0847

Texas

Texas Alcoholic Beverage Commission
5806 Mesa Drive
PO Box 13127
Capitol Station
Austin, TX 78711-3127
Phone: 512-206-3333
Fax: 512-206-3449

Utah (Control State)

Utah Department of Alcoholic Beverage Control
1625 South 900 West
Salt Lake City, UT 84130
Phone: 801-977-6800
Fax: 801-977-6888

Also provides:
Restaurant License (full service)
Restaurant License (limited service)
On-Premise Banquet and Catering License
Private Club License
On-Premise Beer License
Tavern License
Single Event Permit
Temporary Beer Permit

Vermont (Control State)

Vermont Department of Liquor Control
Green Mountain Drive, Drawer 20
Montpelier, VT 05620-4501
Phone: 802-828-2345
Fax: 802-828-2803

Virginia (Control State)

Virginia Department of Alcoholic Beverage Control

Main office:
2901 Hermitage Road
Richmond, VA 23220

Mailing address:
Virginia Dept. of Alcoholic Beverage Control
PO Box 27491
Richmond, VA 23261
Phone: 804-213-4413
Fax: 804-213-4415

Washington (Control State)

Washington Business License Services
Department of Licensing
PO Box 9034
Olympia, WA 98504-3075
Phone: 360-586-2784
Licensing: 360-586-6700
Fax: 360-586-1596

Washington State Liquor Control Board
3000 Pacific Avenue
PO Box 3098
Olympia, WA 98504-3098
Phone: 360-664-1600

Complaints relating to tobacco issues: 1-888-838-3956

West Virginia (Control State)

West Virginia Alcohol Beverage Control Commission
Enforcement & Licensing Division
322 70th Street S.E.
Charleston, WV 25304-2900
Phone: 304-558-2481
Toll-Free: 1-800-642-8208
Fax: 304-558-0081

Wisconsin

Wisconsin Alcohol & Tobacco Enforcement
Department of Revenue
4610 University Avenue
Madison, WI 53708
Phone: 608-266-3969
Fax: 608-264-9920

Wyoming (Control State)

Wyoming Liquor Commission
1520 East 5th Street
Cheyenne, WY 82002
Phone: 307-777-7231
Fax: 307-777-5872

Canada

Liquor Control and Licensing Branch (LCLB)
Ministry of Public Safety and Solicitor General
PO Box 9282, Stn Prov Govt
Victoria, BC
V8W 9J7
Phone: 250-356-9596
Fax: 250-387-1753

Canadian Association of Liquor Jurisdictions
382 Elm Road
Toronto, Ontario, Canada
M5M 3V8
Phone: 416-780-1851
Fax: 416-780-1865

Puerto Rico

Luis Perez-Rivera
Director
Negociado de Bebidas
PO Box S-9024140
San Juan, PR 00904

Distributors and Brokers

This is a partial list of distributors and brokers in the United States. A company's listing here does not constitute a recommendation.

National Distributors and Brokers

The Charmer-Sunbelt Group
60 E. 42nd Street
New York, NY 10165
Phone: 212-699-7000
Fax: 212-699-7099
www.charmer-sunbelt.com

Subsidiaries including Charmer Industries (New York), Premier Beverage (Florida), Reliable Churchill (Maryland), and Ben Arnold-Sunbelt Beverage (South Carolina)

Johnson Brothers Liquor Co.
1999 Shepard Road
St. Paul, MN 55116
Phone: 651-649-5800
Fax: 651-649-5894
www.johnsonbrothers.com

Alabama, Florida, Hawaii, Minnesota, Nebraska, Nevada, North Carolina, North Dakota, South Dakota, Rhode Island, and Wisconsin

Republic National Distributing Co.
See www.rndc-usa.com/about/offices.asp for an office near you.

Alabama; Arizona; Colorado; Florida; Kentucky; Louisiana; Maryland; Mississippi; Nebraska (license pending); North Carolina; North Dakota; Ohio; Oklahoma; South Carolina; South Dakota; Texas; Virginia; Washington, D.C.; and West Virginia

Southern Wine & Spirits of America
1600 N.W. 163rd Street
Miami, FL 33169
Phone: 305-625-4171
www.southernwine.com

Alabama, Arizona, California, Colorado, Florida, Hawaii, Idaho, Illinois, Kentucky, Maine, Montana, Mississippi, Nevada, New Hampshire, New Jersey, New Mexico, New York, North Carolina, Oregon, Pennsylvania, South Carolina, Virginia, Washington, West Virginia, Wyoming, Utah, and Vermont

Young's Market Company, LLC
2164 N. Batavia Street
Orange, CA 92865
Phone: 714-283-4933
Toll-Free: 800-317-6150
Fax: 714-283-6175
www.youngsmarket.com

Alaska, Arizona, California, Hawaii, Idaho, Oregon, Washington, Montana, Wyoming, and Utah

State Distributors and Brokers

Alabama

Alliance Spirits & Wine, LLC
Montgomery, AL 36116
Phone: 334-420-2902
Fax: 334-420-2907

Alaska

Alaska Distributing
Anchorage, AK 99509
Phone: 907-279-3511
Fax: 907-276-1325

Alaska Distributors Co.
Corporate Office
Seattle, WA 98108-1702
Phone: 206-622-7311
Fax: 206-623-9922

Arizona

Alliance Beverage Distributing Co.
Phoenix, AZ 85043
Phone: 602-760-5500
Fax: 602-760-5610

Connolly Sales & Marketing
Cave Creek, Arizona 85327
Phone: 480-488-1665
Fax: 480-488-1812

Arkansas

Barrett Hamilton, Inc.
Little Rock, AR 72203
Phone: 501-565-4641
Fax: 501-565-8561

Central Distributors, Inc.
Little Rock, AR 72206
Phone: 501-372-3158
Fax: 501-372-2461

Little Rock Distributing Co.
Little Rock, AR 72203-3417
Phone: 501-490-1506
Fax: 501-490-0215

California

See Young's Market Company and Southern Wine & Spirits in national listings.

Colorado

Beverage Distributing Corp.
Aurora, CO 80011
Phone: 303-371-3421
Fax: 303-371-3942

Midwest Beverage Company (Beverage Distributing Corp.)
Aurora, CO 80011
Phone: 303-371-0832
Fax: 303-371-8106

Connecticut

Connecticut Distributors, Inc.
Stratford, CT 06615
Phone: 203-377-1440
Fax: 203-377-8960

Eder Bros., Inc.
West Haven, CT 06504-0949
Phone: 203-934-8381
Fax: 203-932-2492

Delaware

Century Wine & Spirits
Wilmington, DE 19850
Phone: 302-324-4100
Fax: 302-324-4110

First State Distributing Group, LLP
Wilmington, DE 19899
Phone: 302-655-5511
Fax: 302-654-4254

District of Columbia

Washington Wholesale Liquor Co., Inc.
Washington, DC 20018-1520
Phone: 202-832-5600
Fax: 202-832-3629

Florida

See national listings.

Georgia

Empire Distributors Inc.
Atlanta, GA 30331
Phone: 404-349-1780
Fax: 404-346-4608
www.empiredist.org

Georgia Crown Distributing Co.
Atlanta, GA 30378
Phone: 404-344-9550
Fax: 404-346-7638

Savannah Distributing Co., Inc.
Savannah, GA 31498
Phone: 912-233-1167
Fax: 912-233-1157
www.gawine.com

United Distributors, Inc.
Albany, GA 31706
Phone: 912-436-9501
Fax: 912-436-7838

Hawaii

Paradise Beverages (corporate office)
Lihue, HI 96766
Phone: 808-245-6938
Fax: 808-245-5208

Idaho

Spirit Distributing
Boise, ID 83706
Phone: 800-457-7280
Fax: 208-377-2616

Illinois

Callison Wholesale Liquor Co.
Belleville, IL 62222
Phone: 618-277-4300
Fax: 618-277-6267

Geneva Bottling
Geneva, IL 60134
Phone: 630-232-0100
Fax: 630-232-0697

Indiana

Olinger Distributing Co.
Indianapolis, IN 46206
Phone: 317-876-1188
Fax: 317-876-3638
www.olingerindiana.com

Iowa

Glazer's Distributing
Urbandale, IA 50322
Phone: 515-252-7173
Fax: 515-252-8681

Hawkeye Wine & Spirits
Urbandale, IA 50322
Phone: 515-252-1665
Fax: 515-252-1708

Kansas

Glazer's of Kansas
Lenexa, KS 66215
Phone: 913-894-2112
Fax: 913-894-1372

Standard Beverage Corp.
Lenexa, KS 66215
Phone: 913-888-7200
Fax: 913-841-9186

White Brokerage Co.
Wichita, KS 67205
Phone: 316-722-9463
Fax: 316-722-3884

Kentucky

Bryant Distributing Co.
Owensboro, KY 42302-1678
Phone: 270-684-8852
Fax: 270-686-8431

Locations in Louisville, Lexington, and Wilder.

Louisiana

Glazer's Companies of Louisiana
St. Rose, LA 70087
Phone: 504-443-8600
Fax: 504-443-0111

The Beverage Agency
Baton Rouge, LA 70802
Phone: 225-343-3451
Fax: 225-383-6636

Maine

United Beverages, Inc.
Concord, NH 03301
Phone: 603-228-6530
Fax: 603-228-6531
www.unitedbeverages.com

Maryland

Liquor Control Board—Worcester County
Snow Hill, MD 21863
Phone: 410-632-1250
Fax: 410-632-3010

Montgomery County Government
Department of Liquor Control
Rockville, MD 20855
Phone: 240-217-1900
Fax: 240-217-1962

Reliable Churchill LLLP
Baltimore, MD 21226-2702
Phone: 410-439-5000
Fax: 410-439-3497

Massachusetts

Gilman/Country Club Wine & Spirits
West Springfield, MA 01089
Phone: 781-278-2000
Fax: 781-278-2250

Horizon Beverage Company
Avon, MA 02322
Phone: 508-587-1110
Fax: 508-587-2714

Merrimack Valley Distributing Co.
Danvers, MA 01923
Phone: 978-777-2213
Fax: 978-774-7487

Premium Coastal Beverage
Ludlow, MA 01056-0409
Phone: 413-583-7845
Fax: 413-583-7850

United Liquors, Ltd.
Holyoke, MA 01040
Phone: 800-719-9463
Fax: 413-532-5682

United Liquors, Ltd.
Braintree, MA 02185-9219
Phone: 617-323-0500
Fax: 508-584-0927

Michigan

General Wine & Liquor Company
Highland Park, MI 48203-3117
Phone: 313-852-3908 or 313-852-0521
Fax: 313-867-4039

Minnesota

Bellboy Corporation
St. Louis Park, MN 55426
Phone: 612-544-8178
Fax: 612-544-0157

Griggs, Cooper & Co.
St. Paul, MN 55104
Phone: 651-646-7821
Fax: 651-646-1497

Quality Wine & Spirits
Minneapolis, MN 55440
Phone: 952-854-8600
Fax: 952-851-0501

Sunny Hill Distributors, Inc.
Hibbing, MN 55746
Phone: 218-263-6886
Fax: 218-263-6111

Mississippi

Alliance Spirits & Wine LLC—Mississippi Office
Madison, MS 39110
Phone: 601-859-9000
Fax: 601-859-4800

Missouri

Glazer's Midwest
Columbia, MO 65202
Phone: 573-474-6153
Fax: 573-474-7313

Locations in Kansas City, St. Louis, and Springfield.

Major Brands
Columbia, MO 65205
Phone: 573-443-3169
Fax: 573-874-1035

Locations in north Kansas City and St. Louis.

Montana

Alliance Spirits & Wine LLC
Bozeman, MT 59718
Phone: 406-587-9032
Fax: 406-522-7756

Nebraska

Nebraska Wine & Spirits, Inc.
Omaha, NE 68124-0265
Phone: 402-339-9444
Fax: 402-593-0209

United Distillers Products Co.
Omaha, NE 68127
Phone: 402-339-9100
Fax: 402-597-7289

Nevada

Blach Distributing
Elko, NV 89803
Phone: 775-738-7111
Fax: 775-738-6731

DeLuca Liquor & Wine, Ltd.
Las Vegas, NV 89030
Phone: 702-735-9141
Fax: 702-732-0684
www.vegasdrinks.com

Silver State Liquor & Wine Ltd.
Sparks, NV 89432
Phone: 775-331-3400
Fax: 775-331-3474

New Hampshire

United Beverages, Inc.
Concord, NH 03301
Phone: 603-228-6530
Fax: 603-228-6531
www.unitedbeverages.com

New Jersey

Allied Beverage Group, LLC
Carlstadt, NJ 07072
Phone: 201-842-6200
Fax: 201-842-6327
www.alliedbeverage.com

Fedway Associates, Inc.
Mt. Laurel, NJ 08054
Phone: 856-234-3200
Fax: 856-778-0160

Fedway Associates, Inc.
Pt. Kearny, NJ 07032
Phone: 973-624-6444
Fax: 973-344-3336

R & R Marketing, LLC
Trenton, NJ 08650
Phone: 609-587-6103
Fax: 609-587-2770

R & R Marketing, LLC
West Caldwell, NJ 07006
Phone: 973-228-5100
Fax: 973-403-8679

New Mexico

Connolly Sales & Marketing
Albuquerque, NM 87120
Phone: 505-899-8825
Fax: 505-899-4031

New York

Charmer Industries
Astoria, NY 11105
Phone: 718-726-2500
Fax: 718-726-4428

Colony Liquor Distributors, Inc.
Kingston, NY 12402
Phone: 845-338-2740
Fax: 845-338-9385

Locations in Albany, Syracuse, Rochester, and West Seneca.

Eber Bros. Wine & Liquor Corp.
Rochester, NY 14624
Phone: 585-349-7700
Fax: 585-349-7720

Locations in Amherst, Guilderland Center, and Liverpool.

Peerless Importers, Inc.
Brooklyn, NY 11222
Phone: 718-383-5500
Fax: 718-389-4209
www.peerimp.com

North Carolina

Alliance Spirits & Wine, LLC
Charlotte, NC 28273
Phone: 704-588-2923
Fax: 704-504-3702

North Dakota

Ed Phillips & Sons
Fargo, ND 58108
Phone: 701-277-1499
Fax: 701-282-8869

Ohio

Allied Wine & Spirits
Dayton, OH 45402
Phone: 937-220-6426
Fax: 937-220-6474

Glazer's Distributing
Columbus, OH 43213
Phone: 614-552-7900
Fax: 614-552-7888

Midwest Wine & Spirits
Cincinnati, OH 45242
Phone: 513-769-5811
Fax: 513-588-3687

Universal Marketing, Inc.
Columbus, OH 43213
Phone: 614-864-3720
Fax: 614-864-1978

Oklahoma

Action Wholesale Liquors
Oklahoma City, OK 73179
Phone: 405-682-8527
Fax: 405-682-8559

Central Liquor Co.
Oklahoma City, OK 73147
Phone: 405-947-8050
Fax: 405-949-1416

Dixie Liquor Company
Hartshorne, OK 74547
Phone: 918-297-0133
Fax: 918-297-0293

Sterling Wine & Spirits
Oklahoma City, OK 73103
Phone: 405-557-1818
Fax: 405-557-1857

Oregon

See national listings.

Pennsylvania

Capital Wine & Spirits Co., Inc.
North Wales, PA 19454
Phone: 267-960-0900
Fax: 267-960-0901

Rhode Island

Providence Beverage Co.
West Greenwich, RI 02817-0026
Phone: 401-392-3390
Fax: 401-392-3478

Rhode Island Distributing Co.
West Greenwich, RI 02817
Phone: 401-392-3390
Fax: 401-392-3478

South Carolina

See national listings.

South Dakota

Sodak Distributing Co.
Sioux Falls, SD 57101
Phone: 605-336-3320
Fax: 605-336-3322

Tennessee

Athens Distributing Co.
Nashville, TN 37208-3144
Phone: 615-254-0101
Fax: 615-254-1749

Best Brands Incorporated
Nashville, TN 37229-0155
Phone: 615-350-8500
Fax: 615-350-8129

Beverage Control, Inc.
Knoxville, TN 37940
Phone: 865-577-5541
Fax: 865-577-6760

Delta Wholesale Liquors, Inc.
Memphis, TN 38104
Phone: 901-272-0276
Fax: 901-722-9210

Horizon Wine & Spirits
Chattanooga, TN 37422
Phone: 423-899-3962
Fax: 423-892-6127

Horizon Wine & Spirits
Nashville, TN 37209
Phone: 615-320-7292
Fax: 615-321-3589

Texas

Glazer's Wholesale Distributors
Dallas, TX 75380-9013
Phone: 972-392-8200
Fax: 972-702-8508

Locations in Abilene, Amarillo, Austin, Corpus Christi, Dallas, El Paso, Farmer's Branch, Houston, and San Antonio.

Utah

Alliance Spirits & Wine, LLC
Salt Lake City, UT 84104
Phone: 801-886-0096
Fax: 801-886-0098

Vermont

United Beverages, Inc.
Concord, NH 03301
Phone: 603-228-6530
Fax: 603-228-6531
www.unitedbeverages.com

Virginia

Alliance Spirits & Wine, LLC
Richmond, VA 23230
Phone: 804-377-8910
Fax: 804-377-8913

Washington

See national listings.

West Virginia

Alliance Spirits & Wine, LLC
Dunbar, WV 25064
Phone: 304-766-8888
Fax: 304-766-8889

Wisconsin

Edison Liquor Corp.
Brookfield, WI 53045
Phone: 414-821-0600
Fax: 414-821-0363

Edison Liquor Corp.
Madison, WI 59714
Phone: 608-246-8868
Fax: 608-246-0863

General Beverage
Madison, WI 53744
Phone: 608-271-1234
Fax: 608-271-8625

General Beverage
New Berlin, WI 53151
Phone: 414-543-3300
Fax: 414-543-4340

General Beverage
Oshkosh, WI 54901
Phone: 920-235-9130
Fax: 920-235-3085

Noelke Distributors
La Crosse, WI 54601
Phone: 608-785-0984
Fax: 608-782-8860

Wyoming

Alliance Spirits & Wine, LLC
Cheyenne, WY 82009
Phone: 307-772-0645
Fax: 307-772-0644

The Pre-Opening Calendar

Starting a bar is more intricate than planning a wedding, and as with undertaking any large project, the more organized you are, the easier it is to make sure you have everything covered.

You are opening a business. You are spending a lot of money. Some may be your own, some may belong to people you know, and some may belong to people who have decided to trust you. Regardless, you need to be able to open your bar without a hitch.

The following pages contain checklists that will help keep you on track. They will take you from conceptualizing your theme to your grand opening. Use this calendar to keep you moving forward toward your dream of starting and running a bar.

Organize Yourself

You will need to keep track of many moving parts, important people, and crucial deadlines over the next year or so. While everyone has his or her own system, we prefer organization that is compact and easy to grab. Using a three-ring binder, copy down the following checklists or use a calendar and put the important deadlines on it. Then separate the notebook into sections, such as the following:

- ◆ Concept development
- ◆ Competition and research

- Business plan
- Financial information/pro forma
- Permits and licenses
- Personnel
- Contacts and vendors

Each section should have a few plastic paper protectors into which you can slip permits, miscellaneous notes, applications, or anything else that may need to be easily accessed during this process.

Now that you're organized, let the countdown begin.

Twelve to Nine Months Before Opening

❑ Go to your local ABC location and buy (then read) the book of laws and regulations that you will need to follow as a bar owner. (See Chapter 2 and Appendix B to help you locate your state's agency.)

❑ Network with bar owners and operators, lawyers, accountants, bankers, and anyone else who will give you the time of day. Build your support structure and find a mentor or two. Ask tons of questions and search for answers. (See Chapter 1.)

❑ Write down what your preliminary vision for your bar is, from the theme to what it will serve to where you think it should be located. Record what you see in your mind's eye.

❑ Start doing your research: What are the demographics of your area? What types of bars (and restaurants) are there and have there been in your area? What is the competitive environment? How many bars are in your area? Where are the voids in the marketplace? How does your vision and theme for your bar fit in? (See Chapter 3.)

❑ Investigate potential ways to secure future funding. (See Chapter 4.)

❑ Visit other bars and assess what you like and what you don't like. Include everything: menu, pricing, décor, and service style.

❑ Spend some time analyzing why the successful establishments in your area thrive while determining why the unsuccessful ones fail.

❑ Start looking for locations. Analyze them for traffic patterns, visibility, space, and accessibility. (See Chapter 6.)

❑ Get a feel for potential costs of buying, leasing, construction, start-up, and so on.

❑ Build preliminary profit and loss forms and guidelines. Put together rough financial statements and projections. (See Chapter 4 for more information and Appendix D for sample forms.)

❑ Start observing your competition's operation and develop your own operation parameters. Frequent other establishments, looking at how they operate. Spend time pinpointing things you like and things you don't.

❑ Build operational "like" and "don't like" sets of lists. For instance, "I like that they frost the beer mugs" and "I don't like the thin unfrozen french fries that come with the grilled cheeseburger."

❑ Try to determine square footage requirements for your facility—what your minimum, maximum, and optimum needs are.

❑ If you are considering serving food or even specialty drinks, begin your recipe file. Remember your theme as you do this. (See Chapter 15.)

❑ Build a network with restaurant equipment dealers and get a feel for the cost of equipment. (See Chapter 10.)

❑ Start your search for lawyers, insurance agents, accountants, and more people who can be of assistance.

❑ Get information about obtaining health permits, liquor licenses, and building permits. Determine how to structure your business legally. (See Chapter 5.)

❑ Talk to restaurant owners and other entrepreneurs about their experiences as business owners.

❑ Analyze your personal strengths and weaknesses and determine a plan of action to develop your knowledge base or hire people who can cover your shortcomings.

❑ Find and catalog associations, trade magazines, and research material for easy access. (See Appendix B.)

Eight to Seven Months Before Opening

❑ Continue to research the industry and the market.

❑ Conduct a complete competitive analysis. (See Chapter 3.)

❑ Determine the market you want to target. (See Chapter 3.)

❑ Finalize your theme.

❑ Put together your mission statement and business plan. (See Chapter 4.)

❑ Spend quality time determining the name of your restaurant. This decision is critical, so spend time asking for input (see Chapter 7). Once you decide on a name, have your logo designed.

❑ Determine what will make you different from your competitors.

❑ Begin to build a site criteria checklist.

❑ Meet with real estate agents and bankers in the area you are considering. Start discussing your theme, your funding needs, and your business plan progress and begin looking at sites.

❑ Get familiar with the area you are considering and its traffic count data. (See Chapter 6.)

❑ Revisit your P&L and projections. Refine your numbers and assumptions along the way. Change as warranted.

❑ Get a good feel for what products and services are offered and at what price in your area.

❑ Continue to collect recipes and edit out those that do not fit your theme.

❑ Contact several vendors and contractors to begin estimating costs, time availability, and requirements.

❑ Select your advisors and support team. You will need an attorney, accountant, and insurance agent as part of your professional support. (See Chapter 5.)

❑ Join trade associations and local chambers of commerce and any local business groups to gain more networking opportunities.

❑ Identify all of your options for obtaining the necessary cash and line up your funding. (See Chapter 4.)

Six to Five Months Before Opening

❑ Meet with all necessary government officials, legal counsel, insurance agents, and accountants to go over application basics: cost, timeline, and the necessary steps to getting the appropriate licenses and permits.

❑ Complete your business plan. (See Chapter 4.)

❑ Set up the restaurant's name and legal entity and obtain a taxpayer ID number. (See Chapter 5.)

❑ Finalize your vision by putting all the details for the menu, décor, music, lighting, signage, etc. on paper.

❑ Narrow down your site choices to one or two that match your needs.

❑ Set up all services, such as electricity, telephones, garbage removal, water, and sewer services.

❑ Check with the local zoning board, planning commission, and health department to ensure the site is (or will be) approved for its intended use.

❑ Discuss plans with contractors, lawyers, mentors, friends, and family to get their input.

❑ Review all financial projections with your banker, accountant, contractors, vendors, and lawyers to ensure accuracy. Determine all cash needs.

❑ Continue to tweak and revise all financial projections and analyses as more information comes to light.

❑ Map out your floor plan for your potential site. (See Chapter 9.)

❑ Determine preliminary equipment needs based on your potential site. (See Chapter 10.)

❑ Select your location and complete the deal. Make sure your advisors walk through every step of this process with you.

❑ Revise your plans where necessary to reflect your new site.

❑ Begin to schedule contractors and vendors. Plan the execution of the opening and steps needed to make it happen. Build a facility construction plan and calendar. The contractor will help you do this. You give him the planned opening date, and he will give you the facility construction plan.

❑ Apply for your health permit, liquor license, building permits, and any other licenses and permits you need.

Four Months Before Opening

❑ Determine silverware, glassware, china, linen, and other miscellaneous needs and prepare your order. (See Chapter 16.)

❑ Finalize your pricing strategy to reflect your theme and your area. (See Chapter 17.)

❑ Finalize customer count and sales forecasts.

❑ Finalize your liquor, wine, and food cost projections and determine the food cost of every item on your menu. (See Chapter 17.)

❑ Begin to write your operations manual and employee handbooks.

❑ Ensure that construction is progressing per the schedule.

Three Months Before Opening

❑ Set up an office and your bookkeeping and accounting systems.

❑ Determine ideal staffing needs. (See Chapter 11.)

❑ Determine what the area demands for salary and wage guidelines.

❑ Finalize projected labor costs.

❑ Make sure you have all of your licenses in hand or have at least filed the necessary paperwork with the proper agency.

❑ Continue to revise and develop all of your financial plans.

❑ Finalize your promotions and marketing and advertising plans. (See Part 6.)

❑ Have all of the appropriate marketing pieces designed and printed. This material includes business cards, letterhead, menu boards, signage, website, and promotional material.

❑ Meet with all your vendors to prepare orders and determine delivery schedules and terms.

❑ Order all equipment, tables, chairs, cash registers, and small wares to be delivered at an appropriate time closer to opening. Ordering ahead of time prevents back-orders from affecting you.

❑ Make changes to your plans if you deem them to be necessary and prudent. Keep in mind, however, that things should be just about finalized at this point.

❑ Plan how you are going to select, hire, and train employees. Who do you need and how soon?

❑ Ensure that the facility construction is progressing per the construction schedule.

Two Months Before Opening

❑ Put in all orders for food and beverage products to arrive three to four days before your open date.

❑ Determine the hours of operation of the restaurant.

❑ Design all cash-handling procedures, inventory procedures, checklists, forms, and control processes.

❑ Finalize the menu. Get the menu designed and printed based on your theme.

❑ Arrange for the acceptance of credit cards and order the necessary equipment and supplies.

❑ Finalize written job descriptions and all manuals, systems, and employee policies and procedures.

❑ Finalize uniform selection for staff.

❑ Arrange to have all insurance coverage to take effect two weeks before your grand opening. Meet with your insurance agent to discuss and plan the schedule.

❑ Finalize your entire operating statement, cash-flow statement, balance sheet, and all projections and review them with your accountant, banker, and lawyer.

❑ Begin the hiring process. Place ads, conduct interviews, offer positions, and determine start dates.

❑ Ensure that construction is progressing per the schedule.

❑ Check on the status of any and all outstanding permits, licenses, and insurance policies.

❑ Begin your Grand Opening Plan. (See Chapter 21.)

❑ Don't change the theme. Modifications become significantly expensive and risky this late in the game. Though alterations do occur, if you prepared properly early on you'll avoid them.

Thirty Days Before Opening

❏ Ensure that construction will be completed and schedule your walk-through of every inch of your establishment with the general contractor and interior designer to ensure that everything is up to par.

❏ Finalize all operating systems, financial tracking and reporting systems, control systems, information and management systems, and ordering systems and test them to ensure they work properly.

❏ Finalize all arrangements with vendors.

❏ Hire staff.

❏ Send out VIP party invitations to community leaders, friends, family, and civic organizations.

❏ Hang banner announcing "Opening Soon."

❏ Aim to be completely ready two weeks ahead of time.

The Final Two Weeks Before Opening

❏ Construction should be finished.

❏ Train staff.

❏ Test all equipment to make sure it is in working order.

❏ Prepare for small wares arriving.

❏ Ensure that your complete order of small wares has arrived per your order.

❏ Make sure you have menus and other promotional materials.

❏ Follow up to ensure all necessary licenses, permits, insurance policies, and tax ID numbers are obtained and properly displayed, as per ABC requirements.

❏ Make a plan with the construction manager to address anything that is out of order or unsatisfactory.

❏ Prepare for your VIP party.

❏ Outside sign should be installed. Make sure that the city signs off with sign permit building codes.

❑ Ensure that all construction punch-list concerns have been addressed and sign off on the construction as meeting your standards and expectations.

The Final Week Before Opening

❑ Hang banner announcing "Grand Opening."

❑ Ensure that your food, beverage, and supplies orders have arrived.

❑ Stage dress rehearsals with friends, family, neighbors, and associates as nonpaying customers.

❑ Make sure all items on previous checklists are complete.

The Night Before Opening

❑ Relax and enjoy yourself. This will be your last night to relax in a while.

❑ Get some sleep.

Checklists, Forms, and Guidelines

License and Permit Checklist

Use this checklist to make sure that you get all the different federal, state, and local licenses and permits you need to acquire prior to opening for business:

- ❏ Basic business operation license from the city in which your business will operate, or from the local county (if the business will be operated outside of any city's limits)

- ❏ Federal employer identification number (EIN), also called a tax identification number (required for almost all types of businesses)

- ❏ Fictitious business name permit (also called DBA or "doing business as" permit)

- ❏ Zoning and land use permits

- ❏ Health department permits

- ❏ Sales tax license

- ❏ Fire department permits

- ❏ Liquor license

Pro Forma

When submitting your pro forma to a potential investor, include a letter that explains how you got the figures in your Profit & Loss (Income) Statement Forecast. You could also duplicate this form for one-year, three-year, and five-year forecasting.

Profit & Loss (Income) Statement Forecast

_____ *Quarter*

Months	July	August	September
Net Sales:	$ (% Sales)	$ (% Sales)	$ (% Sales)
Food	_____	_____	_____
Non-Alc. Beverages	_____	_____	_____
Liquor	_____	_____	_____
Wine/Champagne	_____	_____	_____
Beer	_____	_____	_____
Other (Cover Charges)	_____	_____	_____
Less Returns & Allowances	_____	_____	_____
Total Net Sales:	_____	_____	_____
Cost of Sales:	_____	_____	_____
Food	_____	_____	_____
Non-Alc. Beverages	_____	_____	_____
Liquor	_____	_____	_____
Wine/Champagne	_____	_____	_____
Beer	_____	_____	_____
Labor	_____	_____	_____
Total Cost of Sales:	_____	_____	_____
Gross Profit:	_____	_____	_____
Operating Expenses:	_____	_____	_____
Laundry & Linens	_____	_____	_____
Office Supplies & Expenses	_____	_____	_____
Consumables/Disposables	_____	_____	_____

Paper & Plastic Goods   _____   _____   _____

Promo & Comps (cost)   _____   _____   _____

Entertainment   _____   _____   _____

Contract Labor   _____   _____   _____

Marketing   _____   _____   _____

Printing   _____   _____   _____

Advertising   _____   _____   _____

Web Hosting/Internet Fees   _____   _____   _____

Postage & Delivery Fees   _____   _____   _____

Equipment Rental
(Dishwasher)   _____   _____   _____

Equipment Rental—Other   _____   _____   _____

Small Wares   _____   _____   _____

Gas & Auto Expenses   _____   _____   _____

Bank Charges   _____   _____   _____

Credit Card Charges (@ 2%)   _____   _____   _____

Bad Debt   _____   _____   _____

License Fees   _____   _____   _____

Dues & Subscriptions   _____   _____   _____

Accounting Fees   _____   _____   _____

Other Professional Fees   _____   _____   _____

Liability Insurance   _____   _____   _____

Medical Ins.—Partners   _____   _____   _____

Rent   _____   _____   _____

CAM Charges (Ins.)   _____   _____   _____

Real Estate/Property Ins.   _____   _____   _____

Telephone   _____   _____   _____

Gas   _____   _____   _____

Water   _____   _____   _____

Electric   _____   _____   _____

Sewer Maintenance   _____   _____   _____

Trash   _____   _____   _____

continues

Profit & Loss (Income) Statement Forecast *(continued)*

_____ *Quarter*

Months	July	August	September
Net Sales:	$ (% Sales)	$ (% Sales)	$ (% Sales)
Repairs & Maintenance	_____	_____	_____
Total Operating Expenses:	_____	_____	_____
Operating Income:	_____	_____	_____
Other Expenses:	_____	_____	_____
Depreciation	_____	_____	_____
Amortization	_____	_____	_____
Net Income:	_____	_____	_____
Labor Detail:	_____	_____	_____
FOH—Hourly	_____	_____	_____
BOH—Hourly	_____	_____	_____
BOH—Salary (Chef/Sous Chef)	_____	_____	_____
Salary-Mgmt./Supervisors	_____	_____	_____
Employers Payroll Taxes (@ X%)	_____	_____	_____
Work Comp (@ X% per $100)	_____	_____	_____
Total Labor:	_____	_____	_____

The Hiring Checklists

The following checklists will walk you through the hiring process, from interviewing to offering a position.

The Interview Checklist

This checklist will help you communicate important information to the applicant during the interview process. Following is a list of recommended items to cover during an interview.

Bring:

- ❏ Applicant's resume
- ❏ Job description/job posting
- ❏ Interview questions

Make sure to:

- ❏ Greet the applicant
- ❏ Introduce yourself and other staff members
- ❏ Avoid interruptions or distractions
- ❏ Actively listen and take notes

Discuss:

- ❏ Job description (explanation of duties and expectations)
- ❏ The establishment and your vision
- ❏ Working hours
- ❏ Dress code
- ❏ Parking fees (if applicable)
- ❏ Pay dates
- ❏ Benefits (if applicable)
- ❏ Ask them for references
- ❏ Advise them that the position may require a background check (if applicable)

Ask:

- ❏ Job-related questions
- ❏ Open-ended questions
- ❏ Scenario-based questions

Reference Check

Reference Check

Applicant's name: _____

Position applied for: _____

Employment History

Name of company: _____ Phone number: _____

Applicant's title: _____

Dates of employment: From _____ To _____

Final salary: _____ Eligible for rehire: Yes ___ No ___

Additional comments: _____

_____

Information from: _____ Title: _____

Name of company: _____ Phone number: _____

Applicant's title: _____

Dates of employment: From _____ To _____

Final salary: _____ Eligible for rehire: Yes ___ No ___

Additional comments: _____

_____

Information from: _____ Title: _____

Name of company: _____ Phone number: _____

Applicant's title: _____

Dates of employment: From _____ To _____

Final salary: _____ Eligible for rehire: Yes ___ No ___

Additional comments: _____

_____

Information from: _____ Title: _____

The Offer Checklist

Use this checklist to cover the necessary terms and conditions of employment with an applicant when you offer them a job. Some items may not apply to each position being offered, but it is still a handy guide.

Please tell them about the following:

- ❑ Starting salary (monthly or hourly)
- ❑ Probationary period (if applicable)
- ❑ At-will employment (if applicable)
- ❑ Pay dates
- ❑ Work hours
- ❑ Benefits (if applicable)
- ❑ Required payroll deductions (DCP)
- ❑ Confirm a start date
- ❑ Schedule an employee orientation
- ❑ If a background check is required, advise them the offer is pending the successful results of the background check

The Orientation Checklist

Use this checklist to make sure you orient your new employee quickly and properly. You want to help them feel welcome and introduce them to you and your business in a favorable light. This is also the best opportunity to provide them with all the pertinent human resource information and forms.

- ❑ Introduce them to the staff.
- ❑ Orient them with their work area.
- ❑ Explain their job and give them a copy of the job description.
- ❑ Explain their performance standards.
- ❑ Explain your expectations of them.
- ❑ Provide an employee handbook.

❑ Explain the use of timesheets.

❑ Have them sign W-2 forms, sexual harassment policy, receipt of employee handbook, and any other government forms.

❑ Provide orientation/training on the telephone.

❑ Schedule training sessions.

Shift Schedule

Shift Schedule										
Day_____ Date _____										
Name: Shift	3:00	4:00	5:00	6:00	7:00	8:00	9:00	10:00	Total Hrs.	
___ ___	___	___	___	___	___	___	___	___	___	
___ ___	___	___	___	___	___	___	___	___	___	
___ ___	___	___	___	___	___	___	___	___	___	
___ ___	___	___	___	___	___	___	___	___	___	
___ ___	___	___	___	___	___	___	___	___	___	
___ ___	___	___	___	___	___	___	___	___	___	
___ ___	___	___	___	___	___	___	___	___	___	
# of people scheduled	___	___	___	___	___	___	___	___		
Hours scheduled	___	___	___	___	___	___	___	___		

Shift Swap Sheet

In the bar business, you may give your employees set schedules. For instance, you may give your bartender Ray Thursday, Saturday, and Sunday nights. When you do this, you can make your employees responsible for covering their shifts if something comes up. The following sheet helps make communication clear for all parties involved when shifts are being covered.

Shift Swap Sheet

SCHEDULED EMPLOYEE NAME	INITIALS	SHIFT DAY [(MM/DD/YY), WEEKDAY]	SHIFT TIME	SUBSTITUTING EMPLOYEE	INITIALS	MGR. SIGNATURE OK

Actual Income Statement

Actual Income Statement

For the Period of _____ to _____

	$	Percent of Total Sales
Sales	$_____	%_____
Food	$_____	%_____
Beverage	$_____	%_____
Total Sales	$_____	%_____
Cost of Sales		
Food and Beverage Cost	$_____	%_____
Paper Cost	$_____	%_____
Total Cost of Sales	$_____	%_____
Gross Profit	$_____	%_____
Controllable Expense		
Direct Payroll	$_____	%_____
Indirect Payroll, Taxes, Employee Benefits, etc.	$_____	%_____
Misc. Operating Expense	$_____	%_____
Repairs/Maint.	$_____	%_____
Utilities	$_____	%_____
General Admin.	$_____	%_____
Advertising	$_____	%_____
Total Controllable Expenses	$_____	%_____

Profit Before Occupancy Expense

Rent	$_____	%_____
Taxes	$_____	%_____
Insurance	$_____	%_____
Interest	$_____	%_____
Depreciation	$_____	%_____
Net Profit	+$_____	

Creating a Cleaning Schedule

Use the following form for each area and each item to be cleaned, as discussed in Chapter 20. The information you fill out here will help you create a cleaning manual for your establishment.

Cleaning Schedule

Area to be cleaned _____

Item(s) to be cleaned _____

Frequency of cleaning _____

Materials to use _____

_____

_____

How to clean _____

_____

_____

Precautions _____

_____

_____

Standard of cleanliness achieved _____

Who cleans _____

Checked off by _____

Daily Cleaning Schedules

When it comes to making a great impression, clean is king. Use the following daily cleaning schedules to keep you and your staff on track. These are just samples. Your establishment may or may not have some of the equipment listed here.

Bartender—Daily Cleaning Schedule

BARTENDER—Daily Cleaning Schedule			Date:	
WHAT	WHEN	HOW	WITH WHAT	INITIALS
Bar equipment and food utensils	Every 3-4 hours	Wash, rinse, sanitize	Cleanser, fresh water, and sanitizer	
Bar counters and nonfood contact surfaces	End of shift	Wash, rinse, sanitize	Cleanser, fresh water, and sanitizer	
Condiment containers	End of day	Wash, rinse, sanitize	Dishwashing machine recommended cleaners	
Prep counters	In between products and every 4 hours	Wash, rinse, sanitize	Cleanser, fresh water	
Dish racks	End of day	Wash, rinse, sanitize	Cleanser, fresh water, and sanitizer	
Drain covers	End of day	Clear of debris, wash, rinse, sanitize	Dishwashing machine recommended cleaners	
Dry storage areas	Daily	Sweep/mop per procedures	Quarry cleaner	
Hand sink handles	Every 4 hours	Wash, rinse, sanitize	Cleanser, fresh water, and sanitizer	
Hand sinks and area	Each shift	Wash, rinse, sanitize	Cleanser, fresh water, and sanitizer	

Ice buckets	Each time used	Wash, rinse, sanitize	Dishwashing machine chemicals	
In-use utensils	In between products or every 2 hours	Wash, rinse, sanitize	Dishwashing machine chemicals	
Mixer base and exterior	Between products	Wash, rinse, sanitize	Cleanser, clean water, and sanitizer	
Mops/brushes	Daily	Wash, rinse, sanitize; hang upside down to drip dry over sink	Cleanser, clean water, and sanitizer	
Walk-in	Daily	Sweep, mop floors, organize containers		
Preparation areas	Each use	Wash, rinse, sanitize	Cleanser, clean water, and sanitizer	
Storage bins	End of day	Wipe and sanitize exterior with cloth	Sanitizer	
Reach-in handles	End of day	Wipe and sanitize exterior with cloth	Sanitizer	
Reach-ins	End of day	Wash, rinse, sanitize	Cleanser, clean water, and sanitizer	
Soda	End of day and throughout shift	Wipe clean of soil and dust	Water	
Soda machine nozzles	End of day	Soak diffusers in sanitizer solution, scrub interior	Cleanser, clean water, and sanitizer	
Wells	End of day	Wash, rinse, sanitize	Cleanser, clean water, and sanitizer	

Cocktail Waitresses—Daily Cleaning Schedule

COCKTAIL WAITRESSES—Daily Cleaning Schedule			Date:	
WHAT	**WHEN**	**HOW**	**WITH WHAT**	**INITIALS**
Bathroom mirrors	Each shift	Spot clean	Glass cleaner	
Bathroom equipment and surfaces (other than floor, tiles, and mirror)	End of day	Spray, rinse, and wipe with dedicated, disposable towel	Bathroom cleaner	
Stock bathroom	Each shift	Soap, paper towels, seat covers, toilet paper		
Stock dry goods	Each shift	Cocktail napkins, mixers, straws, etc.		
Cocktail tables and buddy bars	Between each turn and end of shift	Wipe clean of food debris with in-use wiping cloth	Sanitizer and water	
Chairs and stools	Between each turn, if possible; end of shift	Wipe clean of food debris with in-use wiping cloth	Sanitizer and water	

Kitchen Area—Daily Cleaning Schedule

The duties here can be spread out among the kitchen staff, food servers (if you have them), prep people, and maintenance crew.

KITCHEN AREA—Daily Cleaning Schedule			Date:	
WHAT	**WHEN**	**HOW**	**WITH WHAT**	**INITIALS**
Condiment containers	End of day	Wash, rinse, sanitize	Dishwashing machine recommended cleaners	
Cooling racks	End of day	Wipe clean of food debris with in-use wiping cloth	Sanitizer and water	
Front counters/shelves	End of shift	Wash, rinse, sanitize	Cleanser, fresh water, and sanitizer	
Cooler counters/shelves	End of shift	Wash, rinse, sanitize	Cleanser, fresh water, and sanitizer	
Delivery counters	End of shift	Wash, rinse, sanitize	Cleanser, fresh water, and sanitizer	
Prep counters	In between products and every 4 hours	Wash, rinse, sanitize	Cleanser, fresh water	
Dish racks	End of day	Wash, rinse, sanitize	Cleanser, fresh water, and sanitizer	
Drain covers	End of day	Clear of debris, wash, rinse, sanitize	Dishwashing machine recommended cleaners	
Dry storage areas	Daily	Sweep/mop per procedures	Quarry cleaner	
Exterior premises	End of day	Sweep entire areas of debris and trash, check landscaping	Water spray if needed	
Floors	Daily as needed	Sweep/mop per procedures	Quarry cleaner	

continues

KITCHEN AREA—Daily Cleaning Schedule *(continued)*			Date:	
WHAT	**WHEN**	**HOW**	**WITH WHAT**	**INITIALS**
Freezers	End of day	Sweep/mop per procedures; if walk-in, wipe exterior	Quarry cleaner	
Front doors	Throughout shift as needed	Spot clean glass and wipe	Glass cleaner clean other surfaces	
Hand sink handles	Every 4 hours	Wash, rinse, sanitize	Cleanser, fresh water, and sanitizer	
Hand sinks and area	Each shift	Wash, rinse, sanitize	Cleanser, fresh water, and sanitizer	
Hood filters	At the end of every other shift	Soak in degreaser, spray clean with clean water, air dry	Non-caustic degreaser	
Hood grease pans	Biweekly	Empty into grease bin, run through dishwasher	Dishwashing machine chemicals	
Ice buckets	Each time used	Wash, rinse, sanitize	Dishwashing machine chemicals	
In-use utensils	In between products or every 2 hours	Wash, rinse, sanitize	Dishwashing machine chemicals	
Knife holders	Every 3 hours	Wash, rinse, sanitize	Cleanser, clean water, and sanitizer	
Line drawers	End of day	Wash, rinse, sanitize	Cleanser, clean water, and sanitizer	
Line inserts	End of day	Replace with clean, rinse and sanitize dirty ones	Dishwashing machine chemicals	
Mixer base and exterior	Between products	Wash, rinse, sanitize	Cleanser, clean water, and sanitizer	

WHAT	WHEN	HOW	WITH WHAT	INITIALS
Mops/brushes	Daily	Wash, rinse, sanitize, hang upside down to drip dry over sink	Cleanser, clean water, and sanitizer	
Walk-in	Daily	Sweep, mop floors, organize containers		
Pizza oven	Throughout shift	Wipe interior with clean, moist towel	Water	
Pizza oven	End of day	Vacuum soot and debris		
Pizza oven tiles	End of day	Wipe and buff exterior until free of grease	Water	
Preparation areas	Each use	Wash, rinse, sanitize	Cleanser, clean water, and sanitizer	
Storage bins	End of day	Wipe and sanitize exterior with cloth	Sanitizer	
Reach-in handles	End of day	Wipe and sanitize exterior with cloth	Sanitizer	
Reach-ins (and wells)	End of day	Wash, rinse, sanitize	Cleanser, clean water, and sanitizer	
Scales	Between use and every 3 hours minimum	Wash, rinse, sanitize	Cleanser, clean water, and sanitizer	
Slicer	Between use	Wash, rinse, sanitize	Cleanser, clean water, and sanitizer	
Trash receptacles	Daily	Wipe exterior with disposable cloth; rinse interior once emptied	Cleanser, clean water, and sanitizer	
Wiping cloths (in-use)	Every 2 hours	Put in dedicated linen launder bag		

Server—Daily Cleaning Schedule

SERVER—Daily Cleaning Schedule			Date:	
WHAT	WHEN	HOW	WITH WHAT	INITIALS
Service hand sink and handles	Every 3-4 hours	Wash, rinse, sanitize	Cleanser, fresh water, and sanitizer	
Bar equipment and food utensils	Every 3-4 hours	Wash, rinse, sanitize	Cleanser, fresh water, and sanitizer	
Bar counters and nonfood contact surfaces	End of shift	Wash, rinse, sanitize	Cleanser, fresh water, and sanitizer	
Cappuccino machine	Throughout shift, end of day	Wipe and buff exterior, clean steamer and spout	Hot water and sanitizer	
Cleaning room	End of day	Sweep/mop and organize	Quarry cleaner	
Coffee machines	End of day	Wash, rinse, sanitize	Cleanser, fresh water, and sanitizer	
Front counters	Throughout shift and end of day	Wipe clean of food and debris	Cleanser, fresh water, and sanitizer	
Cooler counters	Throughout shift and end of day	Wipe clean and dry, wash, rinse, sanitize	Cleanser, fresh water, and sanitizer	
Dining tables	After each turn and end of day	Wipe clean and dry, wash, rinse, sanitize	Cleanser, fresh water, and sanitizer	
Dining chairs and booths	After each turn and end of day	Wipe clean of food, dust, and debris	Water	
Iced tea dispenser	End of day	Wash and rinse and sanitize or run through dishwasher	Cleanser, fresh water, and sanitizer or dishwashing chemicals	

Master Cleaning Schedule

The following schedule is a housekeeping or maintenance cleaning schedule that will ensure that everything works properly and that your establishment is clean when the health inspector comes. This is only a guide; check with your local health department and add anything else that they review to this schedule.

Master Cleaning Schedule			Date:	
WHAT	**WHEN**	**HOW**	**WITH WHAT**	**INITIALS**
Air Conditioner	Quarterly	Replace		
Bulk dry storage	Monthly	Dishwashing machine	Dishwashing and sanitizing chemicals	
Ceiling vents	Weekly	Dust and vacuum		
Condenser coils	Monthly	Vacuum		
Cooling racks	Weekly	Scrub clean all surfaces and wash, rinse, sanitize	Cleanser, fresh water, and sanitizer	
Cutting boards	Weekly	Inspect for cracks, crevices; bleach or replace as needed		
Tables	Weekly	Inspect for and remove gum from underneath, check leveling and fix as needed		
Dishwashing machine	Weekly	De-lime as needed	Lime Away	
Drains	Weekly	Scrub clean and sanitize	Cleanser, fresh water, and sanitizer	
Exterior areas, such as trash	Weekly	Scrub and degrease	Degreaser	
Refrigerator fan guards	Weekly	Turn off, brush and wipe with damp cloth, turn back on		

continues

Master Cleaning Schedule *(continued)*			Date:	
WHAT	**WHEN**	**HOW**	**WITH WHAT**	**INITIALS**
Ice machine	Weekly	Empty and wash, rinse and sanitize, air dry	Cleanser, fresh water, and sanitizer	
Light fixtures	Weekly	Dust and spot clean	Glass cleaner	
Oven	Weekly	Per manufacturer's instructions	Oven cleaner	
Pizza pans	Monthly	Cure with oil, run through oven twice		
Refrigerators/gaskets	Weekly/Monthly	Defrost and clean	Cleanser, fresh water, and sanitizer	
Reach-ins	Weekly	Empty (placing food in refrigeration), clean off all food debris, rinse and sanitize	Cleanser, fresh water and sanitizer	
Stainless steel	Biweekly	Polish after cleaning	Stainless-steel cleaner	
Trash receptacles	Weekly	Scrub clean and sanitize	Cleanser, hot water, and sanitizer	
Walk-in	Weekly	Clean doors, gaskets, shelves, and walls	Cleanser, fresh water, and sanitizer	
Walls	Monthly	Wash	Cleanser, fresh water, and sanitizer	

Par Sheet

THE AMOUNT ON HAND (INV)–WHAT YOU NEED TO BUILD TO
(PAR) = AMOUNT TO BE ORDERED (ORDER)

PAR SHEET		Day: Date:			Day: Date:			Day: Date:		
ITEM	UNIT	PAR	INV	ORD	PAR	INV	ORD	PAR	INV	ORD
Example	#	3	2	1	3	2	1	3	3	

Inventory Tracking Sheets

Use the following forms to keep track of your "gold." Remember, all the liquor, beer, wine, and food in your bar is money. Using these sheets, even if you have a point-of-sale system, aids you in tracking your inventory.

Inventory Sheet

Inventory Sheet

Area:

Date:

Performed by:

ITEM	UNIT (BY WEIGHT VOLUME, EACH)	NUMBER OF ITEMS	COST PER UNIT	$ AMOUNT ON HAND
EXAMPLE:	BOTTLE	3	$7.00	$21.00

Cost of Sales Sheet

Cost of Sales Sheet

Period:

AREA	COST OF ITEMS	ACTUAL SALES	COST PER SALE THIS PERIOD	LAST PERIOD
LIQUOR				
OPENING INVENTORY	$____	$____	%____	%____
ADD SPILLAGE/ BREAKAGE	____	____	____	____
SUBTOTAL	____	____	____	____
LESS CLOSING INVENTORY	____	____	____	____
TOTAL COST FOR PERIOD	$____	$____	%____	%____
BEER				
OPENING INVENTORY	$____	$____	%____	%____
ADD SPILLAGE/ BREAKAGE	____	____	____	____
SUBTOTAL	____	____	____	____
LESS CLOSING INVENTORY	____	____	____	____
TOTAL COST FOR PERIOD	$____	$____	%____	%____

continues

Cost of Sales Sheet *(continued)*

Cost of Sales Sheet

Period:

AREA	COST OF ITEMS	ACTUAL SALES	COST PER SALE THIS PERIOD	LAST PERIOD
WINE				
OPENING INVENTORY	$____	$____	%____	%____
ADD SPILLAGE/ BREAKAGE	____	____	____	____
SUBTOTAL	____	____	____	____
LESS CLOSING INVENTORY	____	____	____	____
TOTAL COST FOR PERIOD	$____	$____	%____	%____
FOOD				
OPENING INVENTORY	$____	$____	%____	%____
ADD SPILLAGE/ BREAKAGE	____	____	____	____
SUBTOTAL	____	____	____	____
LESS CLOSING INVENTORY	____	____	____	____
TOTAL COST FOR PERIOD	$____	$____	%____	%____
TOTAL COMBINED AREAS	$____	$____	%____	%____

Breakage Log

Breakage Log

Date:		Shift:	
Bartender:			
ITEM	**TALLY**	**TOTAL**	**MGR SIGNATURE**
Vodka: Well			
Vodka: Call (specify)			
Vodka: Call (specify)			
Vodka: Premium (specify)			
Rum: Well			
Rum: Call (specify)			
Rum: Call (specify)			
Rum: Premium (specify)			
Scotch: Well			
Scotch: Call (specify)			
Scotch: Call (specify)			
Scotch: Premium (specify)			
Tequila: Well			
Tequila: Call (specify)			
Tequila: Call (specify)			
Tequila: Premium (specify)			

continues

Breakage Log *(continued)*

Breakage Log

Date:		Shift:	
Bartender:			
ITEM	**TALLY**	**TOTAL**	**MGR SIGNATURE**
Brandy: Well			
Brandy: Call (specify)			
Brandy: Call (specify)			
Brandy: Premium (specify)			
Whiskey: Well			
Whiskey: Call (specify)			
Whiskey: Call (specify)			
Whiskey: Premium (specify)			
Gin: Well			
Gin: Call (specify)			
Gin: Call (specify)			
Gin: Premium (specify)			
List any specialty liquors as pulled:			
Beer: (list below as pulled)			
Wine: (list below as pulled)			

Complimentary Drink Log

Complimentary Drink Log

Time Period:_____ Shift:_____

Bartender:_____

Date	Product or Item	Amt	Wine Cost	Liquor Cost	Beer Cost	Mgr
____	____	$____	$____	$____	$____	____
____	____	$____	$____	$____	$____	____
____	____	$____	$____	$____	$____	____
____	____	$____	$____	$____	$____	____
____	____	$____	$____	$____	$____	____
____	____	$____	$____	$____	$____	____
____	____	$____	$____	$____	$____	____
____	____	$____	$____	$____	$____	____
____	____	$____	$____	$____	$____	____
____	____	$____	$____	$____	$____	____
____	____	$____	$____	$____	$____	____
____	____	$____	$____	$____	$____	____
____	____	$____	$____	$____	$____	____
____	____	$____	$____	$____	$____	____
____	____	$____	$____	$____	$____	____
____	____	$____	$____	$____	$____	____
____	____	$____	$____	$____	$____	____
____	____	$____	$____	$____	$____	____
____	____	$____	$____	$____	$____	____
____	____	$____	$____	$____	$____	____
____	____	$____	$____	$____	$____	____
____	____	$____	$____	$____	$____	____
____	____	$____	$____	$____	$____	____
____	____	$____	$____	$____	$____	____

Spillage Log

Spillage Log

Date:_____ Shift:_____

Bartender:_____

Date	Product or Item	Amt	Wine Cost	Liquor Cost	Beer Cost	Mgr
____	_____	$____	$____	$____	$____	____
____	_____	$____	$____	$____	$____	____
____	_____	$____	$____	$____	$____	____
____	_____	$____	$____	$____	$____	____
____	_____	$____	$____	$____	$____	____
____	_____	$____	$____	$____	$____	____
____	_____	$____	$____	$____	$____	____
____	_____	$____	$____	$____	$____	____
____	_____	$____	$____	$____	$____	____
____	_____	$____	$____	$____	$____	____
____	_____	$____	$____	$____	$____	____
____	_____	$____	$____	$____	$____	____
____	_____	$____	$____	$____	$____	____
____	_____	$____	$____	$____	$____	____
____	_____	$____	$____	$____	$____	____
____	_____	$____	$____	$____	$____	____
____	_____	$____	$'____	$____	$____	____
____	_____	$____	$____	$____	$____	____
____	_____	$____	$____	$____	$____	____
____	_____	$____	$____	$____	$____	____
____	_____	$____	$____	$____	$____	____
____	_____	$____	$____	$____	$____	____
____	_____	$____	$____	$____	$____	____
____	_____	$____	$____	$____	$____	____

Index

X-Y-Z

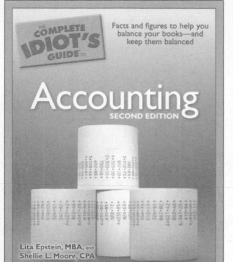
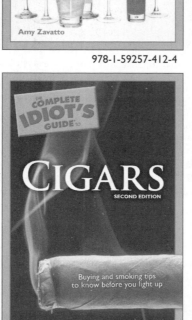
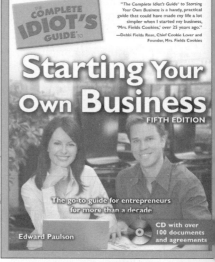

BIBLIO RPL Ltée

G – JUIN 2008